DIRT McGIRTT

The Man Florida Loved to Hate

ROBERT G. MAKIN

Copyright © 2016 Robert G. Makin
Printed version ISBN: 978-0-9887553-0-7
Kindle version ISBN: 978-0-9887553-1-4

All rights exclusively reserved. No part of this book may be reproduced or translated into any language or utilized in any form or by any means, electronic or mechanical, including photocopying, recording or by any information storage and retrieval system, without permission in writing from the publisher.

Library of Congress Catalogue-in-Publication Data
Makin, Robert G.
Dirt McGirtt

Front Cover Design by Robert G. Makin

This is a work of historical fiction. Any resemblance between contemporary characters herein and actual persons is purely coincidental. The author and publisher shall have neither liability nor responsibility to any person or entity with respect to any loss or damage caused or alleged to be caused directly or indirectly by information contained in this book.

Other books by Robert G. Makin:
    Return to Masada
    Strathnaver
    The Faces of Inanna
    Aleister through the Looking Glass
    Where the Clouds Sleep

Sons of Aaron Publishing

Palm Coast, Florida
www.sonsofaaronpublishing.com

Having been educated in American social history, I harbor a real passion for the epic that made our country what it is today, and I love a rattling good yarn. Mr. Makin has accomplished both of these in his latest novel, DIRT MCGIRTT. Set in and around St. Augustine in the late 1700s, Mr. Makin weaves a wonderful web of adventure centering on the fictitious and at the same time real character of Daniel McGirtt. History did not always shine a positive light on the real Daniel McGirtt. Many saw him as a villain, a ruffian at best. Mr. Makin paints another side and the reader flows through the story anticipating the next adventure and apprehensive of Daniel's fate in the latest situation. I think Mr. Makin did a brilliant – and I do mean brilliant – job of weaving "Dirt's" story into the context of the history of Northern Florida. He is a masterful storyteller. I thoroughly enjoyed reading it. It was both informative and exciting.

    Dr. Richard O. Salsgiver
    Professor Emeritus
    California State University, Fresno

This book is dedicated, with hearty thanks, to Daniel McGirtt, variously spelled McGirtt, McGirt, McGirth, McGirit and most lately spelled by his descendants "McGuirth."

I am proud to have known him, through the historical writings of his enemies, and the scanty but loving anecdotes of his friends.

Contents

Preface 1
1 3
2 12
3 22
4 30
5 40
6 48
7 56
8 62
9 68
10 77
11 86
12 96
13 108
14 121
15 134
16 147
17 158
18 169
19 182
20 191
Author's Note: 196
Bibliography 198
Acknowledgements 201
About the Author 203

DIRT McGIRTT

The Man Florida Loved to Hate

ROBERT G. MAKIN

Preface

Writing this history of Daniel McGirtt presented some interesting complications and problems. That he lived so long ago means that there is not much information about him anywhere that is easily accessible. Historical accounts parrot one another, but sometimes with conflicting dates and accounts of the events described. Further complicating matters, the McGirtt family had a propensity for naming their children after immediate family. So James McGirtt, Daniel's father, and James McGirtt, Daniel's brother, are easily confused because historical accounts never distinguish which is which. Daniel's brother James named one of his sons Daniel and that Daniel made a name for himself as well. Accounts of Daniel's imprisonment in El Castillo de San Marcos in the 1790s fail to distinguish which Daniel was imprisoned and why. The account of Daniel's second wife, Susannah Ashley, appears to relate to the son of Daniel's brother James, not to Daniel the son of the British Officer James. Accounts of the death of Daniel McGirtt argue with one another, debating whether he died in 1789 or 1804. One account claimed his death took place around 1812, but it seems that death is of Daniel the son of the brother. Comparing the different accounts led me to conclude that the 1804 date is probably correct.

Finding Daniel McGirtt's grave proved even more challenging. That he was living under an assumed name in South Carolina during his last years meant that I would not find him under a tombstone with the name Daniel McGirtt written on it. On the other hand, there is a Daniel McGirtt buried in St. Marys, Georgia, who is apparently the son of Daniel's brother James and the husband of Susannah Ashley. At this writing, I still have not located Daniel's grave, but the trail has led me to Sumter County in South Carolina. I think I will ultimately find it there.

For me, historical fiction means that the events described in the story are historically verifiable and true. It is fiction from the perspective that no one could possibly know who said what and when. Fleshing up the historical events required developing an understanding of the character and an attempt to grasp his motivations and drives. For example, why would Daniel travel all the way from Maxton Island to St. Augustine to steal eight slaves from Samuel Farley? If he wanted to steal slaves, there were plenty elsewhere who were more easily accessible. That he did it on the night of the inauguration of Vincente Zespedes as Governor of Florida smacks of its being a statement as much as a theft, if it was even Daniel who stole the slaves. The allegation was never proven, but comes down to us as fact. Applying an understanding of his motives in situations like this is where the fiction (or speculation) part of this historical fiction comes into play.

Very few of the characters in the story are inventions. Some of those real life characters, as colorful in every respect as Daniel McGirtt, probably deserve histories of their own. Francisco Xavier Sanchez (1736-1807), twenty-seven years old at the beginning of the British Period, remained in British Florida to manage his family's substantial assets. He survived the British Period nicely and continued his businesses well into the Second Spanish Period, finessing the various governors and governments with the skill of a polished statesman. He lies with many of his family members in the Tolomato Cemetery on Cordova Street in St. Augustine.

The superior officer who tried to confiscate Daniel's horse is one pivotal character whose name I was unable to learn. That the event took place at Fort MacIntosh, Georgia, is speculation. The exact location of the event is never adequately clarified in the historical accounts. The later destruction of that fort is dramatically hyperbolized. I found it interesting that, not very far from the Fort MacIntosh location, another site is referred to by the local people today as "Burnt Fort." It's on Burnt Fort Road where it meets the Satilla River. That is probably the actual location of the event.

Writing *Dirt McGirtt* gave me the feeling that I actually knew the man. Someone recently asked me if I could have lunch with anyone I wanted to, living or dead, who would it be? Without hesitation I answered "Daniel McGirtt."

R.G. Makin, St. Augustine, Florida

1

1775 marked the beginning of Britain's first war with the Marathan Empire on the subcontinent of India. There were three of these wars, lasting well into the nineteenth century. Trouble was brewing for Great Britain on the continent of North America as well, stemming from what the American Colonists regarded as unfair taxation practices. This began with the Stamp Act, enacted by Parliament on March 22, 1765. The Stamp Act taxed the North American Colonists for every piece of printed paper including cargo manifests, newspapers, even playing cards. Under British law, this was not legal since only the colony's representatives in their own governing bodies could enact taxes other than taxes regulating commerce. Additional taxes enacted in this way by Parliament further angered the Colonists. The Tea Act of May 10, 1773, was the straw that broke the camel's back of unfair taxation. The ultimate protest of the Tea Act, known in history as The Boston Tea party, took place in Boston on December 16 of that same year. Thomas Jefferson later remarked in his autobiography that if there had been no Boston Tea Party, there would have been no American Revolution. In 1773 and 1774, the Colonists began organizing formal resistance.

Other news from 1775: James Cook left on his second voyage around the world and for the first time, the Marine Chronometer was in use, enabling Cook to find his longitude.

Southeast Georgia, 1775

The first blow struck with a loud smacking sound, drawing blood and leaving a long angry welt at the upper and lower ends, where it touched his skin. Shirtless, Daniel McGirtt gritted his teeth, unwilling to grant his persecutors the satisfaction of even so much as a groan. Kneeling with his hands tied in front of him, in the center of a large crowd of onlookers, he steeled himself for the next blow. The Scottish were not given to forgetting such outrages and Daniel, a first generation Scottish American, could see in the eyes of his brother James, at the edge of the crowd, the same fury he himself felt with each agonizing lash. Almost on cue, biting flies began attacking Daniel's exposed and bloody back.

"Make the twenty lashes slow, so he has time to relish each one." Captain John Barker of the Patriot forces at Fort MacIntosh stood five feet nine inches tall, a full five inches shorter than the ruddy-faced, carrot-topped and very muscular Daniel McGirtt. Barker's family hailed from Sussex, south of London. Barker was actually born there, an immigrant and a damned traitor to his nation.

Daniel tried to clear his mind of the anger and outrage welling within. *We're far too outnumbered here,* he told himself. *Ten of us only among over four hundred of Barker's men.* The second blow struck with ferocity equal to the first. Daniel's back bled freely. The biting flies gathered for a feast disturbed only by the third blow from the horsewhip that Barker selected for the punishment. *My father, British Colonel James McGirtt, was right.* "The patriots are barely organized rabble with no discipline or honor. They don't stand a chance against Great Britain. Britain always wins." *Is my father always right? Not necessarily.*

Choosing the Patriot cause had proven hard for Daniel. The British Crown had been good to his family. A pension for his father, land in South Carolina – at Camden – good fertile land and slaves to work it. They had good neighbors, too. They were the Cantey, Boykin, Chesnut and James families, living closely together on or near the Great Neck of the Wateree River. The dwindling Wateree Tribe which once possessed the land no longer represented a problem. Life was good. His wife, Mary James, sister to John James, filled his life with joy and children. Leaving all that was harder for Daniel than he thought it would be. The parting gift from his father, a horse named Gray Goose, nearly moved him to tears every time he thought of it. Gray Goose stood seventeen hands. Her finely muscled long legs and small head suggested Arabian stock. She was the envy of all, especially Captain John Barker who believed that his right of command included the right to claim McGirtt's horse.

Wrong! Daniel's objection to the confiscation of his horse came to blows that landed both of them in the mud. Barker withdrew after having McGirtt arrested for insubordination. Bathed and in fresh clothing, he soon returned and ordered that Daniel be flogged. "Twenty lashes with a horse whip. What do you think of that, McGirtt? I want to make sure you remember me." Barker brushed a fleck of dust from his clean shirt, smirked at Daniel's muddy clothes and pressed the issue. "I think I'm going to call you Dirt McGirtt. I hope you enjoy your whipping, Dirt."

Daniel's response rung in Barker's ears and would ring again, in time. "Making me remember you is not something you should want, Barker. For remember you I will!" Those witnessing this exchange discussed at length whether it was the look in Daniel's eye when he said that, or the words he said, that caused Barker to step back, almost fearfully, tripping over a misplaced piece of firewood and falling again in the mud.

The fourth blow from the horsewhip broke Daniel's train of thought. *The sting of the lash doesn't seem to be as bad as the first ones. Maybe old Ben Swiller, the man with the whip, is feeling merciful.* Ben's large belly seemed an impediment to his use of the whip. His thinning, nearly black hair and round face struck Daniel as being that of a kindly sort, with a wife and children at home, a man who had no taste for such exercises, neither the strain nor the intent. Before bending in for the fifth blow, he stopped and adjusted his suspenders and wiped a bead of sweat from his forehead.

"Keep going, you lazy bastard," Barker shouted at him. "Lay it on good or you'll be kneeling on the ground, next." Barker glanced around in surprise as he heard a low murmuring arise among the onlookers.

Daniel waited for the next blow and just before it came, he could her old Ben mutter, "I'm so sorry, Daniel."

Why did I come here? The thought repeated itself over and over. Visions seemed to force themselves on him, memories of his days fishing on the Wateree River with Hampton and Cantey at Jumping Gulley. Jumping Gulley's narrowness almost forced the river to become rapids there, if it could be said the Wateree River had a rapids anywhere. Its slow meandering through the low hills of Kershaw County found no place for the water to fall fast enough for a real rapids. *I wish I never had to leave that place.* There in the rapids it was easy to catch bass, perch, Arkansas Blue Catfish, crappies. Bait was easily available at night when the night crawlers stuck their heads out of the ground to breed. There was nothing like coming home with a basket full of bass and perch for the kitchen. Warmed by the laughter of family and friends all around and feasting on fresh fish those nights, they drank home brewed beer and consumed fresh bread, still warm from the oven. It made for the best of times.

Crack – another blow from the whip. *I'll be surprised if there is any skin left on my back at all when this is done. Barker, a bloody English Man, should remember that Scots never forget. Our feuds last thousands of years; the hate passes from father to son for generations. The head patriot in this place is going to pay for this as will his movement.* The visions came back. *Ah yes. Jumping Gulley.*

"Do you think any horse could actually jump that gap?" Hampton's question was more of a challenge than a question. Daniel knew what Hampton really meant was, 'Do you think YOU could jump a horse over that gap?' Daniel was sure he could, with the right horse and under the right conditions.

"Yes," Daniel answered with a smile. His look assured Hampton that he understood the challenge, but Daniel confirmed the suspicion with, "and some day, I'll do it and prove it to you." His memory brought a smile to his lips, just as the next lash from the horsewhip struck his naked and bloody back again.

"Hit him harder!" Barker shouted at old Ben Swiller. "Your blows are so light that he smiles when you hit him!"

"I don't want to kill him." Ben protested.

"I don't care if you do. Hit him harder. See if you can break some bones with that whip!" Barker, again surprised at the murmur that went up around him, noticed that some of the crowd of soldiers appeared to be moving in closer. Angry looks from most of them cooled his zeal for blood, at least for the moment. "On the other hand, Ben, let's stop the flogging for now. We can finish in the morning."

Daniel did not cry out during the beating, but when Barker suspended it, and he rose to be escorted back to his imprisonment, he directed a question. "Say, Captain Barker. What penalty do you mete out for horse thieving? Where I come from, we hang them."

Barker reacted as if stung by the very lashes that just laid McGirtt's back into a bloody mess. "Dirt McGirtt! Are you calling me a horse thief?"

"That fact is self-evident, sir. What would you call it?"

Barker, not about to be trumped by Daniel's accusation announced, "Tomorrow, you get twenty more lashes and on your sore back, I think you will find that particularly unpleasant. Until tomorrow, then, Dirt. Maybe you will even die of the festering of your sores!" Daniel noticed with satisfaction that Barker had two black eyes and his bent nose still bled freely.

As the sun descended in the west, mostly hidden by the dense foliage, the mosquitoes began buzzing around Daniel's head. With no fire nearby to smoke them away, they began feasting on Daniel's blood. The ready invitation of the exposed wounds on his back lured most of the insects, especially the flies but others chose instead the exposed skin around his neck, ears and face. With no extra shirt or jacket to shield himself, he sat there on his log, stoically waiting for morning. Two armed guards stood at the entry to his log circle lock-up. A few hours into the darkness, he glanced up at the sound of voices. "We've been sent to relieve you. We'll watch him. Go get some supper."

The voices were familiar to Daniel but through his misery he failed to identify them, thinking they were only some of the soldiers he had met earlier, while they were setting up their bivouac. Moments after the relieved guards disappeared into the darkness, his replacement guards seated themselves on either side of him. They were Daniel's brother James McGirtt and his friend Patrick Alcorn. "Daniel. Can you ride? Speak softly. We don't want anyone to notice we're talking with you, although in the darkness, it's unlikely anyone will see."

"What's going on?" Daniel could barely see through the swelling caused by the mosquitoes around his eyes.

"We're leaving. All of us," James told him. "Gray Goose is saddled and ready to go. All of us are ready as soon as you say you can ride."

"Let's go, then," Daniel stood, stretching his legs. "It'll be a day or more before this starts getting really sore. Until then, I'm good for the saddle."

Most of the camp was asleep. No one expected any visits from the English since the existence of the camp was mostly a secret. Fort MacIntosh, on the Satilla River, would not be completed for at least another year. Winn's men would proceed to capture Cockspur Island and a British schooner anchored in the Savannah River, and history would report little more about it.

After all were mounted and most of the men had ridden out of the camp, Daniel couldn't resist shouting, "Hey Barker! Barker! Bark at this, you dog! You will hear of me again and you will see me again and when you do, you will rue this day!" With that, Daniel galloped out of the camp behind his nine men. He could hear the camp stirring as he turned his back on American Patriotism for all time. One lone musket blast came from the camp, the ball tearing through the leaves overhead. The wild shot missed by a wide margin and by the time others were ready to fire, all of McGirtt's party were out of sight and probably out of range. Daniel could still hear the shouts of "Deserters! Cowards!" One call caused Daniel to smile grimly and fuse his determination. It was Barker. "Dirt McGirtt! Get back here and face your music! McGirtt!"

"We're going to Florida," James announced when they were far enough away to no longer fear pursuit. "It's not far and Florida is British. We'll be safe enough there."

"But we joined the Colonists," Daniel objected. "We could be hanged."

"They don't need to know that," was James' rejoinder.

Daniel winced with every thrust of his horse's hooves as his wounded back stiffened. "Maybe the King's cause is the just one after all. It seemed the right thing to do, to join the Patriots and fight against the unfair taxes and the tyranny of no representation in London. But George is King, isn't he? He has the right to tax. We are just colonies of the Mother Country. I will fight for the Crown."

☙ ❧

They rode slowly through the rest of the night. The trail they followed led somewhat west of straight south, away from the coast. At first light, James called a halt to rest and feed the horses. "Tonight," James announced to Daniel, "we will cross the Suwannee River and tomorrow we will be in Florida. There we will rest and get you well."

The prediction was close to true but when they crossed the Suwannee, they found themselves surrounded and badly outnumbered by a large band of Indians, all heavily armed, some on horseback. Without exception, all ten of them raised a hand in greeting and James, with a broad smile, called out, "Hello, there, friends. We are glad to see you." Daniel couldn't keep himself from smiling at the obvious deception. Glad to see the Indians? Maybe not so much.

A very stern looking man, not tall, but husky with a deeply tanned face and long coal-black hair hanging loosely down his back walked up to James, who appeared to be the leader. The man carried a long spear. A knife, obviously of European manufacture, dangled from a rope around his waist. He stopped not far in front of James. He did not smile. "¿Ustedes Españoles?"

"My name is James McGirtt," James answered. "We do not speak Spanish. We are British."

The man smiled, lowered his spear and answered in English. "Then you are welcome. I am Payne, the son of Ahaya, Chief of the Oconee in this place. I invite you to come to our home, the village of Cuscowilla. We have food and my father will wish to welcome you himself. Puc-Puggee is there. You may know him. He is also British."

"I don't know any man whose name is Puc-Puggee, but it will be a pleasure to meet Ahaya and Puc-Puggee. Payne, my friend, my brother is injured." James motioned at Daniel who was slumped in his saddle, a grimace of pain frozen on his face.

Payne approached Daniel, walked slowly around Gray Goose, frowning at Daniel's bloody shirt, the stains of blood darkening the area under his belt, staining his pants red. "Who did this to you?"

James stepped in and answered for Daniel. "A horse thief captured him and overpowered him. Then he had him flogged for refusing to give up his horse. They were colonists at Fort MacIntosh on the Satilla River. Daniel needs to rest and get some sort of treatment for his back. I'm afraid the festering will spread and it may be bad for him."

Payne whistled at some of his fellows and they quickly approached. Before Daniel knew what was happening, they had him on a litter with handles that could be carried easily by two men. A pretty Indian woman cut off his shirt and after washing the broken skin, smoothed an ointment over his wounds. "This we get from the pine tree," Payne explained. "And mixed with some other things, it will prevent the spreading of the soreness that comes from wounds. We always carry some with us. We must go to Cuscowilla. There we can care for your brother much better."

Daniel slept most of the way to Cuscowilla. He woke on a platform three feet above the ground, suspended on poles. The dwelling had open sides. The roof consisted of woven palmetto leaves. The man seated beside him, fair-complected, obviously European, had thinning hair on top, hanging lower on the sides of his head. His long straight nose overhung thin lips that seemed perpetually on the verge of smiling. He had a steaming cup of some drink beside him and he was smoking tobacco in a white clay pipe. His clothing, Daniel guessed, was handmade by Indian squaws from skins captured in the wilderness that surrounded him. The man's most prominent feature, his eyes, glanced fiercely around, almost continuously, with a characteristic look of imminent discovery. "Oh. I see you're awake," the man said. "How are you feeling, Daniel?" Dan tried to sit up, but the pain in his back and the dizziness in his head stopped him from doing more than leaning on one elbow. "Please don't try to get up, my boy," the man told him. "From what I've seen of the work of these people, you'll be just fine in a few days, but for now, you must rest. Sleep if you can. The body heals nicely when it's asleep."

Daniel eased back onto the bedroll that now captured his curiosity. As he examined it he said, "I'm afraid you have me at a disadvantage, sir."

"Oh. I apologize for not introducing myself immediately. The Alachua Oconee call me Puc-Puggee. The name is quite quaint. It means 'Flower-Hunter.' I am what you might call a naturalist. I'm studying the plants and their nature in this wonderful place called Florida. That's what brought me here from Pennsylvania. This is a charming country, and what a diversity of horticulture! At home, I am called William Bartram. Call me Bill, please. I stay here at Cuscowilla from time to time, between expeditions. This is such a charming and sweet people, the Oconee Creeks. Knowing Chief Ahaya is an adventure in itself. I should alert you to the fact that chief Ahaya hates the Spanish. He has sworn that he must kill one hundred Spanish men before he dies, so that he can have peace in the afterlife. So far, he has killed only 57 and he is angry that the Spanish left, for the most part, twelve years ago. He mourns that he has not killed a Spanish man in that length of time. Perhaps he will get his chance; although I do not support this ambition, I can certainly understand it. The Spanish treated him and his people shamefully. He is a very fierce man both in friendship and in war. I am sincerely happy that he doesn't see me as an enemy."

Daniel had fallen asleep again. His sleep only lasted until he moved when the pain would awaken him, rudely and sharply, but then he would slip back into his dreams. The dreams were also fitful, with the face of John Barker appearing prominently, interspersed with visions of his wife, Mary and their children. Then the thought would return, *Why did I come to this place? Why did I not follow my father's advice and accept a commission from the British?*

When he woke again, it was to a gentle nudge from his brother James. Daniel was surprised to find a very unique Indian man with him. Daniel estimated his age to be around fifty years. His hair, hanging over his shoulders, showed signs of gray. His lined face reflected wisdom and passion. Daniel found the man's direct attention disconcerting, to say the least. The Indian man spoke first. "I am Wakapuchasce. The people call me chief. You have found my hospitality adequate?"

James answered for his brother. "You have been most kind to us. Daniel is healing nicely. How can we ever repay you?"

"When you kill the Spanish, do that in my name. I have only killed fifty seven. I must kill more but there are so few now."

"Father," an Indian woman standing behind them interjected, "you think only of killing. There are babies to raise, food to be found and cared for, clothing to be made. Life goes on."

"My name is Wakapuchasce," the man repeated. "When we came here we found many wild cattle. I had my people capture them and we raise them as pets. We have thousands. Sometimes we eat them.

Because of the cattle, my people have begun to call me Ahaya. In your tongue it means Cow Keeper." Wakapuchasce grinned. Daniel was amazed at the man's perfect teeth, but said nothing.

"Wakapuchasce says we must go to St. Augustine," James said.

Ahaya cut in. "There you must meet my good friend Governor Patrick Tonyn. He will help you."

2

In St. Augustine the widow woman, Mary Evans Peavett, had just finished the addition of a second floor living area to the house she purchased across from the British military barracks on St. Francis Street. Moving her family to the second floor, she brewed beer on the first floor which she sold to the soldiers for a nice profit, along with home cooked meals from food she acquired from local merchants and farmers.

The indigo plantation established by Andrew Turnbull and his many indentured servants, on the banks of Spruce Creek, seventy miles south of St. Augustine, were undergoing horrendous hardships, not the least of which was the harsh treatment they received from their new masters. News of the many deaths from yellow fever, malaria and Indians was bad enough but the thought of their starving proved too much for the Peavett family. Supplies to the plantation were intermittent and sometimes did not arrive at all. Mary Peavett initiated a fund, based on donations from the soldiers across the street, to supply food. Francisco Sanchez volunteered the use of some of his boats to deliver the supplies to the indigo plantation, seventy miles south of St. Augustine. Those shipments from Sanchez often included some of his own beef. With permission from Governor Tonyn, a number of the soldiers volunteered to accompany the deliveries to protect them from the incursions of Indians who sometimes raided such vulnerable enterprises.

Other news from 1775: Francis Salvador became the first Jew to be elected to public office in America, in South Carolina, on January 11.

Pope Pius VI began his two-decade reign on February 15.

George Washington assumed command of the Continental Army, Cambridge, Massachusetts, on July 3.

King George III proclaimed the American Colonies to be in open rebellion on August 22.

Portland, Maine, was burned by the British on October 16.

Lord Dunmore, the last Royal Governor of Virginia, promised liberation to any male slaves who joined the British military on November 7.

American troops captured Montreal, November 13.

The Northern Hemisphere was in the middle of "The Mini-Ice Age" in which the Thames River froze over every year from about 1700 until 1804. This may be what gave The Snow Campaign its name in December 1775.

January 1775

Francisco Xavier Sanchez never rode the trails north from St. Augustine without a company of at least six armed men. The trail, always filled with surprises like Charlie Walker's ragtag refugees from Georgia or Indians looking for something easy to take, lacked unexpected events this day. That in itself surprised Francisco and made him uneasy. The overcast sky, chill January air and a brisk northeast wind rustled the palm branches and blew the guajaca from the large old oak trees. *Spanish moss, the Johnny Bull call it. Funny – we used to call it Englishman's Beard. Then they called it Spaniard's Beard. It's still just guajaca.* Francisco, although he resisted it with all his might, enjoyed the ride north today: cool, quiet and winter. Seagulls could be seen wheeling overhead. *Our winter visitors are here.* Francisco smiled at the thought.

"*¡Hoa, Espera!*" (Wait!) Jorge Espinosa, riding in the lead called out. *"¿Que es? ¡Mira!* (What is that? Look!) Jorge and those behind him stopped to wait for Francisco to overtake them. Ahead, under the leaves of a palmetto bush, on the side of the trail, colors that didn't belong there disturbed the green of the plants that should be covering the ground. Francisco could feel the fear and revulsion rising in his gorge. *What has happened now?*

As Francisco grew closer, he could see that they were looking at the body of a man. He wore a dirty white homespun shirt, a red bandana around his neck. His long tangled black hair half covered his face. His cotton pants were drenched in blood which came from a gaping wound in his stomach and another one higher up, on his chest. His once deeply tanned skin was a ghastly shade of gray. "It's Pablo," he announced, quietly. "He's dead." Pablo Giutterez worked as Francisco's head honcho at the Diego Plantation, Francisco's first North Florida Hacienda. He now had three such haciendas, scattered down the St. Johns River, of a thousand or more acres each. His father Jose Sanchez had received the original grant, the first thousand acres, from the King of Spain to raise cattle and horses, to supply lumber and food for the people of St. Augustine. The operation had since grown to include shipments to Cuba, the Bahamas, the Windward Islands and even Spain. Now with Great Britain back in charge, shipments to Cuba had become clandestine. His larger sales now went to supply British garrisons up north. That Francisco Sanchez was a rich man did not dull his sense of humanity or his friendships with those who worked his haciendas. He ruled his slaves as a father more than an owner, allowing them to stay or leave as it suited them. He did not sell them, split up families or abuse them. If his slaves chose to leave, he helped them reach Ahaya's settlement to the west or join others of the Indian communities in North Florida. His paid help like Pablo were, to him, co-workers, friends. The loss of Pablo would be a blow to his operations but more than that, the loss of a well-loved companion across the dinner table with the rest of his family: Maria Piedra, his mulatto concubine and their children.

Pablo had often been a welcome guest in their home on St. Charles Street as well as an overseer of his properties. His first reaction at finding Pablo dead of a violent act was grief, quickly crowded out by apprehension. "Who did this?" His voice began rising in anger, louder with each repetition, *"Who did this? Why?"*

Francisco slung Pablo's body over his horse and walked ahead, leading the animal. The path to the hacienda, about a mile ahead, led through fields where Francisco expected to see cattle grazing, but there were no cattle. He expected to see slaves in the fields, at least a few people, watching over the cattle or mending fences and tending to the hundreds of other chores that required doing, but he saw no one. The sudden lack of the accustomed chatter among his party emphasized their dread of the unknown catastrophe. Francisco found the silence deafening, adding to his apprehension. At almost a crawl, they crept up on the hacienda, having no idea what to expect. What they found was silence and emptiness. The cattle were gone. None of the slaves was present. They found one more body at the foot of the steps to his front porch. Diego de Palma was still alive, but barely. Diego oversaw matters of his home, acquiring food, directing its preparation. In another place and another time, he might have been referred to as a butler.

"Who did this?" Francisco demanded of the man. "Who did this to you? Where did they go? Where are they now?" Diego could barely get enough breath to talk. He had obviously been lying on the porch for hours. His shirt was deeply stained with his blood. The dust on the porch had become a sort of red mud. Francisco's dog, at the foot of the porch was growing stiff and cold. *They even killed my dog!* "Diego! Can you tell me? Who?"

"Raiders from Georgia," he managed to gasp out. "They took everything."

Francisco began issuing orders, first to attend to Diego – "get him into a bed. Get him cleaned up. Wash his wounds. Get him water. Let's try to save him. It might be possible!"

Francisco's barn smoldered in ashes. His horses were gone. He motioned to Pablo and Roberto. "You two. Come with me! Let's see if we can make any sense of this! There must be three hundred head of cattle missing, a dozen horses. They even took my chickens!" Francisco fumed, kicking things out of his way as he walked toward the smoldering remains of his barn. *I wonder why they didn't burn the house?*

"Jaime!" Francisco called over his shoulder. "Please ride back to St. Augustine and tell Governor Tonyn about this. I've heard of raids like this but this is the first one I've seen with my own eyes. We must put a stop to this! This cannot happen again! I was about to ship those cattle to the Islands. Now where will I get three hundred head of cattle to fill my contract?" *Thank God Maria and the children are in the city. They could have been taken as well ... and the children and Maria herself are of color. They would be taken as slaves!* The thought of his mistress and their children being forced to Georgia and impressed into slavery maddened him even more. He swore loudly and viciously as he kicked debris out of his path.

As the day wore on, Francisco found many more valuable items missing. Diego de Palma died late that afternoon. Francisco would have been proud to prepare dinner for him himself, but all the food supplies were gone, driving Francisco into another rage that ended with "Pablo, Roberto. See if you can shoot some rabbits for our dinner. There may be some potatoes in the ground behind the house. We can at least eat, after we bury these two valiant friends, Pablo and Diego. Tomorrow we will ride to my next hacienda to the south and retrieve some supplies to start over here. We will need a bull and as many cows as possible – and some chickens, *Por Diós!*" He kicked away a chair that had been standing on the front porch of his house. It clattered to the ground with one leg broken.

CG 80

Morning came quietly to Francisco Sanchez. There was rain. The freshening wind drove the rain into his face at a sharp angle. More guajaca lay on the ground from the large oaks that surrounded his Diego Plantation. *What would my father do in this situation?* Jose Sanchez, Francisco's father, had never faced such civil unrest or raids from the colonists. He had made friends with them by making his goods available to them in St. Marys and other small towns near the border. He treated them fairly and honorably. They, in turn, treated him honorably. *They were his friends. They are MY friends! I have done the same. Where could these pícaros have come from? They are not from St. Marys. They must be others from farther west.*

After a breakfast of palm cabbage and rabbit flesh left over from the night before, he announced, "We must see if we can track these raiders. Maybe we can get some of the cattle back, or the slaves. Maybe we can even recover some of our chickens!"

The trail led north and west toward the Welaka (now the St. Johns River). *Could these fools be thinking of using the ferry at Cow Ford?* Not much conversation took place among Francisco and his six armed men on horseback. All were wary, watching and listening for any sign of others ahead. "They couldn't have gone far, driving three hundred head of cattle. There will be wagons with broken wheels and other things to slow them. We'll likely catch up around midmorning or maybe close to noon."

Jorge Espinosa, again riding in the lead, raised a hand to signal a halt, his horse dancing slightly at the sudden stop. "Someone is coming," he passed the whisper back to Francisco.

Francisco responded, "Get ready for a fight!" He rode slowly ahead to take the lead in whatever bloodletting was about to take place. The men waited in silence, muskets at ready, swords loose in their scabbards. A pileated woodpecker swung through the trees overhead, stopping to peck at old dead oak limbs along the way. Francisco loved to watch them on the rare occasions when they appeared, but this time, he gave it only a single glance. A gray squirrel raced up a tree ahead of them, probably a signal that whatever is coming was almost here.

The first thing to make an appearance made Francisco gasp sharply. Tensely he nudged his horse forward, only to see many more fire cracker cows, some with their young chasing a nipple as they walked. *My cattle! What the hell?*

Behind the lead cattle came numerous negro men and women with sticks, prodding the cattle toward the Diego Plantation. Some of the negroes had young with them as well, all equipped with sticks to help direct the cattle along the path home.

"¡Hola!" Francisco called out, waving. "¿Que pasa?" The slaves waved back, indicating others were following. Puzzled, Francisco and his men urged their horses against the flow of the cattle and worked their way to the end of the line. There, to his surprise, he found wagons loaded with caged chickens, tools, food supplies and more slaves. Pulling the wagons, Francisco was pleased to see, were his stolen horses. *This is almost a full recovery! IF, that is, they intended to come home and aren't just lost in the forest.*

Now he could hear voices. They were speaking English, not the perverted cockney of the south Georgia farmer but of the north lands of Great Britain. *I never thought I'd be glad to hear a Scottish accent!* He didn't know whether to smile or grimace. Then he saw them. By their clothing they could not be identified as belonging to any special group, but they all wore the same kind of hat. *A militia of some kind?* Francisco stopped his horse and signaled his men to put down their arms and wait with him. The riders came closer and one of them stopped beside Francisco.

He sat tall in his saddle, a squarely built man of ruddy complexion, carrot red hair, a curly beard and intense blue eyes that studied him closely. "And who might you be?" The ruddy-faced man demanded.

Francisco felt that the question was a fair one. "I am Francisco Xavier Sanchez, a real Floridano. I supply food to St. Augustine, and cattle and horses and lumber and sometimes slaves. These cattle, wagons and horses you are driving are mine, recently stolen at the cost of the lives of some of my people! And who might you be?" Francisco felt anger rising again, but restrained it because he was so badly outnumbered.

The red-headed man took off his hat, ran his fingers through his matted hair, scratched his beard and said, "I am Colonel Daniel McGirtt of the East Florida Rangers. We found this ragtag group of raiders driving these cattle toward Cow Ford. I guess they thought we would let them get away easily. When they saw us, they dropped everything and ran for it. Some of them fired on us. They won't do that again." Daniel's eyes grew fierce as he said it and Francisco knew that he himself would never fire on this formidable man, either.

Only a month ago, at the behest of Governor Patrick Tonyn, Colonel Daniel McGirtt had become a colonel in the East Florida Rangers, tasked with patrolling Florida's borders to stop just such attacks on Florida's civilian population. McGirtt held out his hand in greeting. "I'm glad to meet you, Francisco Xavier Sanchez. I have heard of you."

Francisco, still nonplussed from the unexpected turn of events, accepted McGirtt's handshake which he found overly strong. "Colonel McGirtt, I am profoundly pleased to make your acquaintance. I apologize that I have not before heard of you but you can be assured, I will never forget you."

CB ED

John Cantey, of Cantey Lane, five miles south of Camden, South Carolina, puffed on a corncob pipe as he rocked on his front veranda and looked over the fields of cotton that stretched beyond his vision to the wooded rise beyond. He had found his dinner very satisfying, cooked by his house slave, Savannah. Savannah was pushy, for a slave, even bordering on the smart-aleck, but she knew he could have her whipped if she went too far. Of course he never did, but when she pushed too far, he would threaten to sell her to old Ebram Havaleck, down in the next county. Havaleck had a terrible reputation for the way he treated his slaves and Cantey would never sell anyone to such a master. He believed Savannah knew that, and when he made such a threat she would hand it back with, "You do that an it's no more elderberry pie for the likes of you, Mr. John."

Cantey smiled at the memory of the exchange as he opened the package he had received from his Aunt Dinah in Atlanta this morning. It was a copy of one of the local newspapers with a letter about how things were shaping up with the war effort in that part of the country. There was the usual diatribe against the imposition of British taxes and the incredible audacity of the king and parliament who used the "sweat of our brows and backs to fund wars overseas that have nothing to do with us." After reading her letter, he opened the newspaper. He frowned at the headline and his frown deepened as he finished reading the article. Cantey called out to his wife.

"Elizabeth? Elizabeth – can you come out here for a moment?" Elizabeth arrived with a small tray carrying two cups of tea. Smiling, she set the tray on an end table between them and sat down. "What is it, husband?"

"Your brother Daniel is making quite a name for himself. Look at this article." He handed her the newspaper. The headline said, "Kershaw County South Carolina's Daniel McGirtt Kills Three in Raid of Georgia Farmers." The article named the three men who had been killed while transporting a herd of cattle and assorted property they had legitimately purchased from a plantation in North Florida.

"McGirtt maliciously swept down upon them with a vast number of bandits collected from the rabble and woods of the North Florida swamps and viciously killed three men trying to protect their legally purchased property. He made away with a herd of cattle numbering some two hundred head, thirty five slaves, dozens of horses. This outrage is beyond imagining, that such people can exist in civilized times."

The article went on to describe the events at Fort MacIntosh where "McGirtt viciously attacked a superior officer for no reason, then fled to avoid his just punishment."

Elizabeth folded the newspaper and laid it beside the teacups. She chose one of the cups, lifted it and took a sip. "I wonder if Mary has seen this."

Cantey's eyebrows went up slightly as he turned to answer. "You mean his wife? Isn't she the sister of John James down in Stateburg?"

"She is." Elizabeth answered. "That's where she's staying, under an assumed name, I'm told. I wondered why she wasn't using her own name. I guess this is why."

"What kind of man is your brother?" Cantey crossed his legs and took a sip of tea.

"My brother – no – my brothers *both* are honorable and decent men. There is something missing in this article. Neither James nor Daniel would ever be a part of something like this, much less at the head of it. As for the incident at Fort MacIntosh, I believe there has to be more to that story too. Daniel would never attack another without plenty of provocation. In fact, I bet those men from Georgia stole those cattle and horses and Daniel stopped them. That's what I think!"

03 80

March 1775

Daniel McGirtt sat uncomfortably in a stiff wooden chair by the open window at Maria's in St. Augustine. The brazier in the center of the room filled the room with smoke. Daniel was thankful for the open window, where, from time to time a whiff of fresh air would puff its way inside. His order of beef stew, boiled potatoes and whatever greens Maria had available was cooking in the outside kitchen while Daniel sipped

Maria's homemade beer and waited for Francisco Sanchez to show up. Daniel watched in amusement as Maria moved rapidly around the room, refilling cups with beer, taking orders for food, avoiding the adventurous hands of the British soldiers who were her main clientele. Her buxom figure was far more agile than it appeared to be and her manner, a combination of flirtatious and coy, became commanding and stern exactly when needed to fulfill the role she had chosen at La Taberna de Maria.

Across the room, near another window, a group of dogged bumpkins, carried away with their own exuberance, felt compelled to share it with any and all, and demanded more of Maria's attention than she seemed willing to share. Maria was not about to be intimidated. In a loud voice she announced, "Hands off, you fools! If you don't settle down I'll have your asses thrown into the mud road out front!"

"Smokey in here!" Francisco commented loudly. Daniel had been so wrapped up in the show on the other side of the room that he had not seen Francisco come in.

Daniel straightened up in his chair in surprise. "Yes. It's supposed to keep the mosquitoes out. It seems to work. I don't know if I'd rather have the mosquitoes or the smoke, though. What do you think?"

Smiling, Francisco took a seat and said, "The mosquitoes might make us sick, but then, so might the smoke. I don't know which is better. What's new with you?"

Daniel took a sip of his beer as Maria stopped at their table. "Ready for another? And how about you Don Francisco?"

Francisco indicated he would have some beer and added, "I'm not a don, but thank you."

With Maria on her way to fetch the beer, Daniel answered Francisco's question: "More of the same. A lot of people are fleeing the colonies, those loyal to the Crown. When they get here, they have nowhere to go, no means of support, no shelter. They're desperate and I'm afraid this is just the beginning. Worse yet, there is a lawless factor in west Georgia, more or less away from the action of the revolution. They think Florida is fair game. They think they can ride in here and take whatever they find and justify it as part of the war effort."

"It's not," Francisco's lean, weathered face hardened at the recent memory of his own experience with this kind of robbery.

"More plantations have been sacked. Governor Tonyn just told me the Padamaran Plantation has been burned and looted. He set me on the trail of that bunch. I'll be leaving at first light. What's new with you, my friend?"

Francisco was carrying a folded newspaper. He shoved it across the table to Daniel. "I found this in one of the shops. It's a few months old but I thought you'd like to see it."

Daniel opened the paper and on the front page he found the same article his sister and her husband had read a few months before. When he finished, he closed the paper and shoved it back across the table to Francisco. "You know what they say, my friend. History is made by those who write it."

Francisco frowned. "These people are writing your history, my friend. If you don't find someone who will tell the truth, this will be your history."

3

July 4, 1776, was a momentous day in the history of the nascent United States. Delegates of the Second Continental Congress in Philadelphia adopted the Declaration of Independence, denouncing the tyrannical rule of King George III of England. The birth of the new republic was celebrated throughout the northern colonies. On July 2, the Continental Congress had formally declared the name of the new nation to be "The United States of America." This replaced the term "United Colonies," which had been in general use.

In Florida, the celebration of America's birthday was a dud. Settlers carried on with normal life in the two British Floridas: West Florida, centered around Pensacola; and East Florida, with St. Augustine as its capital. They were unaware of the turbulent uprisings to the north. When news of the rebellion finally reached them on July 20, Floridians were outraged. Very few joined in the festivities, and those who did were ridiculed. In fact, rioting against British authority in Florida was viewed as nothing less than treason.

Florida folks denounced the challenge to British rule by burning effigies of John Hancock and Samuel Adams in the public square in St. Augustine and by drinking to the health and success of King George.

Floridians were mostly loyal to the British crown. They were comfortable with the authority of the British Parliament and approved of the political state of affairs. Taxation was never an issue because for years the territory had been reaping the benefits of English taxes. Money raised through the Stamp Act and other taxation by the British government had been spent generously throughout La Florida.

Other news from 1776: Adam Smith published Wealth of Nations. On July 12, James Cook sailed from Plymouth in a repaired Resolution to search for the Northwest Passage and to return Omai to his home on Huahine in the Society Islands.

    The Padamaran Plantation consisted of ten thousand acres lying on the west side of the St. Johns River immediately south of Maxton Island, a.k.a. Ortega. The grant went to Jacob Wilkerson, a London merchant, a gift from the King of England, George III. Wilkerson hired Alexander Grant to develop it, and develop it he did. The only way McGirtt could get to it was by the ferry at Cow Ford. It took several days to get there. *"Es un hacienda magnifico,"* was all Daniel could get Francisco Sanchez to tell him about it, but Tonyn filled him in.
    "Alexander Grant arrived about seven years ago. There are several houses including the plantation house, if it's still there. They're raising indigo, primarily, and rice, but Grant has a respectable herd of cattle. He breeds horses, too. If you are to recover the stolen property, you must hurry."
    McGirtt's ragtag crew consisted of volunteers he was able to muster, including a little over a dozen Creek Indians that Ahaya sent to help him. The rest, except for half a dozen men who came with McGirtt from South Carolina, were roustabouts with nothing to do but get into trouble; Tonyn threatened them with prison if they didn't join the Rangers. McGirtt barely trusted them; forty six men in all, armed and on horseback including his friend, Patrick Alcorn, from Camden, a former neighbor. McGirtt approached Padamaran from the north. Before they were even within sight of the plantation, musket balls from a dozen or so muskets went buzzing through the trees all around them and over their heads. Two of the roustabouts dropped from their horses, shot. The rest scattered into the palmetto bushes on either side of the path, braving the snakes and spiders, McGirtt and Alcorn with them.
    The short-lived encounter ended with Ahaya's men slipping behind the musketeers. There were eight. Thanks to the Indians, only two

survived, escorted out of their cover at knifepoint for questioning. The Indians' only disgusted comment was, "No Spaniards."

McGirtt's fury, like a red aura, preceded him as he approached the two. With his Skyn Dhu, the black handled dagger his father taught him to never be without, in hand he approached the two men. Their ragged clothes and bare feet shocked him. *A white man has to be a fool to go bare footed in the Florida woods!* Even the Indians were well shod with their deerskin and leather moccasins. The first man shook his shaggy sandy hair out of his eyes to face his death. McGirtt placed the tip of the knife on the skin of the man's throat. A tiny trace of blood appeared. Daniel's voice sounded more like a growl than the voice of a human. "All it will take is a very slight pressure. Where did you people come from?"

"Georgia," the man rasped.

"Where in Georgia?" McGirtt growled.

"Hell! I ain't tellin' you!"

The knife drew ever so slightly deeper into the man's throat. The drop of blood became a thin trickle. "If you don't talk to me, you'll be talking to Jesus in just another minute. *Where in Georgia?*"

"Our farm is halfway up the west side of the Okefenokee on the west side the Suwanee River."

"Is anybody else waiting for us?" McGirtt withdrew the pressure on the Skyn Dhu, but the thin trickle of blood didn't stop.

The man strained to lean backwards, away from McGirtt's dagger. Shaking his hair again, he said, "Just us."

McGirtt withdrew the knife and put it back into its sheath. "If that's not true, I'll be back here very shortly to finish the job I started on your throat." Glancing over his shoulder, he called out to the men behind him, "Tie them up good. One of you stay here to watch over them. If they get too restless, kill them. They tried to kill us and actually managed to kill two of us. When we get finished checking the plantation, a couple of you men can take these two prisoners back to St. Augustine to be charged and hanged."

The remainder of McGirtt's crew followed him, walking their horses carefully toward the Padamaran. They came out of the heavy tree cover into open fields, planted as far as they could see with indigo. "Just look at these blue flowers!" Alcorn exclaimed. "Beautiful!"

McGirtt gazed to the south over the vast fields. "It looks like they're ready to harvest. I wonder if anyone will be here to do that. There must be two thousand pounds sterling in this field. It's a shame to leave it to die. Do you see any buildings?"

"I do not." Alcorn answered. "But there appears to be smoke in that direction." Alcorn pointed southeast.

Back on their horses, McGirtt and his men rode in the direction of the smoke. Several buildings were in ashes and still smoldering. "That appears to have been a house." McGirtt indicated a tall brick chimney that had survived the fire. "And that, over there, a large barn of sorts."

"There are some other buildings farther south. See them?" Alcorn pointed. "But wait. Look there."

A white man, seated on a stump, watched them from behind what was once the plantation house. Around him, four dark-skinned men and two women of the same color sat on the ground and other stumps. McGirtt approached them on horseback, walking slowly. As McGirtt drew near, the man raised both his hands and called out, "There's no point in comin' in here. Everything's already been stolen. You're a day late and a penny short."

Daniel introduced himself and learned the man's name was Alexander Gray, the overseer of the plantation. "When they came here, me and these darkies were way down there in the woods looking into clearing more land, maybe sell the lumber and plant a larger indigo crop next year. I guess we won't be doing that."

"Have you anyone to harvest the crop you have?" McGirtt asked, politely.

"I have not," Gray replied, lowering his head. "It'll be lost and I may lose my job."

"For a half share," McGirtt began, "I think I can find you labor to harvest and refine the dye. Will you agree to pay a half the crop to harvest all of it?"

"Where you gonna find enough slaves to do this? It has to be done in the next few days, or it'll be too late."

"I have a friend who may be able to help you. Francisco Sanchez is a good man but maybe not so good as to supply this much labor without a share. I think he'll accept fifty percent. If he has the men available, I'm sure he'll send them. You will know in two or three days. I realize fifty percent is a substantial loss to you, but better that than lose all of it. Aye?"

03 80

The ride north into Georgia led McGirtt and his party through sand hill and swamp, slapping mosquitoes and yellow flies the whole way. Alcorn, usually a chatterbox of cynicism and wit, remained very quiet. McGirtt didn't mind the break in the chatter but after the second day he grew curious. "What are you so quiet about Alcorn? You haven't said a word except swearing at the mosquitoes and yellow flies for almost two days."

"What we're doing just seems so futile." Alcorn resumed his silence for a few minutes. McGirtt agreed in his heart but didn't want to encourage the sentiment. "The raiders from Georgia are overwhelming," Alcorn finally continued. "The Padamaran isn't the only plantation that was raided and burned in recent months, just the biggest one. It seems that every few weeks someone else is getting burned out and robbed. What we're doing is like trying to put a tiny patch on a sinking ship. We go after maybe one in ten of these incidents. Yes, we bring back the property, we do a little payback in the place where the stolen goods have been taken, but they only come back the next week and do it again. What are we really accomplishing? To guard Florida's borders, we need troops and lots of them."

"We aren't the only ones out here, you know," McGirtt remonstrated. "Colonel Cunningham has a large force, as does Mayfield, and there are others. The East Florida Rangers is not just us. Florida's Governor Tonyn is doing the best he can under the circumstances."

"Georgia is British." Alcorn wasn't satisfied. "They could be doing more, there in Georgia, to put a stop to this. One British colony raiding another British colony just doesn't make any sense to me. Why are they doing this?"

Daniel rode in silence for a few minutes. Then, clearing his throat, he began, "Great Britain kept Georgia as a sort of buffer between the colonies to the north and Spanish Florida to the south – a buffer that was intended to encourage the Spanish to stay in Florida. But even with the buffer, the Spanish were raiding as far north as South Carolina clear back to the seventeenth century, over a hundred years. James Moore, one of South Carolina's old governors, went to Florida and burned St. Augustine to teach them a lesson, but they didn't learn anything. They continued raiding. James Oglethorpe took up the crusade a few years later and HE burned St. Augustine, too, but the raids from the Spanish continued. Georgia is just a buffer; it doesn't even have its own government. It only has a few cities and most of them are right on the seacoast. Most of the colony, and it's the biggest colony Britain has, is wilderness, populated by Cherokee, Choctaw and Creek Indians. Most of them aren't even friendly to us. Ahaya with his band of Creeks is a real blessing."

"I see what you mean," Alcorn replied.

"Most of those raiding Florida plantations are miscreants who fled civilization and they're living in the woods, like Indians. When they manage to steal some cattle or slaves, they take them to Savannah or Augusta and sell them there. They use the money to get drunk, entertain some women, buy supplies and go back to their shacks in the wilderness. They're wild men, criminals. Some of those criminals even came from the Tower of London – hardened criminals. We're acting as Florida's police."

The encampment where McGirtt and his party found the Padamaran's raiders was just as McGirtt described it – shacks and filth. "This is nothing but mud and swamp!" Alcorn was disgusted. "How do people survive in such places?"

The fight was brief. The cattle, horses and slaves were many. Only two men and four women were present to resist McGirtt's party and the women fought as hard as the men. McGirtt's party killed all but two. Driving the cattle and horses back to the Padamaran was easier because of the slaves' willingness to help.

"I hate this." McGirtt muttered loudly enough that Alcorn, riding next to him, could hear. His face twisted with remorse. Then he turned to Patrick and continued. "These people are dirt poor with no education and no one to help them. They take what they think they can and we go and kill them for it. Their lives are one desperate fight after another. If it isn't disease or hunger, it's alligators and snakes and then when things just start to look a little better for them, the East Florida Rangers show up with muskets blazing and swords flashing. I hate it! How many people did we kill back there? For what? Their husbands, sons and wives will come back and find their family dead, their shacks burned, their stolen property gone. They will hate us. They may even come looking for us, when we aren't wary enough to fight them off or with numbers too great for us to fight alone. We are making bitter enemies, Patrick. I hate it."

"It is as you said." Alcorn spit to the side of his horse. "We are Florida's police. We're doing what we can in support of the king's interests. We are only a few but if we continue, maybe we can make a difference.

☙ ❧

Governor Patrick Tonyn took great pleasure in sipping his tea on his high, east facing balcony at Government House. The bigger ships arriving at St. Augustine had to anchor at sea because the shallow channel coming into the harbor didn't provide enough depth. Two of Francisco Sanchez's brigantines rested at anchor in the harbor, with shallow enough drafts to navigate the inland waters. *Nice for him,* Tonyn mused. *He can transport cattle and lumber to us from the Diego Plantation in those things.* It always amazed Tonyn when he saw Francisco's large boats sailing south on the Tolomato River from the north. "How your people can find their way through the sand bars and wandering bottoms of that river always amazes me," Tonyn once told Sanchez.

"Our best people can't do that. I can't tell you how many times we had to rescue some small vessel run aground five or ten miles north of here. We quit trying, but you seem to breeze through as though the bottom opens for you."

Sanchez had chuckled. "I grew up here. I've been sailing these waters in all manner of craft since I was a boy. My family has been in St. Augustine forty years. I know the rivers and so do my men." Tonyn smiled at the memory. His attention today, however, focused on entertaining General Prevost.

Prevost's age showed in his lined and weary face. Clothed by many years' habit in the heavy woolen uniform of a British general, he waved off the hot tea indicating that he was warm enough already. "Waiting for an invasion that may not come is growing tiresome," he said to Tonyn after the preliminaries of admiring the view from Tonyn's balcony. "The action is all way up north. I yearn to get into it, but I wonder if perhaps my years may be a hindrance. Wars like this are for younger men."

Tonyn, not unsympathetic to the general's complaint, commented, "You have plenty of troops here. Cunningham, Mayfield and McGirtt who are policing Florida's borders have all made the observation that your help would be most appreciated. McGirtt says the few East Florida Ranger regiments are little more than a cork in a leaking ship. Raids of Florida plantations from rabble in Georgia are coming faster than they can stop them and what little effort they are able to make is a mere token to what is needed. Can you help them?"

Prevost shuffled his feet, crossed then uncrossed his legs. He shifted his weight in his chair, furrowed his brow and said, "My superiors have ordered me to keep my troops in St. Augustine and not endanger them with forays into the Florida forests. An organized effort on the part of my 60th Regiment of Foot might alert the colonists to the fact that British reinforcements are waiting in Florida and that may spur them on to try to attack Florida. If the war moves closer, I'm sure General Campbell will summon me."

"Some of our Florida Rangers are getting a lot of public attention in the southern colonies. Have you seen any of the news about Daniel McGirtt?" Tonyn handed a large leaflet to the General. "I don't know why McGirtt is getting all the attention. The news flyers ignored the fact that Colonels Cunningham and Mayfield are doing exactly the same things as McGirtt. Every time McGirtt crosses the Georgia border to retrieve stolen cattle and slaves, another of these stories appear. Look at this one!"

The news was from Columbia, South Carolina: "McGirtt – up to his tricks again. In a vicious raid on the Samerson ranch on the west side of the Okefenokee, McGirtt and his desperadoes stole hundreds of head of cattle and left six dead. Will this man's depredations never end?"

Tonyn shook his head. "The cattle they are referring to here were stolen by the Samerson ranch people when they came from Georgia and raided and burned the Padamaran Plantation, killed several people there and burned most of the plantation's buildings. McGirtt followed his orders. He followed the raiders to their lair and recovered the stolen property. He went further than that. He arranged for the labor to be supplied to harvest the standing crop of indigo and virtually saved the plantation from total ruin. This is the kind of pay he gets – defamation in his old home country of South Carolina. It's not fair."

Prevost smiled as he read the leaflet. "Maybe McGirtt is more aggressive than the others. Do you think?"

"Tonyn put down his tea cup. "I think," he began, "McGirtt is just more recognizable than the others because of his flaming red hair and his size. He is a very big man. I also think that any time a red headed man is seen in that part of the country or does anything unseemly there, McGirtt gets blamed."

Prevost, unable to come up with an appropriate answer, shook his head and said, "I guess McGirtt will just have to plan on making Florida his home. With all this being said about him in South Carolina, he can never go home.

4

1777

May About 439 indentured servants of Andrew Turnbull arrived in St. Augustine. Of the original number, 1,403, 964 had died of malaria, yellow fever and various other ailments including starvation, Indian attacks and vicious mistreatment by Turnbull and his overseers. Governor Patrick Tonyn recognized that their terms of indenture had expired. Turnbull refused to release them and forced the Minorcans to sign new letters of indenture or be severely punished. In addition to that, Turnbull had stopped paying the Minorcans their agreed-upon wage, although the indigo plantation had been immensely profitable. Tonyn released them from their indentured servitude, welcomed them to St. Augustine and gave them land.

The largest invasion of Florida by the continental Army was planned. The invasion fell apart because of poor discipline, communication and organization. Two leaders of the invasion, Lachlan MacIntosh and Button Gwinnet, quarreled before the invasion and subsequently fought a duel in which both were wounded and Gwinnet died. Florida Rangers burned Fort MacIntosh near modern-day Atkinson, Georgia.

1778

South Carolina law required that all adult males take the oath of loyalty to the United States or suffer confiscation of their properties and expulsion. This resulted in a huge immigration to Florida, Nova Scotia and the British Caribbean. A large number of Loyalists under British military training and pay, realizing the inability of Great Britain to fulfill its goals, began deserting in large numbers and immigrating to Florida – known as the March of the Scopholites.

1778

Patrick Alcorn lounged against the back of his stiff wooden chair at La Taberna de Maria. His mug of beer half empty, he smacked his lips after one more quaff and said, "What does 'furlough' mean anyway? We got a week off in a place where there is nowhere to go and not much to do except swill beer at Maria's or go fishing. Sightseeing takes about five minutes. There's nothing to see here except muddy streets, primitive houses and the wildlife that never seems to have left the city even with all the people and buildings. Just this morning I had to shoo an alligator out of my doorway. It was a small one, but its mama could have been anywhere nearby. I wonder if they're any good to eat?"

"We never ate them in South Carolina," McGirtt offered, "but the Wateree Indians did."

Francisco Sanchez started laughing. Daniel McGirtt, in the third of the table's four chairs, chuckled as well. Francisco put down his beer mug and said, "The Minorcans are an amazing people. They've only been here a year and already they know everything that's edible. They eat the alligators' tails. I've tried it. It's tough and chewy, rather like over cooked, oversized clams. Alligator tail is all right if you're hungry enough. They also eat turtles, turtle eggs, and that boney thing that swims in such large schools. They call them mullet. I watched old Jose Manucy weave a net out of cotton string that he then cast out over the water to catch them. The net worked very nicely. After he smoked some of them, he gave me one. The meat was very tasty and it peeled right off the bone after it was smoked long enough."

The three were near the window again because of the smoke from the brazier. McGirtt felt distracted and although the fellowship with these friends was always uplifting, the coming assignment gave him a queasy feeling. He glanced out the window and began watching a mockingbird hunting for worms and insects beside the mud road. Alcorn followed his gaze and drifted into the same concerns Daniel was feeling.

Francisco completely understood. "Have another beer, fellows. Just because Prevost has been ordered to Savannah and he wants you to come along, doesn't mean the world is ending. You've been complaining for the last few years that you've seen none of the war. Well, you're about to. Now that France has entered the fray, things are looking up a little bit for the American adventure. Isn't this what you wanted; a desperate adventure in support of a desperate cause? Be careful what you wish for."

"The American adventure, as you put it," McGirtt rose to the bait, "is doomed. Great Britain hasn't lost a war in a long time. It has the best navy the best soldiers the best weapons and ships in the world."

"It would appear," Francisco defended his position, "that the Americans are doing quite a job of defending themselves from the British. The British have suffered defeat after defeat..."

"...And some major victories as well, "McGirtt cut in."

"Whichever way it goes," Alcorn interjected. "Florida is where we have cast our lot and Florida is British."

"We used to think that way." Francisco got a faraway look in his eyes. "Florida was Spanish from 1565 until 1763 – that's almost two hundred years. My countrymen had estates here, haciendas. We believed Florida would always be Spanish. We had cattle, farms, houses that had been in our families for generations and suddenly the land was - *British*. We were astonished. People had to give up their homes that their families had built with their own hands. They were more or less forced to leave. Like me, they had been born here, raised here – real Floridanos and now? Who knows where they went."

"How did you manage to stay?" Daniel wanted to know?

"I requested it and I swore allegiance to the British Crown. I am not a Spaniard. I am a native born Floridano. Florida is my country, whether British, Spanish or American or whatever comes after that. I am a Floridano. My father, Jose, was born in Ronda in Spain. He went to Cuba and then he came here in 1736, the year I was born. I was born in Florida."

A disturbance at the far side of the room distracted the men. A large woman with long wavy black hair, blessed with a voice equal to her in volume, returned their glance. Then she continued her argument – if that's what it was – with Maria. "I ordered pork, not beef. Don't you have any pork?" She tossed her long hair out of her face, glanced back at McGirtt's party again, crossed her ample legs and raised her eyebrows in query as she looked back up at Maria.

Maria, ever the gracious hostess, removed the plate from the table that she had evidently just placed there and said, "I'm sorry Salamanca. I thought you ordered beef. I'll be back in just a few minutes. Do you want that spicy or plain?"

Salamanca puckered her thick lips as though considering the question, then answered, "I haven't had a proper ham since I left Dublin. Can you manage boiled cabbage and potatoes with that ham?"

"We're fresh out of cabbage," Maria said, "but the potatoes and ham we can do. The roasted pork is especially good today. I can add datil peppers if you want it spicy. "

"Datil peppers?" Salamanca furrowed her brow, which she shouldn't have done because it cracked the makeup she had on. "What in bleeding hell is that?"

"It's a new kind of hot pepper the Minorcans brought with them from Spain. They like it very much. Maybe you will too, but it is very hot. Your pleasure is my pleasure. What will it be?"

Salamanca smiled and said, "I think I'll try the roasted pork with the datil peppers. I'll try it, but please bring it over there." She indicated McGirtt's table. "I'm going to move my seat, if you don't mind."

Alcorn practically stared as Salamanca heaved herself to her feet. Francisco, with furrowed brow and lowered head, gazed fixedly at his drink from beneath his bushy eyebrows. McGirtt simply watched in astonishment as Salamanca walked across the floor, swaying her hips in what she apparently believed to be an enticing manner, a well-practiced grin stamped on her face, revealing through her thick lips uncared-for teeth that made McGirtt feel slightly nauseous. When she reached their table she said, "I see you gentlemen have an empty chair. Do you mind if I join you?" She didn't wait for a reply. She pulled the empty chair from under their table and seated herself immediately next to Daniel. "I have some food coming," she continued. "I would really rather not eat alone. Have you gentlemen had your meal yet?"

Daniel slid his chair back to increase the distance from her. Alcorn's bafflement amused Daniel but he said nothing. Francisco, on the other hand, glared at the woman and said, "Go away, Puta!"

At that point, Maria showed up at their table, fists on hips and a frown on her face. "Salamanca! We have had this conversation before. You may not do business in my store. It's time for you to leave."

Salamanca tried to look offended, first at Francisco who had called her a whore and now at Maria. "That's not very polite. I'm a good customer and I did not try to *'do business'* with these men."

The door to La Taberna de Maria stood propped open to encourage the circulation of air inside the building and to help clear the dense smoke from the brazier. Once Salamanca had completely disappeared from the door, the men looked at each other and sniggered. McGirtt looked at Patrick Alcorn and said, "Alcorn, I thought you were going to knock her down and take her right here and now."

Alcorn started laughing. "I'd think I'd be afraid of getting lice or some other dread illness."

Francisco couldn't resist adding, "I guess since the French are once again the enemies of Great Britain it will be acceptable to refer to that as 'The French Disease.'"

McGirtt started laughing again, remarking, "The French used to call it 'The Spanish Disease.'"

"I take exception to that," Francisco chortled. "We used to call it 'The English Disease.' No one knows for sure where it came from."

McGirtt grew silent for a moment, withdrawing into his own thoughts and memories, not paying attention to the quips and jests that continued about Salamanca. Finally he said, "My wife Mary fears I'll be tempted to stray during this long separation. I don't think that's going to happen. I miss her."

"What's she like?" Francisco asked.

McGirtt took a long breath, stared through the window a moment, then turned back to Francisco. "She's tall, not as willowy a she once was, before the birth of our children. When she lets her hair down, it is thick, auburn, with just a hint of the Scottish red and it hangs below her waist. Her manner is gracious and wise. She was educated by her grandfather with the help of many. She's well read and has the wit to view history and the humanities with humor and insightfulness. I don't know if I love her mind most or her body. I hope I can see her again before we both grow old."

The conversation lasted through two more beers each. On parting, Francisco slapped McGirtt on the back and said, "Don't forget , my friend. If you find any more unharvested indigo, be sure to contact your friend Francisco. That was a nice arrangement… and it netted you five hundred pounds of British Sterling."

"You shouldn't have paid me," Daniel asserted. "I didn't do that to get paid. I did it so those people wouldn't lose their entire crop."

"Whatever your reasons," Francisco rationalized, "it was a welcome bargain that I would be happy to enter into again."

ങ ഌ

The Battles of Georgia

"Wars and rumors of war. " McGirtt sat high on Grey Goose, headed in the direction of the so-called fort where he had been humiliated. The cool weather sat well with him as it did for the rest of his merry men. There were dispossessed South Carolinians, freed slaves, trained British troops, fifty or so Creek Indians whom Wakapuchasce had insisted he bring with him with the comment that if they found any Spanish that his braves could do the killing in his name. Daniel's mind wandered. In the Colony of Georgia, his men were bound to the north for Savannah, named for the Savano Indians who, farther north, were known as Shawnee. But Daniel's mind was in Camden where his wife Mary was staying with Daniel's sister Elizabeth and her husband John. His comment stemmed from a fleeting daydream about the last time he sat in church. The Minister, that day, read from Matthew 24:6.

Patrick Alcorn rode beside him that day. Daniel glanced over at him; Alcorn seemed to be reading his thoughts, because he finished the passage: "...See that ye not be troubled: for all these things must come to pass, but the end is not yet."

Alcorn was obviously the worse for wear; his once immaculately clean uniform now bore smudges of dust from his horse's sides, mud from the endless east Georgia muck and the occasional splatter of blood where he had killed attacking mosquitoes. Aside from the discomforts of the trail, Alcorn's demeanor was light and happy, except when he spoke of the fighting ahead. "So. We're going to ambush the Continental Army just south of Midway, are we? I hope they haven't heard about it and are waiting to ambush us."

McGirtt turned his attention back to the trail and the horses and men ahead of them. This action was being directed by Lt. Colonel Thomas Browne, whom McGirtt disliked and distrusted. Brown suffered from continual headaches. In his small community, north of Augusta, the patriots who called themselves The Liberty Boys took issue with the fact that Browne chose to remain a Tory. They scalped him, hanged him, burned him and shot him. He nearly died but, defying the inevitable, he escaped to Florida where Tonyn, thrilled by Browne's hatred of the patriot cause in Georgia, made him a Lieutenant Colonel in the Florida Rangers and sent him to Georgia to fight for Great Britain. *Since Georgia is his battleground, we are under his direction.* "Hey Alcorn." McGirtt looked to his side again. "Do you think Browne is insane?"

Alcorn shifted uncomfortably in his saddle. "I don't think this is a safe subject. I just think he's in pain much of the time and his nasty attitude stems from that rather than from some mental disorder. Of course, constant pain can make a man a little crazy. Do you think he's insane?"

"I don't know." Daniel felt uncomfortable with the subject, too. "I think he's certainly obsessed with defeating the Americans. Maybe that's what it takes be successful in such an enterprise. Tonyn certainly likes him."

Having arrived at their destination on the shores of Blackbeard's Creek, they bivouacked their horses. In the general silence of the place, they could hear movement approaching from the west. The order quickly circulated to remain absolutely quiet and take up positions behind the large live oak trees and prepare to fire from cover. The Florida Rangers had profited from hard experience with the Native Americans about how to fight in forest cover, but these Patriot troops, under the command of a former British officer, had obviously not yet learned. Traditionally, British troops lined up with row after row of soldiers with single-shot muskets. The front row would kneel and fire. Then the next row would step through their line while the first line reloaded, presenting an almost constant line of fire with a systematic advance. The second line would then kneel and fire after which the next line would step ahead and fire while the previous line reloaded. Although effective in Europe, this battle technique positioned them like ducks in a shooting gallery, allowing seasoned guerilla forest fighters like McGirtt, Browne, Cunningham and Mayfield to pick them off one by one. The Creeks were naturals, almost instinctively flanking the enemy's barrage attack to snipe viciously from the rear and sides. Patriot General Screven's men didn't stand a chance. Screven himself took eleven musket balls but amazingly didn't die until the next day. The Patriots retreated and Sunbury became British once again.

⌘ ⌘

McGirtt perched unhappily on a log in front of a small campfire, toasting a cotton-tail rabbit on a stick over the fire. Cunningham and Mayfield sipped coffee as they sat on "natural stools;" tree stumps that were hard on the butt, a bit damp, and either too tall or too short. Mayfield, a thick, stocky man of Liverpool with black curly hair on the sides of his head and bare skin on top, wore a hat "to keep the bugs off my head." His plantation was situated on the west side of the St. Johns River, just north of Pilotaikita where a very convenient trading post handled the purchase and sale of the vast amounts of indigo from Mayfield's farm. Cunningham's land skirted the east shore of the river, far south of Maxton Island, the land Tonyn had promised to McGirtt, if the adventure was adequately profitable. Cunningham's interest focused more on cattle and lumber, and he devoted a lot of energy to experimenting with manufacturing of pine tar and turpentine which he sold to boat builders as wood preservative and sealant. Cunningham's vast pine forests on the banks of the river were continually tapped for their juices much as sugar maples are tapped farther north for their sweet syrup. They were farmers all: King Cotton, Indigo and Pine trees joining hands to fight a common foe, liberty seekers from the monarchy of Great Britain, traitors to the crown. *On the other hand,* McGirtt pondered, *the Crown has been exceptionally good to us in return for our loyalty. They have become landed gentlemen, as I will be if the campaign is successful.*

Mayfield broke the silence. Standing and stretching, he yawned, spit and said, "So where we going next, boys? Savannah? I hear General Prevost already has that secured so if we go there we won't have much of a fight."

None of them wanted conversation this early in the morning. McGirtt ignored the question and continued roasting his breakfast. Cunningham, after coughing a few times offered, "Browne wants to go inland on the way and engage Fort MacIntosh. Of course, that's a bit to the west so it will be a couple of extra days travel time to Savannah."

This got McGirtt's interest. "What does he want with Fort MacIntosh? There's nothing there to speak of, just an isolated outpost on the Satilla River."

Cunningham replied, "Colonel Browne says it blocks transportation up the River. It's not a major trade route but it *is* a trade route and we need it to get supplies on the way to Augusta. The Continental Army still holds Augusta, but it won't for long, especially if we can get supplies up the Satilla to support troops. Fort MacIntosh is a roadblock on the Satilla River. We're going to end that."

McGirtt turned his rabbit over the fire to roast the other side. The browning meat looked good to him but it wouldn't be ready to eat for a little while longer. He glanced at Alcorn, who was in the process of consuming some concoction he had made using thick crusted bread and salted meat he brought with him. "What do you think, Patrick? Will we find Captain John Barker there?" McGirtt smiled at the thought.

☙ ❧

Fort MacIntosh stood in a compromised spot. The desire was to guard the approaches on the river from both directions, on a bend of the river, but the land was too low, marshy and subject to flooding when the heavy rains came. The higher land stood too far back from the river to afford the views of the approaches, so the fort stood in between the marsh and the higher land, where the view wasn't quite as good, but it would not flood except in the heaviest of weather. That its location was lower than most of the surrounding land gave advantage to the Florida Rangers who slipped in quietly with their Indian companions. As part of his war effort, Cunningham had insisted on bringing a short two wheel wagon, pulled by a donkey, all the way from his plantation on the St. Johns River. Getting the wagon across the various rivers the army had to traverse made the trek more difficult, but Cunningham insisted that the wagon continue with them.

"What's in the donkey cart?" McGirtt asked Cunningham when they first met, at the St. Mary's River, just north of St. Augustine. "Why do we have to muscle that across every stream and gully? We have enough food in our packs and we can replenish it easily, most of the time."

Cunningham smiled at the question. He looked up at McGirtt and, smiling more broadly, replied, "Turpentine, my friend. Turpentine. It's stored in glass wine bottles, and each bottle is wrapped nicely so they won't bump into each other and break."

"We have no ships to paint in Georgia," McGirtt quipped. "Why the turpentine?"

Cunningham turned, but before he walked away he said, "You'll see."

Now McGirtt saw. The Rangers crept up on the fort in the wee hours of the morning. There was a sentry posted on each corner of the fort that they could see from the higher elevation. Three of the sentries appeared to be asleep while the fourth one had his eyes fixed on the river. Cunningham softly called for his donkey cart, stopped a respectful distance from the overview so that its noise wouldn't alert the sentries. Two bottles at a time, Cunninghams' men brought the bottles to the front. Others circled around to the sides of the fort, each carrying two bottles of turpentine. Cunningham's signal was the first bottle. He removed the cork from the bottle, inserted a short piece of cloth that he allowed to soak up some of the liquid. Then he touched a glowing ember to the soaked cloth and heaved the bottle with great strength over the wall of the fort. When it landed, the bottle broke, releasing the turpentine, which virtually exploded into a large wild fire. As soon as the light from the wick began its trajectory over the wall, numerous other bottles from the two other directions followed suit. Shortly, many streams of light could be seen sailing through the air from the forest around fort. In seconds, Fort MacIntosh was engulfed in flame.

Screams of the men inside the fort were testimony to the brutality of the attack. The fort's drawbridge came crashing down with men surging out upon it before its far end even hit the ground. Their escape, thwarted by musket fire from the hundreds of Florida Rangers stationed in front of the building, completed the destruction of this outpost. The only ranger who received an injury had burned his fingers by getting some of the turpentine on them before he lighted the fuse.

Not very many Patriots survived to surrender, but those who did were seated meekly on the banks of the Satilla River, not far from where their fort once stood. When the fire subsided enough, McGirtt, Alcorn and Mayfield entered the burned-out structure. The smell of turpentine, replaced by the odor of burning wood and flesh disgusted McGirtt. "This is sickening," McGirtt said over and over as they counted the bodies of the men who had burned to death in their attack. "Sickening!"

Lieutenant Colonel Thomas Browne entered the fort behind them to appraise the results of the attack. On hearing McGirtt's lamentation he snapped. "This is *war*, McGirtt. Our job is to kill the enemy. That's what our job is. We did a good job. Killing is always sickening. But you'll get used to it."

5

1779-1879

Great Britain was at war in South Africa: The Xhosa Wars with the Boer settlers.

1779

February 3 – Patriot Major General Moultrie defeated the British detachment at Port Royal Island in South Carolina.

February 14 – Patriots Andrew Pickens and Elijah Clarke defeated the British at Kettle Creek, Georgia.

March 3 – British Lt. Colonel Jacques Marcus Prevost defeated the Patriots under General John Ashe at Brier Creek, Georgia.

May 11-13 – Major General Augustine Prevost (Brother of Jacques) broke his siege of Augusta at the approach of Patriot Major General Lincoln.

June 20 – Patriot Major General Lincoln inflicted extensive casualties on British troops at Stono River, South Carolina, in an indecisive battle.

June 21 – Spain declared war on Great Britain, joining the Patriot cause. The Siege of Gibraltar began.

September 23 – John Paul Jones, aboard the *Bonhomme Richard*, captured the British man-of-war *Serapis* off the British Coast.

September 28 – The Tappan Massacre – "No Flint" Grey killed thirty Americans by bayonet.

October 9 – American attempt to recapture Savannah failed.

Savannah, 1779

Mud paths, giant live oaks, huge old long needle pine trees, mosquitoes and snakes provided an exciting passage. The approach to Savannah compared nicely with the rest of the land north and south as far as McGirtt could recollect. The North Florida land he remembered as more marshy with gently rising sand hills, populated by that amusing bird with the harsh, hooting call - the red headed sand hill crane. "This is more like home," McGirtt remarked to Alcorn, riding next to him on a tall chestnut mare. "The land is higher, drier and rockier, but where's this famous City of Savannah. Is it small and primitive like St. Augustine? What are we to expect?"

A mockingbird swooped out of a nearby tree, taking a peck at McGirtt's hat and hissing like a cat. McGirtt chuckled at the bird's audacity and kneed his horse to a slightly faster pace to get out of the bird's territory. With that, the bird took a swipe at Alcorn before retiring to the treetops. "The mockingbird is a Patriot," Alcorn quipped. ..."a rebellious, insignificant colonist, taking potshots from a safe distance."

"They may seem like that." Smiling, McGirtt glanced back over his shoulder to see where the bird had gone. "But if there are enough of them, they can put up quite a defense or even an offensive."

"Then they run and hide," Alcorn added.

"The Colonists have had some major victories over us." McGirtt stopped smiling as he turned his face to Alcorn. "George III has his hands full with this one. He's fighting in South Africa, North Africa. He just won a very expensive war against Spain a few years ago and now Spain has thrown its hat in the ring with the Colonists. So, we're at war again with the French and the Spanish as well the colonies in Africa and the Americas. George has his hands full."

Alcorn continued in silence for a few minutes, then almost as though talking to himself, muttered, "This rebellion wasn't George's fault. It was Parliament that enacted the Stamp Act and the Townsend Duties.

That's what started making everyone so angry."

"Yes," McGirtt sighed. "But it was the Tea Act that really set them off - like a powder keg. And now there is a war and we are sent to defend King George's City of Savannah. There she is, by the way." They stopped to peruse the scene. The view, partly obscured by the many oak trees planted at the order of James Oglethorpe some years ago, revealed colorfully painted two story homes with cedar shingled roofs, neatly cared for gardens and dirt streets, as far as they could see. "We can't see much of it because of the contour of the land and the foliage. I wonder how they're going to receive the motley crew that we are. Take a look at us."

Alcorn and McGirtt glanced back at the troops, such as they were, following them. Ahaya's braves, clad in deerskin and homespun, mixed freely with the cotton clothing of the refugees from the northern colonies who had joined them when the Banishment and Confiscations Acts of Georgia, South Carolina, North Carolina and Virginia were passed. These acts of the Colonial legislatures, at the encouragement of the Continental Congress, provided for any and all remaining loyal to the crown to be evicted from the colony and their goods confiscated. Some, like Colonel Browne, had been tortured and threatened with hanging when they refused to leave. "The idiots actually scalped Browne before he got away, and fractured his skull, so he says. He suffers from severe headaches even yet." McGirtt shook his head in disbelief. Quite a few of the refugees fled to British Florida and, being destitute, joined the East Florida Rangers. Others hid out in the swamps and became bandits and robbers, living like Indians, off the land. Governor Tonyn quaintly referred to them as "banditti." "Right now, it's still summer," McGirtt remarked. "But when winter comes, those men are going to have to find warmer clothing than they now have. North Florida gets cold enough, but this is Georgia. There may even be snow."

The Cock and Bull Inn stood defiantly under Savannah's stony bluff overlooking the bay. Its walls, cut from the sandstone quarries not far away, supported a steep wooden hip roof covered in slabs of wood for shingles. Tall ships, some merchantmen and some built for war, rode at anchor on the gentle chops before them. McGirtt could see a frigate, in the distance, standing for the inner bay with four masts blossoming in white and a gentle bow wave of white spume rising beneath its bowsprit. Men hung over the rails trying to get a better glimpse of America's Georgia metropolis. Half way up the main mast a watchman shouted steering commands to the helmsman. McGirtt could almost hear his voice. Other sailors scurried like monkeys up the ratlines readying themselves to reduce sail. McGirtt turned his attention to the

Cock and Bull Inn.

The sign, bearing the image of a rooster perched on the horn of a bull's head, dangled precariously above the door. Sounds of loud voices and laughter poured from the entrance and open windows. The smell of stale spilled beer wafted through the air. Cigar butts, broken glass and pottery littered the stone-paved street beneath McGirtt's feet. He turned to his companions, Patrick Alcorn, William "Bloody Bill" Cunningham of the turpentine farm and Charlton Peabody Fenton from Glastonbury in the Somerset Hills. Fenton, a tall, lean, pale-faced man with a short goatee, had just received a promotion to major and seemed determined to prove himself worthy. McGirtt and Cunningham treated the fact that Fenton invited himself to join them with tolerant amusement. Alcorn knew the dynamic of the situation but kept silent to see how this was going to play out, his eyes twinkling and no smile on his lips.

As they entered the establishment, a portly waiter with a towel over his shoulder and a tray of beer mugs called out to them, "Seat yourselves, boys," as he hurried past. His long greasy hair and stained clothing spoke of a certain consistency with the architecture and overall ambience of the dining room. Kicking litter out of the way, McGirtt carefully picked a path to an empty table not far from a window. With a round of beer on the table, served in tall stoneware mugs, McGirtt leaned back for a moment, relieved that the journey was over for the time being and that a moment of respite was finally at hand. "The beer is good, despite the surroundings," he chuckled.

He lifted is beer and quoted, "Here's to the breezes that blows through the treeses, lifts the girls' skirts above their kneeses and shows the spot that pleases all over the land of the freeses, by Jesus."

After a round of howling laughter and a heavy quaff of the local brew, Cunningham raised his glass and continued the toasts. "Here's to you and here's to me and may we never disagree but if we do, piss on you. Here's to me."

Following another round of laugher and another heavy quaff, Fenton chimed in with, "Friends my come and friends may go, and some just peter out, you know. But peter out or peter in, may you always be my friends."

The laughter was interrupted by a voice heavily accented and obviously from south London. "Who's the bloody Scot? I heard the goddamn brogue. Is it you?" He indicated McGirtt. McGirtt's party stopped laughing and watched in amazement.

McGirtt, not to have his good time spoiled by stupidity, graciously answered. "I was born in South Carolina but learned the language of the King at the knees of my parents. They were born and raised in Renfrew in the bonnie land of the thistle and the heather, but we're all British subjects, here, my friend. Allow us to buy your table a round of beer?"

"Screw your beer, you bloody bastard. My family was robbed by yours and I'll have none of your kind too close. By the way, Scotty, I never did learn what a Scotty keeps under his kilt. Would you mind tellin' me? I bet there's nothin' there!"

McGirtt was growing disgruntled. "If you must know or you must check," McGirtt's voice was growing into a gentle snarl, "you'll discover what we carry is the bagpipe. If you had a set, you'd probably be more mannerly. I've heard that men from London can't even sound the pipes. Care to show us if that's true?" Alcorn said nothing, but he suspected when he saw Daniels right hand slip quietly under the table what was about to happen.

The Londoner, it could be clearly seen, took a moment to process the insult. After a few seconds his eyes grew wide in fury and he said, "You son of a bitch."

McGirtt, not to be found wanting for speech, immediately replied, "I'm sorry sir. You are mistaken. I am not your brother."

The drunk Londoner stood taller than McGirtt by several inches – and he did so suddenly. With one movement, he swept his sword out of its sheath. He was ruddy-faced, sandy-haired, portly and big. The sword continued its ascent until he held it over his head with both hands. He lunged toward McGirtt, swinging the sword down with all his considerable strength. Daniel stood just as suddenly. With his left hand he raised his chair, sweeping it up and to the left, violently blocking the sword thrust aimed at his head. With his right hand, he thrust his Skyn Dhu into the man's midsection, aimed slightly up, under the ribs, to touch the heart. The man's mouth dropped open. His eyes bulged. He stood there stunned for just a few seconds before collapsing to the floor.

The room was immediately silent with all eyes turned to McGirtt, chair in one hand, black handled dagger in the other, staring at the dead man on the floor, then at the others at the dead man's table. Daniel put the chair back on the floor, leaned over, wiping the blood from his Skyn Dhu on the dead man's shirt before returning it to the sheath under his cloak. "How about that round of beer I offered to buy?"

Savannah was a rough place in those days. It is yet.

☙ ❧

Brigadier General Augustine Prevost sat contemplatively studying the view of the Savannah River and the access to the sea through the Savannah Inlet, far to the right of his direct view. His swivel chair, upholstered with shining leather and obviously heavy cushioning, faced the windows. Daniel McGirtt, observing him from the entrance to Prevost's office, smiled at the luxury the general was enjoying, consisting of a few moments of leisure, a comfortable chair, a clay pipe with, no doubt, Virginia tobacco. One of the two armed guards outside the General's office door softly cleared his throat to get Prevost's attention. Prevost swiveled his chair around to face them. It was a wizened face, lined and weary. His wig sat just so on his probably baldhead. It was sitting back far enough to reveal a deep indentation on the left side of Prevost's forehead. McGirtt remembered his father talking of Prevost's wound.

"He was shot right in the head," Colonel James McGirtt had related. "We thought he was dead for sure. It was a musket ball, but he must have one hell of a hard head. The damned thing bounced off, but it left a big dent. He wears it like a badge of honor, and it surely is."

The guard introduced the visitors. "Brigadier General Augustine Prevost, may I present Lieutenant Colonels Daniel McGirtt, William Cunningham and Stephen Mayfield of the East Florida Rangers?"

Prevost rose from his chair, nodded his head politely and said, "Please come in, gentlemen. I have heard so much about you." Daniel felt that Prevost's crooked smile was genuine but with an edge, lips favoring one side over the other. After they were all seated, Prevost went into the small talk warm-up required by polite meetings. When he was satisfied that he had been polite enough he went to the subjects at hand.

"I understand two of you, McGirtt and Cunningham, have something interesting in common, aside from being refugees to Florida and subsequent members of the East Florida Rangers."

"What would that be, sir?" Cunningham queried.

Prevost smiled, leaned back in his chair and continued. "Both of you at the onset of the war signed on with the Continental Army, our enemies. Both of you were whipped for insubordination; McGirtt because a superior officer tried to commandeer your horse and Cunningham because your terms of recruitment were being violated. Both of you escaped your confinement and both immigrated – I'm trying to avoid the word 'fled' – to East Florida. There you agreed to serve the King, as you should have done in the first place. I'm particularly surprised at you, McGirtt. I know your father, James. We served in the Seven Years War on the French Indian front in Canada. He's certainly an honorable man and certainly loyal to the country of his birth. Why did you choose to side with the Colonists?"

Cunningham cleared his throat quietly and spoke up. "May I be so bold, sir, as to answer for both of us?"

Prevost raised his chin slightly, turning his attention from McGirtt to the other and said, "Please do."

"Like most of the colonists, we felt the taxes enacted serendipitously by Parliament to be not only illegal but gratuitously unfair. King George did not approve the taxes nor condone them, but the law was the law and we were forced to obey. Both of us were carried away by popular sentiment and felt we had to play a part. Both of us immediately realized our error, recognizing through profoundly dishonorable treatment, that the Colonists had been away from civilized society for too long. They were becoming wild men. Both of us came to our senses under the sting of the lash and retreated to land governed under a more gentile and sensible manner. Since then, we have served the Crown with distinction, according to our superiors, sincerely regretting our former indiscretions."

Prevost was not a boy. His smile hinted to McGirtt that this man knew bullshit not only by the sound but by the smell as well. Daniel glanced at Cunningham in surprise, not only at the well-turned phrase but at the cheek of the man. Well, maybe what he said was at least partly true. The truth was that the outrages perpetrated on the two demanded retribution. The rationalization was true too, but a rationalization, nevertheless, for what they both really wanted – revenge. For a passing moment, it amused McGirtt to understand, at least fleetingly, that both of them had come to believe in the rationalization. Were things good under British Rule? Yes. Would things be better with the United States of America acting as an independent nation? Who could tell? From what Daniel had seen and Cunningham had seen, the answer was "perhaps not."

The brigadier general turned his attention, now, to Daniel. "Does he speak for you?"

Daniel smiled before answering. "He does, but I think it's only fair to add that the outrageous treatment we both received would never have occurred under more civilized rule. We were both treated unfairly, villainously and unconscionably. To acquiesce to it by remaining loyal to that service was out of the question."

Prevost seemed either satisfied with their answers or weary of the subject; maybe both. "I have orders for you. I have requested to be relieved of duty and to be permitted to retire. Brigadier General George Garth is being sent to replace me. He is a very capable commander. I'm sure you will appreciate that once you get to know him. In the meantime, we must carry on the war. I have been ordered to send forces north, crossing the land between here and Charleston. We are to fight a war of devastation. The intention is to remove the ability of the rebels to support troops and to so demoralize them that they either come to their senses and return to the Crown or they flee into the wilderness and disappear. Either way, it removes the threat that they become a factor in the defense of their cause.

"I have chosen you three to lead this effort. You will march at the end of the week or sooner if you're ready. You will burn every house, village, church, blacksmith's shop – everything between here and Charleston. Once you have passed, nothing should be left standing, especially crops. You will confiscate all property including cattle, horses, slaves, gold, books, silver plates that they eat off of and the cutlery they use for eating. You will leave no gold, silver, art works, antiques – nothing. Kill anyone who resists – with prejudice. No excuse will serve for resisting. No quarter will be granted for any reason. Burn everything. Confiscate everything. Do you understand? – all the way to Charleston. You will be like land based privateers. You may keep the value of one quarter of what you confiscate. The rest you will deliver to us here at Savannah. From here we will dispose of the property as the King sees fit."

The three men wore shades of gray in their complexions as they left the general's office. What horrendous orders! *We are to lay waste to the lives and property of thousands of people!* McGirtt did not like the idea.

"By the way, McGirtt," Prevost called to them as they left the office. "Quite a turn of the phrase, there at the Inn, you know. Can he sound the pipes or not?" As they turned down the hall from the General's office, they could still hear him laughing.

6

1779

September–October – American Forces failed to recover the city of Savannah held under the authority of Brigadier General Augustine Prevost.

1780

May 12 – British captured Charleston, South Carolina

August 6 – Patriots defeated the Tories at Hanging Rock, South Carolina.

Augustine 16 – British, under Cornwallis, defeated Americans at Camden, South Carolina.

October 7 – King's Mountain, South Carolina: Patriots defeated Major Patrick Ferguson and one third of Cornwallis's army.

October 14 – Washington named Nathaniel Greene commander of the southern armies.

Patriot installations directly across the river from Savannah persuaded McGirtt and Cunningham to make their way west, to where they could cross the river without dodging gunfire. The resistance wasn't heavy, but, "there's no point in taking fire while we're defenselessly riding barges out in the open. I prefer to choose my battles more carefully." Feathery seeds floated in the air, everywhere. McGirtt brushed some off his shirt as he spoke. "What kind of seeds are these, anyway?"

Cunningham rode beside him with several thousand troops behind them. The troops were freed slaves, Creek Indians from Wakapuchasce's villages as well as others who had joined the British forces. Others of the Rangers' warriors included planters from Georgia and South and North Carolina, driven from their land by the angry sentiment of their neighbors, the Patriot Colonists. Those rode their own horses, carried their own guns and brought enough of their own food to last a week or longer. None were pleased with the orders but all understood.

"Let me see if I got this right," Alcorn asked, as they rode out of Savannah. "Charleston is held by the Whigs. Augusta is held by the Whigs. Both of these cities are supplied with food and other things from the plantations in the surrounding area that are owned by their fellow rebels. Am I right so far?"

"Yes." McGirtt's answer was brief.

"Our job is to make sure that those plantations that are supplying the Whigs in these cities can no longer do that."

"That's right," Cunningham answered. "But not only that – Prevost wants us to make sure they are completely dispirited. He wants us to crush their will to fight by destroying their lives. That is exactly what we are going to do."

Alcorn furrowed his brow, imagining what was to come. He noticed McGirtt, head lowered, frowning at the ground. Alcorn barely heard McGirtt muttering, "May God forgive us."

On the north side of the Savannah River, Bloody Bill Cunningham and his men rode west and north. McGirtt and his forces turned east, picking their way along the cart-paths and trails along the river. The first chore was to remove the snipers on the north side of the Savannah River. Resistance was scattered and light. "They take a shot and run," McGirtt complained.

"Like Indians, hiding behind trees," Alcorn agreed. "One shot and they're gone, mostly to another tree, down range where they can take time to reload and wait for us." Alcorn had experienced a near miss. Just after a limb was shot out of a tree next to his head, he heard the bang of the musket. "Duck when you see the puffs of smoke. It's all the warning we're going to get before the ball arrives."

McGirtt sweated under the hot July Georgia sun. They all did. "I don't know which is worse; the yellow flies, the mosquitoes or the musket balls. Which bite is fiercest?"

"The mosquitoes seem to bring disease." Alcorn answered. "The yellow flies bring pain and distraction as we try to swat them away. The musket balls, I think, are the fiercest. It's lucky they don't have wings like the other pests." Another musket ball whizzed between them.

McGirtt dismounted, signaling those behind him to do the same. "It will be better if we walk our horses instead of providing such wonderful targets, mounted on their backs."

It took little more than a few minutes to overcome the resistance at the wharf across from the city, resulting in seventeen dead Colonists and one wounded Florida Ranger. It was Jeffrey Mickler from the San Mateo area, across the St. Johns River from Pilotaikita, as the Creeks called Palatka in those days. The first plantation to be burned stood just north of the river with lands fronting the rivers and bays, north of the city. McGirtt and his men rode onto the land at a slow walk, waiting for resistance to appear. When none did, after searching the houses for people and valuables, they set fire to everything and waited to make sure nothing would be left standing. McGirtt's forces waited for his signal to continue north and east, but Daniel sat there on Grey Goose, arms crossed, almost as though he were hugging himself. Alcorn rode up beside him and Daniel acknowledged him with a grunt. "There's plenty of cotton and indigo in those fields," Daniel indicated with a wave of his hand. "Order the men to set fire to those as well."

"Whose place do you suppose this is, Daniel?" Alcorn, not as overcome with the destruction as Daniel obviously was, frowned at the heavy smoke and waited.

"There's no name on the gate." Daniel glanced at the path to the plantation's grand entrance. "It must belong to Loyalists who fled to Florida as we did. I wonder if they'll ever come home to this. At least, no one else will be able to use it to support the fight against us. We'll make camp for the night once we get away from this smoke."

The next plantation, only a mile north, had vegetables, cattle, vast fields of cotton, indigo and marsh dammed off for rice. Slaves in the fields wielded rakes and hoes. They were loosening the soil around the plants, doing general weeding and some were picking ripe produce. "Round up the slaves," Daniel ordered. "Have them leave their rakes and hoes and shovels on the ground where you find them. We don't need gardening tools. Collect them outside the plantation fences and hold them over there."

Just then a man emerged from the plantation house, easily visible ahead of them. He was unarmed. Behind him, several women and more slaves appeared from the house and waited behind while the man approached. McGirtt spurred Gray Goose toward the man.

"Exactly what the hell do you think you're doing with my slaves?" The man wore a long sleeved white shirt with a ruffled collar, straight slacks and highly polished leather boots that McGirtt decided he must have bought in England. *They certainly don't make boots like that around here.*

"And who might you be?" McGirtt inquired politely.

The man drew himself up to his full height and forced to look upward at McGirtt sitting on his horse announced, "I am Evan MacRoe. I own this plantation and the slaves you are removing. I demand that you release them so they can return to their labor."

"I am very sorry, Mr. MacRoe," Daniel replied with tight lips. "I am Lieutenant Colonel Daniel McGirtt of the East Florida Rangers and I have been ordered by Brigadier General Augustine Prevost to lay waste to this area. That means, if you value your life and the lives of your family, you will immediately vacate the premises and never allow me to lay eyes on you again, for if I do I will surely lay waste to you as well. Leave the house slaves. Take only your family."

MacRoe's eyes grew wide in fury. His face went from its tan to a much darker shade leaning violently toward red. "Get the hell off my land, you son of Satan or I'll tear your head off with my own hands." A dagger appeared in the man's right hand. MacRoe began to approach McGirtt with rapid steps that were halted suddenly at the sound of a musket shot from just beside Daniel. McGirtt glanced to his side, annoyed that MacRoe had been cut down. *Maybe he could have been saved.* The musket smoked in the hand of one Private Bradley Stevens, who with a dozen others, had followed McGirtt as he approached the main house.

"I'm sorry, sir. We're here to make sure you are safe. He had a knife and was coming for you."

Daniel dismounted Gray Goose. "Be at peace, soldier. I understand you did your duty." MacRoe lay belly down in the reddish soil, his face to one side. He was gasping. The musket ball had left an exit wound in the man's back that poured red, staining the already reddish soil. Daniel knelt beside the man and said, "I'm sorry, MacRoe. This has to be done."

MacRoe, still full of fight, although not so full of strength, managed to gasp, "I'll be with God's army when He comes for you, you vile bastard."

Daniel remained for the last few minutes it took for the man's eyes to glaze into the stare of death. At the sound of the shot, a woman came running from the porch. The house slaves kept the children with them at the main dwelling. Her shrieking drew Daniel's attention from the site of the death's last gasp. "Private Stevens. Restrain that woman until she calms down. Please don't shed any more blood unless you absolutely must. We aren't here to kill civilians. We're here to demoralize them. We want them to come to their senses and return their loyalty to the Crown, not to die."

"Yessir." Stevens, with a wave of his hand, took three others to help him.

At the east end of the property, Daniel could see a wooden tower. He shaded his eyes to look more carefully. "Hey, Alcorn. What do you suppose that is? It looks like an observation tower. Do you think they can see the ocean from here?"

The tower stood some sixty feet above the cotton field below. At the top, McGirtt and Alcorn strained their eyes to the east, over the trees. "It was certainly decent of MacRoe to provide us with this tower," McGirtt remarked. "From here we can see the layout of the land pretty well. Look to the north. There are more plantations scattered out as far as we can see. What's that to the east?"

Alcorn, still obviously shaken by the violence of MacRoe's death, answered in grim tones. "I think it's what they call Hilton Head Island, discovered by Captain William Hilton under sail for King Charles II. To the south is Daufuskie Island. At least, that's what my map says."

"Look at the fields on Hilton Head. I suppose we're going to have to go over there and to the other island, as well."

Alcorn shuddered. "This is grim business."

"Grim indeed," McGirtt muttered. "These people won't forget my name for hundreds of years. It's too bad it isn't the name of the man who ordered it that will be remembered, Brigadier General Augustine Prevost. But he did what he had to do. Now we will do the same. King and country. George will prevail."

"At what cost?" Alcorn had begun the descent from the tower.

"Blood and treasure," McGirtt responded. "Blood and treasure. That is the price of all wars."

McGirtt remained on top of the tower for a few more minutes, gazing to the west. The smoke was so thick in the distance that it struck him as the heavy clouds of a gathering storm. *I can see Cunningham is doing the same as I am. It's thick where we just were and thick where he is. South Carolina will never be the same.*

The next plantation stood just a mile north of MacRoe's. The house, a gracious two story frame structure with a wide porch and ivory painted columns had fresh, sky blue paint on its clapboard sides. From the second floor roof sprouted a small round tower which, if the house had been closer to the sea, would have been called a "captain's walk," or a "widow's walk," depending on who was home at the time. Numerous outbuildings included a cookhouse; a blacksmith shed; two large barns, one for livestock and one for storing grain and the produce collected at harvest time. At the far side of the field behind the main house, slave cottages lined the border – *far enough away,* McGirtt frowned at the thought, *that they wouldn't have to smell them from the main house. It's a shame the slaves can't be provided with bathing facilities like their owners have.*

Resistance presented itself clearly in the form of the plantation owner and three young men, probably his sons, on horseback, armed with swords and muskets who rode out to the gate to meet them. The muskets were respectfully pointed at the ground, but clearly cocked and ready to fire. The older man looked vaguely familiar to McGirtt and as he approached, Daniel knew him. "Well," McGirtt called out as soon as he felt he was within earshot. "If it isn't my old friend, Captain John Barker!"

"Dirt McGirtt! By the gods! You're making quite a name for yourself, Dirt. News travels fast around here."

"Indeed, Barker. The clouds of smoke you see to the south are from my campfires. When we burn your place, we'll have a barbecue." Barker's face grew even darker than it had been when he recognized McGirtt. "Choose!" McGirtt told Barker. "Poverty – or death to all of your family. What will it be, Barker? You and your sons best uncock those muskets and do it very gently and immediately."

Barker glanced around at the more than fifty men who were kneeling all around McGirtt, their muskets focused on him and his sons. He knew, and McGirtt could see the shift in his expression as it happened, that this battle would be hopeless. "So dismount your horses, you and your sons. Go back to the house and collect your families, under guard of course. I will permit you to walk away unharmed, but if you provide resistance, I will happily order you shot, all of you."

"Do as he says, boys." They uncocked their weapons and dismounted. They unbuckled their swords, dropped them on the ground and with three armed British soldiers each, they walked back toward the tall blue house where there were women and children watching apprehensively from the veranda.

Turning to Alcorn, McGirtt ordered, "Have all the cattle, horses and slaves collected, over there just beyond the front gate. Have the cattle and horses driven to the meeting point we discussed on the next river, north. Sanchez should be there in a few more days with one or two of his brigantines to transport these spoils of war to market." McGirtt dismounted from Gray Goose and, leading the horse toward the house muttered, still within Alcorn's hearing, "Francisco will have to be protected from Ahaya's men. There are quite a few of them with us."

Alcorn glanced to the next field where the braves of Wakapuchasce, very experienced in handling cattle, were herding the livestock of Captain John Barker to join what had been taken from MacRoe and the other plantations that had been burned in the last few days.

McGirtt ordered that Barker and his family be kept near the gate, within sight of the house as they burned it and all the outbuildings. He stayed with them for a short time before releasing them to go wherever they could find shelter, if they could. "How can you do this to us, McGirtt? Do you hate me so much? You were insubordinate. What did you expect?"

"Barker," McGirtt's lips were drawn tight and his speech came in clipped tones. "If it were just me, I would not do this to you and your family. I would not even kill you. But I would beat you to within an inch of your life for the whipping you gave me. I still feel inclined to do that, but in view of what I have been ordered to do to you, I will allow you to go away uninjured, unless you force me to take some other action by resisting us. If you do that, I will take grim pleasure in the result."

The family watched in horrified silence as the roof on their beautiful two story plantation house collapsed onto the second floor, then that floor collapsed and the fire roared suddenly high enough that they could feel the heat even as far away as they stood watching it. Barker's wife sobbed pitifully. His sons stood helplessly watching, all still under armed guard. McGirtt mounted Gray Goose and rode away with a contingent of soldiers behind and beside him. Alcorn rode at the rear.

As McGirtt rode away, he heard Barker shouting loudly, "McGirtt! I'm going to hunt you down and kill you, if it's the last thing I ever do!"

McGirtt reigned in Gray Goose and turning in his saddle, he called back, "Barker, if you try, it might *be* the last thing you ever do!"

The days wore on. Fire after fire burned their way into McGirtt's mind. Elegant plantation house after house littered the ground in ashes. Burned crops, burned cooking houses, barns and slave cottages filled his days and haunted his nights. Lowing cattle, the voices of confiscated slaves, the sounds of devastation, heartbreak and ruin of hundreds of people hardened him. At first, he would lose his meals. He had little appetite for what he was doing or for food. Alcorn chided him about losing weight. "Your face is growing lean. Your clothes just hang on you. You must eat!" So eat he did.

"Butcher another one of those steers," he would say, "and make sure the slaves eat as well as we do!"

Francisco Sanchez rode aboard the first of the brigantines that arrived in Port Royal Sound to collect the booty. McGirtt was glad to see him. Not as tall as McGirtt, Francisco was obviously astonished when he saw the herds of cattle and the vast number of slaves to be transported. "This will take many trips and more ships," he observed, mumbling to himself, computing the logistics of the situation. "We'll load up the slaves first," he said. "They have by far the highest value. I can sell them in the West Indies. I'll send three more ships for the cattle, but they will have to make multiple voyages to accommodate all of them. Then there are the horses and the gold and silver articles. You have several wagons loaded with such things, I see."

McGirtt frowned in silence for a moment before replying, "Yes. And this won't be the last of it. We have many more miles to go before we will be too close to Charleston. There the Continental Army is strong and we will have more on our hands from them than we can handle. We also have yet to raid and burn Hilton Head Island. Then we must go to the next island – Daufuskie – and see what must be done there. We should be finished by the end of the summer. Then, Prevost wants me to join Brown in taking Augusta. So we will burn our way to Augusta, at least until we run into Cunningham. I'm told he's driving his cattle, horses and slaves overland back to Florida. We're cleaning out South Carolina, at least this part of it. I hope we don't have to go to Camden. I will not burn out my own family. And I will not allow Cunningham to do that, either. I hope they're safe."

Francisco studied his friend's face before answering. "The path to Augusta from Charleston will take you very close to Camden. If you go in a straight line you will pass just south of Columbia and I believe you have family near there, as well, do you not?"

"I do. My wife, Mary James, is in Stateburg with her brother, just outside of Columbia."

7

1780

May 29 – The Waxhaw Creek Massacre, South Carolina. American Troops surrendered to Lieutenant Colonel Banastre Tarleton. Tarleton proceeded to slaughter them at bayonet point while they were under the flag of surrender, earning for himself the name "Bloody Ban Tarleton."

August 16 – The Battle of Camden resulted in a British victory with Cornwallis, Tarleton, Rawden and James Webster's troops defeating General Gates, Mordecai Gist and Johann de Kalb. Camden was subsequently occupied by the British.

    Brooding, Daniel McGirtt leaned back on his saddle, propped conveniently on the ground, and watched as a crackling campfire heated food for a late dinner. His intense stare, fixed unwaveringly on the fire, framed by furrowed brows, downturned, angry lips and a week's growth of reddish beard, worried Patrick Alcorn. *I haven't seen a smile out of him since we left Savannah.* The slaughter and destruction had left its mark on Alcorn as well. *We've burned a lot of people out of their homes.* The thought continually haunted him. *So many people, now homeless, destitute... But Daniel had to give the orders. He thinks he's the only one responsible. Harder for him.*

"So, Daniel." Alcorn thought he might be able to break into Daniel's sulk. "Is God on our side or not? He must be, since he allows us to continue burning and pillaging."

Daniel sat with his arms crossed, legs stretched out in front of him on the ground with crossed ankles. Before answering, he opened a skin bag he had tied to his belt, dipped out a dab of dark goo which he smeared on his neck, face and ears. "This stuff Ahaya gave us works pretty well against the mosquitoes. I wonder what he puts in it." He closed the bag, re-crossed his arms and continued glaring at the fire. "Hard to say whose side God is on, if He even chooses sides. The rebels think God is on their side. Those loyal to the crown think God is on their side. The Ottoman Muslims think God is on their side and that justifies their raids of the coast of Spain and Italy, their enslavement of whoever they capture there. Europeans think God is on their side and wonder that He allows the unimpeded raiding of Christian communities and the enslavement of their populace. We'll never solve that puzzle."

"But the King rules by divine ordinance, does he not? God must be on his side." Alcorn found himself getting caught up in the question.

Daniel shrugged. "King George, like British Kings going back hundreds of years, received his orb and scepter from the hand of the Archbishop of Canterbury, who then placed the crown on the king's head. He was not made king by God, but by the Archbishop of Canterbury – a man."

"Well," began Patrick, "It was a very good man; a man of God."

"Whatever that means." Daniel's voice sounded coarse. "All those people we burned out, even John Barker, believe in God, believed that God would protect them from us, on whose side God stood, at least on that day. What about tomorrow?"

The morning brought sunshine and one of the hottest days of the summer. Daniel had the remaining cattle driven back into the forest, away from the coast where they could be found easily should the Patriot forces head in that direction. It would be a few weeks before Francisco's next ships could arrive for the remainder. By then, there would be more. "We have more plantations to burn on the way to Augusta," Daniel observed. "Let's get on with it."

Remaining far to the north of the Savannah River, McGirtt's troops began working their way toward Augusta. Cunningham's troops remained on the south side of the river, heading in the same direction, both leaving enormous clouds of black and white smoke behind them. The plantations hugged the river because it represented their source of transportation for crops and supplies, so veering too far from the river led McGirtt and his troop only into wilderness. Almost half way to Columbia they came upon a particularly nice farm with a sign on the gate post that read, "Bravo Fields Plantation." The crop, mostly cotton with smaller fields of vegetables, stood half grown. Black slaves scattered through the fields tended the crops, weeding, hoeing, replanting. Daniel was surprised to find, standing directly in front of him, a tall, very well-muscled black slave, wearing a torn straw hat, homespun cotton shirt and trousers cut half way down the calf. This barefooted man held a four pronged pitch fork in front of him in a most threatening manner. "And who might you be?" The man demanded to know. "I am Jonas. The Master left me in charge to protect the property."

McGirtt pulled up sharply. Gray Goose snorted at the unexpected halt, danced a few steps backward, almost bumping into Alcorn's horse. "Well. Good afternoon to you, Jonas. I am Lieutenant Colonel Daniel McGirtt of the East Florida Rangers. I am here to burn the plantation, confiscate all horses, cattle and slaves, including you, to be sold in the West Indies and elsewhere. You will like the West Indies. It doesn't get as cold there and they have fruit to eat that is not available here. So why not put down the pitch fork and give us a hand?"

The slave stood quietly dumfounded for a moment. Then he spoke. "You going to burn my home, the crops we worked so hard to raise, steal the cattle, horses and all my people and you want me to help you?"

Daniel smiled under a threatening frown. "Yes, Jonas. And there may be some valuables in the house. We'll check on that before we burn it. Is your master available? We will allow him and his family to quietly leave or violently die. Are they here?"

Jonas, backing slowly away, lowered his pitchfork. "The Master has gone to fight for Baron De Kalb up at Camden. His lady and the children have gone to Columbia to stay with her parents until this trouble is over."

"Camden?" McGirtt practically leapt on the word. "Why has De Kalb gone to Camden?"

"Master said Cornwallis and Tarleton are coming down from up north and they're going to burn Camden."

McGirtt sat silently on Gray Goose, eyes wide, mind racing. "Jonas, if you help us, I will take you and your people with me. When we get to Florida, I'll give you your freedom. Maybe I'll even be able to help you get land of your own. Would you like that?"

Jonas plunged the pitchfork's prongs into the soil. "Master McGirtt, what black slave wouldn't like to hear such kind words? I'll gather my people and we'll fetch you some torches. There are forty-six of us, not countin' the babies. Are you sure you can handle so many?"

☙ ☙

Mary James McGirtt lounged in an easy chair, next to the rear window of the home of her sister-in-law Elizabeth and husband John Cantey. The house, two story brick, overlooked fields of cotton, the main crop, in front of the house. Behind the house, Mary had planted vegetables which she took great pleasure in tending. She had okra, lettuce, tomatoes, cabbage and a host of other things including her favorite flower, climbing roses, on trellises surrounding the garden. Mary liked the long summer evenings, in particularly because the longer days meant she could read by natural light for an hour or more after the evening meal. Tonight, she was re-reading Edmund Spenser's *The Faerie Queen* and wondering if her husband, Daniel was like the Red Cross Knight – a gentle knight, pricking on a plain. The news she had about him was all bad, horrible, outrageous, unbelievable. *Daniel? Do those things? I don't think so. If Daniel is pricking on a plain, his dented armor is his dented honor. I wonder what he'll have to say for himself, if I ever see him again.*

Cantey's house faced south and Mary was reading in a room on the north side. As the light grew more dim, she moved to the front veranda where the light was still strong enough to continue reading. When it faded, Mary closed the book, but she remained on the porch watching the clouds in the sky, still lighted by the sun which was now below the horizon.

"Hey, Mary," Elizabeth called from inside, "come on in. The bugs'll eat you alive."

"They aren't bothering me, darling," Mary answered. "If I stay out here, maybe I'll see the smoke from one of Daniel's fires."

Elizabeth appeared in the doorway, hands on hips, a frown on her face. Her red hair, a sure sign of the McGirtt heritage, had come undone. She shook it out of her face and said, "Mary, why so cynical? We know he's fighting on the side of the Crown. He's a soldier. That's what soldiers do. We can only hope he isn't as much of a monster as that Tarleton is supposed to be, killing prisoners and men under a flag of truce. How awful!"

Mary looked behind her at Elizabeth, standing in the doorway. "He was always kind and gentle to the best of my knowledge. He had a streak of the adventurer in him. He couldn't resist racing a horse, trying to jump the horse over higher and higher hurdles. You should have heard some of the stories he told me. It's a wonder he lived to grow up. In his last letter, he said he expected to get some land in Florida and he wants me to join him. I don't know. I'm not the adventurer type. I've never seen an alligator and I hear there are lots of them in Florida. Gives me the shivers."

"Mary!" Elizabeth said suddenly. "Listen!" They stopped talking.

Over the sounds of crickets, night-birds and the few cattle in the barn, they could hear the steps of a horse approaching along the path from Cantey Lane. "Get John," Mary whispered urgently. "Let's get inside!"

Inside the front room, Elizabeth reminded Mary, "John has gone north with Kalb and the others to fight Cornwallis and his crew. He's not here."

"Good Lord," Mary fussed. "What are we going to do?"

"Hello the house," a familiar voice called out from not far away. "Hello the house."

"My God, Elizabeth! It's Daniel!"

03 80

Having safely moved Mary, Elizabeth and Elizabeth's children from Camden, which was about to be embattled and occupied, Daniel felt free to return to the war. His family would be safer at the home of Elizabeth's brother John James in Stateburg, and Stateburg was on his route back to where Daniel would rejoin his men and move on to Augusta. Daniel headed west. Instead of a British uniform he wore a cape, and an animal skin cap he had received as a gift from one of Ahaya's Creek Indians. For all practical purposes he was not recognizable as a soldier at all, much less a British soldier. As soon as he got past Columbia he changed back into clothing that would enable him to function in a British military camp without being challenged. It was Daniel's intention to stay on the road to Augusta until he was about a day's ride from there, then veer south to meet his men. He was about to turn south when he spotted a British military contingent heading east, toward him, apparently coming from the area of Augusta. Instead of turning south, he continued toward them, where they were in the process of setting up a camp for the night.

He fell in with them as though they were long lost friends, although he knew not a man among them. They accepted him as a fellow soldier, companions of the road, and invited him to dine. As they ate, they swapped war stories, which was how Daniel got himself updated on the latest news. Augusta still remained in the hands of the British under Lieutenant Colonel Brown of the Rangers. The regiment hosting Daniel had taken prisoners whom his dinner mates pointed out to Daniel, bivouacked next to a wagon on the edge of the camp. The dinner they were given would hardly be enough for a man to march on. Daniel felt sorry for them. *Prisoners of war – damned and to be hanged in Charleston, he had been told.* Daniel found the companionship of the other Brits satisfying and pleasurable but with the black cloud hanging over his head of having to burn more people out of their homes

After the camp quieted for the night and most of the soldiers were asleep, Daniel rose. Quietly, he strolled to the edge of the encampment, as though to relieve himself. Once out of sight, he began creeping quietly as few knew how to do, toward the prisoners. He found them asleep. Quietly, he slipped his hand over the mouth of one of them who awakened, turning suddenly to look at Daniel. His eyes grew wide as he watched Daniel put a finger to his lips signaling for silence. The man relaxed. Daniel removed his Skyn Dhu from its sheath and cut the ropes around the man's wrists and ankles. With a motion of his hand indicating the man should follow him, he slipped silently along the edge of the camp until they came to the end. Finally, far enough away to be out of earshot, McGirtt whispered to the man, "Anthony Hampton! How did you get captured by these people? I thought you'd be able to ride off and escape them."

Hampton, a man similar in age to McGirtt remarked. "Thank you, Daniel. I don't suppose you have a horse for me, do you?"

Daniel smiled. "I do. I do."

"Why are you doing this?"

McGirtt looked off into the night before answering. "Do you remember fishing together along the Wateree River? We were boys. We swore to always be friends. My word is good, Anthony. Here's your horse. Please ride slowly and quietly until you're well out of earshot lest you wake these men and they come after you. I don't think I have to warn you to stay off the main trails. Be careful."

Gray Goose stood beside the mount Daniel provided for Hampton. "I think I'll be on my way as well. None of those men know my name. There will be no trouble."

8

1781

Spanish settlers founded the City of Los Angeles and Spain recaptured west Florida from Great Britain..

March 2 – the Articles of Confederation were adopted.

June 6 – American forces recaptured Augusta, Georgia.

September 15 – The French fleet drove the British fleet out of the Chesapeake Bay.

October 19 – Cornwallis was surrounded on land and sea by American and French forces. He surrendered at Yorktown, Virginia.

    The George Galphin House, about twelve miles south of Augusta, served as a trading post between whatever nation happened to be in charge at any given time, and the local Indians, especially the Cherokee nation. The British happened to be in charge on May 21, 1781. This lightly guarded center of frontier commerce was protected by a twelve-foot stockade and held a good supply of food including ground corn, dried vegetables, salted beef and pork. The house also had on hand an accumulation of hard cash in the form of gold. Banks were not easily reachable from this remote location and lacked the safety which banks have since come to provide. So money representing transactions for the last several months lay hidden on the site.

Captain Zachariah Cantey, riding in the ranks of General Andrew Pickens, found himself unsurprised that the trading post fell in minutes. The few British troops on hand surrendered directly with only a few casualties. The Patriots had no casualties. Captain Cantey *was* surprised when he was summoned to the tent of General Pickens. Pickens had a long face, accentuated by a narrow, curved nose, ruddy cheeks and a bare, hairless pate. His eyes were cold and assessing. After studying Cantey for a full minute, he said, "I have a job for you. Sit down."

Pickens proceeded to describe the terrain between Augusta and Charleston as rolling hills, none very high, but high enough to hide a brigade. "The land is under agricultural use for the most part. There is corn, wheat, soy, but the chief crop is cotton. Much of the land is cattle-producing, but since the raids by the Florida Rangers and Prevost's men, most of the cattle are gone. The only British stronghold in the area is at the village of Ninety Six. That's way up north of here. There is British strength north of Columbia as well, at Camden." General Pickens rose from his camp chair and strolled to the door of his tent. "Come and see this, Captain."

Outside the tent stood several wagons hitched to teams of horses. Pickens continued, "I want you to take these wagons to General Francis Marion. General Marion is in need of supplies. The front wagon, you may have noticed, contains a chest. That chest is about half full of gold pieces. Marion has need of the money as well. See that he gets it."

Cantey scratched his head and turned to General Pickens. "How will I find 'The Swamp Fox,' sir? His stock in trade is being elusive."

"He'll find *you*," Pickens snorted. "Take the trails north of Charleston to Goose Creek. From there, a road meanders east through the swamps. He'll find you there."

Captain Cantey chose to drive the wagon loaded with the gold chest. The other wagons followed as they slowly made their way toward British-held Charleston, South Carolina. His scouts told him, "There is a trail north from Charleston that we'll reach long before we get near the city. We can stay on the Charleston Road till we reach it."

Cantey, 26 years old and a Captain in the Continental Army, was, perhaps, more sure of himself than he should have been. He felt secure with his platoon of fifty soldiers, all armed to the teeth, trained and battle hardened. Some riders appeared late the second day out from Galphin's Trading Post. They overtook his party, but were riding well off to the left of the trail, in the cultivated lands. Cantey scanned behind him, to the left, trying to assess who they were and what sort of a threat they might represent. The riders outnumbered his party by at least double. *I hope there isn't going to be trouble.*

When the lead rider reached a point abreast of Cantey's wagon, a voice rang out, saying, "Hello the wagons!"

Cantey guessed that the riders were British militia of some sort. He knew his party was badly outnumbered and that they didn't stand a chance in a direct confrontation. He passed the word, "Don't fire upon these riders unless fired upon and then only on my order." He ignored the greeting.

His second in command, Bill Lafferty objected. "We have the road, but they have numbers. If they attack, we'll all be killed."

Cantey drew his lips into a tight, grim line and said, "They aren't going to attack."

Lafferty rebutted, "How can you be so sure? They evidently know what we're carrying and they mean to have it."

The lead rider called out again, louder, "Hello the wagon!"

Cantey fixed his eyes on the road again and issued another order: "Ignore them."

Lafferty quickly passed the order through the platoon, then turned angrily to Cantey. "We have to surrender. If we don't surrender, we'll be killed. You remember what Tarleton did at Waxhaw! These brutal bastards have no mercy."

Cantey kept his eyes fixed forward on the tail of the horse ahead of his wagon. "I said ignore them."

The rider leading the troops to their left called out yet again. "Hello the wagon! I know you can hear me. I know what you have there. Leave the wagons and go in peace, otherwise I will be forced to cut all of you down and take what we want."

Cantey withdrew his fixed stare from the tail of horse in front of him and turned to his left. He glared fearlessly at the lead rider and after a moment he called, "Take your men and your horses and just leave. You will not have our wagons nor will you have what they contain. If you want peace in your life, you will do as I am telling you."

The argument continued for over an hour. As the day wore on, Cantey was growing slightly hoarse from carrying on the conversation in a raised voice. The rider to his left called out again and again. "I know you have a chest of money in that wagon. We have need of that money. Drop the chest on the side of the cart path and ride off, if you value your life and the lives of your men."

"Over my dead body!" Cantey shouted at the rider. "Over my dead body. Now ride off and leave us!"

Daniel McGirtt called back in final answer. "You're a damned fool, Zachariah Cantey and you're damned lucky you're my nephew." With that McGirtt signaled his men to turn about and waited for the wagon train and platoon to pass.

ଓ ଡ

Patrick Alcorn, mounted on his tall chestnut mare, sat wide-eyed and open mouthed. "Who is he?"

McGirtt spit into the dust, obviously angry. "He's the son of my sister and his home is where my wife was hiding until just a few days ago. He's right. If I want peace in my life, I best not harm him." But then McGirtt smiled. "He's one brave lad. I can hardly wait to tell his mother how he faced me down. Did you see that? He was stern and unmoved in the face of an overwhelming force. That's the McGirtt blood in him, by God!"

Daniel filled the rest of the ride to Charleston with tales of Zachariah Cantey as a boy and when he ran out of tales about Zach, he filled in with stories about his own children. If he wasn't talking about his children, he rambled on about horses he owned, races he'd won, hurdles his horses had leapt. Alcorn was glad to see the rooftops of Charleston appearing in the distance. As they drew nearer and entered the city, their pace slowed considerably because none of them had been there since before the British took it back from the Americans the year before. "I haven't seen a single dwelling that doesn't have at least one hole in it from cannon balls." Alcorn's shock was well shared by the others.

"This was a beautiful city," Daniel muttered. "The people here want no part of this war. They've made it a point to say, many times, they don't care who is in charge, just leave them in peace. Now look at the place!"

"Some of these houses look like they've been blown up..."

"Or burned," Daniel added. "We have exploding shells now. General Lincoln was completely overwhelmed with some fourteen thousand British troops against his five thousand. I have to hand it to the guy, though. He held out for over a month."

Alcorn quietly observed shattered house after shattered house as they made their way into the city. "This is where General Pickens was captured, during the siege, is it not?"

"Yes," Daniel sighed. "They should have hanged him, but instead, they allowed him to go home on parole, on the condition that he promised he would fight no more. So there he was at his farm in Georgia when Bloody Bill Cunningham showed up and burned him out. His cattle were confiscated. And his horses and slaves. His house was ransacked for valuables... all taken from him. Cunningham should have killed him. Pickens claimed 'violation of parole' and returned to the war. It was Pickens and others who just took Augusta from us. Brown escaped, I hear."

McGirtt learned with surprise that he was ordered to Savannah to report to Brigadier General Prevost. Crossing so much land that he had recently burned and pillaged did not lift his spirits. On the way, he even learned he had missed a few places, so he stopped along the way to burn and pillage those places. His passage along this route proved in time to meet with Francisco Sanchez who had just arrived in the Harbor River to collect the rest of the cattle and slaves McGirtt had left from his earlier rampage. "I have money for you," Sanchez called out to McGirtt with a grin.

"Did Tonyn get his fair share of the cattle and horses?" Daniel wanted to know. "And what about his share of the gold? Did he get that?"

"Yes. Yes," Francisco answered, anxious to get beyond that subject. "*Señor* Patrick is very pleased. I think when you see him, he has some special reward for you."

"And what about the forty-six slaves from the Bravo Fields Plantation? Where are they?"

Francisco smiled with his eyebrows raised. "I don't understand why you took such a liking to them. They're just slaves."

"Well, where are they? I promised them their freedom if they helped me and they did. I owe them." Daniel liked and trusted Francisco but his tone was growing a little more irritated.

"Be at peace, Daniel. They are waiting for you at my hacienda, Diego Plantation. I put them to work for the time being but I have provided housing and food. They are well and they complain daily that you have not come to honor your word to them."

Grim lipped, Daniel responded, "Tell them you have spoken with me and that I will come as soon as I can."

ଔ ଌ

Brigadier General Augustine Prevost looked older. The lines in his face had deepened. The hole in the left side of his forehead lacked the pink of the rest of his face and throbbed when his passions arose. "I had hoped to be home in Geneva by now," he commented when McGirtt inquired after his health. "I was officially relieved of duty and to be replaced here by Brigadier General George Garth, but the war put a stop to that. I wonder if I'll survive to see my wife Anette again. She's waiting for me in London."

"I'm sure you will," McGirtt answered in good cheer. "You seem to be in the pink and the war will surely wind down soon."

Prevost ran a hand across his brow, shuffled his feet under his desk and answered, "I don't know, Daniel. The war runs badly for us this time. I just learned that Lord Cornwallis surrendered at Yorktown. Our fleet has been driven from the great bay by the French. Things look grim. We barely survived the siege here in Savannah in '79, but we managed, and here we are in 1781, still managing. I fear the worst. We've suffered other defeats elsewhere and our victories have been small ones."

Daniel concealed his distress at Prevost's dire predictions. "Great Britain can still be victorious. This isn't over. With fools like Button Gwinnett and 'Lackland' McIntosh killing each other over women, I don't see how the Americans could ever stand up to a professional military like ours. They are disorganized, unruly rabble. We will prevail."

Prevost smiled. "I wouldn't be so hard on McIntosh, Daniel. He owns land near the mouth of the Altamaha River and raises rice there."

"But he bought the land. It's not his family's. He was a bloody clerk, raised as an orphan. He only did well because of his loud mouth. People are afraid of offending him, especially after he shot down Button Gwinnett. If they had any organizational sense, they would have fought their battle, then shot each other."

Prevost laughed at Daniel's passion. "Be that as it may be, Daniel, this is what I want you to do. Tonyn is screaming for help in St. Augustine. I have a letter from him that came in just a few days ago. He says that people loyal to the crown are being expelled from the northern colonies and their property in the colonies is being confiscated and sold. They are arriving in Florida by the thousands, nearly destitute. Tonyn says it's a mixed blessing. He needs people to populate the area, plant the fertile soil and establish British civilization in that wild place. Many of the old Spanish estates still lie abandoned, many complete with houses and outbuildings, standing nearly ready to resume their old industries. The main crops there, as you know, are still indigo and rice, but there are other valuable commodities being produced in Florida including turpentine, lumber and cattle. Tonyn's problem is feeding these people while they get settled. His additional problem is that since these people are hungry and unemployed, they turn to crime. For food, they rob existing plantations, including your friend Francisco Sanchez. He has his own standing army, of sorts, to protect his properties. Tonyn needs you and the troops you have from the East Florida Rangers. How long do you think it will take you to get there?"

9

1782

March 20 – Lord North resigned as Prime Minister.

July 11 – Brigadier General Prevost and his British troops evacuated Savannah.

November 30 – The Americans and the British signed the Preliminary Articles of Peace. Separate treaties were signed by Great Britain with Spain, Holland and France. The treaty with Spain returned the territories of Florida to Spain without distinct boundaries. The boundaries were settled in the Treaty of Madrid in 1795.

December 14 – The British evacuated Charleston, South Carolina.

    Juan Andreu's small brown eyes contrasted against his wide smile and his thick, now graying, black hair. Hardworking, industrious and indefatigable, he baked his bread, biscuits and cakes, "almost non-stop," his neighbors and friends insisted. A Minorcan who nearly starved to death at Turnbull's indigo plantation along the Spruce Creek, he now worked, saved and invested "so when I die, my children can have a little property and not be poor like me."

    One of Juan's first acquisitions was the old house across the street and a little bit west of Maria's Taberna. He rented it from Jesse Fish, with an agreement to buy within twenty years. This is where Juan sold many of his baked goods whenever he had anything left over from supplying the British Barracks. Although Juan's English was quite good, with a heavy Spanish accent, the sign in front of his shop said, "*Panadero y Panaderia,*" (Baker and Bakery). I may be a British citizen now," he said, "but we mustn't forget the old ways and where we came from and what we've been through." So, he sang and whistled while he worked. The songs were from the Island Minorca, the Fromajada and others.

One of Juan's projects included adding a second floor to his new building where he had two rooms that he could rent to affluent visitors who needed a place to sleep. It was a sturdy frame structure, erected on top of his masonry bakery, where he himself lived with his family. Wrapping around the north and the west facing walls, Juan built a covered balcony where his guests could sit outside and watch the sun descend into the western sky. "If I make the place nice," he reasoned to his family who objected to the additional cost, "I can charge more rent for those rooms." The balcony, he added, could only be described as expansive. The ceiling consisted of cut boards that Juan painted a light green, "to keep the mosquitoes off the guests," he said. "They'll be attracted toward the ceiling by the color of plants." The roof sloped steeply, encouraging St. Augustine's torrential rain to run cleanly off the roof to the ground. Enough overhanging soffit would keep his guests dry enough if they wanted to sit out here and watch the torrents. Except for Maria's across the street and closer to the river, the land to the north and the south produced crops of vegetables planted by others of the townsmen. To the west, live oak trees decorated the skyline with twisting branches sometimes laden with acorns, gray squirrels, mockingbirds, blue jays and the occasional pileated woodpecker, the huge bird with the red head and the raucous voice.

To complete the picture, Juan dug a three barrel well on the west side of the house, covered it with a decorative roof and added a few benches nearby. The draw cord, with a small bucket at the end, was controlled by a crank that coiled a rope around a board that it turned to draw water. This is where McGirtt stood at the moment, turning the crank to draw water for his chamber pot and other toiletry devices provided in the room Juan rented to him for a few nights. Daniel didn't like St. Augustine's water, *smells like the waters of hell – full of sulphur ...and the mosquitoes hanging around this water source won't encourage guests to sit on any of these benches –that's for sure!*

Daniel enjoyed the covered balcony. He pulled his chair to the northwest corner where he could look north and west and watch the day's light fade into night. The evening had been pleasant enough. Maria's Taberna wasn't the only eating establishment in the community, but so far as Daniel was concerned, it was the best.

For dinner companions, he was pleased to enjoy Francisco Sanchez, his aide and companion Patrick Alcorn, William "Bloody Bill" Cunningham and a new visitor in St. Augustine who had been introduced to Daniel by East Florida's Governor Patrick Tonyn: Captain John Elphinstone, Captain of the HMS *Magnificent*, a seventy-four gun ship of the line. "We're serving His Majesty's cause in the West Indies," Captain Elphinstone explained. "I had some hush-hush business with Governor Tonyn necessitating my visit here for a few days. We were thinking of taking on water, but after tasting St. Augustine's water, I'm having second thoughts." Elphinstone stood five and a half feet tall and weighed, according to him, sixteen stone. His notable features included extremely large fierce eyes, oversized slightly pointed ears and a very long nose. "From the Orkneys," he told them. In answer to the teasing about his family name he said, "No we are not elvin. My father says we are half dwarf and half elf, hence the "Elf" and "Stone." I never took him seriously, of course. He was a great tease." Growing fiercely serious and changing the subject, he addressed a question to Francisco. "What sort of cattle are we acquiring from you, Señor Sanchez? I'm told the breeds vary widely. The smaller the size of the animals, the more we can carry, but the smaller breeds will bring less per head because of the size and weight."

After discussing the cargo Elphinstone was to escort back to the Islands, Alcorn brought up the Spanish soldiers Tonyn had been holding in the *Castillo*. "Señor Sanchez, do you still have those soldiers that were captured? I heard you were feeding them and making sure they had adequate clothing for their stay at the old fort. I wonder how Tonyn feels about that?"

Francisco smiled and lowered his eyes to his plate for the moment. The barbecued pulled pork smothered in datil pepper sauce was a favorite of his and it was quickly becoming a favorite of Daniel McGirtt's, as well. He looked at Patrick and said, "I had confusing feelings when Spain came into the war and sided with the American cause, against my new country. It was hard enough when Great Britain took over Florida from Spain back in '63. I was young then. I hated it, but we have property here and Britain allowed us to stay if we wanted. Only two families stayed and swore allegiance to Great Britain. They were my family who came to *La Florida* in 1736 from Cuba and the Solana family, who came to La Florida with Pedro Menendez, long ago. This is their home. We are not Spanish. We are *Floridanos*. When the Spanish soldiers who were captured in the islands were brought here, I felt sorry for them. They are from the place where my father was born – *España*. I had to help them. They are like family. Because I helped these enemies of Great Britain, Governor Tonyn does not trust me any longer. Maybe he is right to not trust me. I am not here for Great Britain. I am here for my family and for La Florida. To stay, I promised to be loyal to Britain. I have been as good as my word to him. I have been, uh, untested, but am otherwise loyal."

Sitting on Juan Andreu's balcony, Daniel smiled at the exchange. He could see how torn Francisco was about helping his former countrymen, now enemies of his new nation. Daniel himself shared some of those feelings. Most of his own family had remained true to the Patriot cause against Britain while he, rebelling against Captain John Barker more than the Patriot cause, itself, returned to the side of King and Crown. He understood Francisco's conundrum more than he cared to tell.

The chat with John Elphinstone brought back memories of tales from the Wateree Indians; those of The Elves of Darkness who protected mankind by keeping dangerous things trapped underground. The tale of Glooskap creating the Oonahgemessuk, another Wateree Indian name for elves, caught his imagination when he was a boy and stayed with him as an enjoyable fable from childhood. As his daydream led him through the skips and trips of childhood and his memories of the Old Indian who told the stories to Daniel and his friends, he watched a man appearing from the corner of his eye, from the direction of Maria's. *Looks like Elphincap or Elphenrod – what was his name?* Daniel paid little attention but was aware of the man as he approached the well in the side yard, stood there with his back to Daniel for a moment, then turned and walked quickly away, just after Daniel thought he heard the sound of a soft splash. *Odd that he didn't draw any water. Did he drop something in the well?* The thought was interrupted by a loud thunk on the wall right beside Daniel's head. The loud *thunk* was followed by the sound of a musket shot. *Someone took a shot at me!* Daniel dropped to the floor of the porch on his stomach, so he could peer out through the railings in the direction of the shot. Patrick Alcorn suddenly appeared from the room next to Daniel's. A loud "What the hell?" came from Captain Elphinstone, still near the edge of the side yard.

"Get down," Daniel said to Alcorn. "That shot just barely missed me."

"Who's shooting at you?" Alcorn, still too stunned to act, seemed to Daniel to be waiting for the next shot.

"Get down!" Daniel hissed, but didn't take his eyes off the field of datil peppers across the street. "There goes one. Let's get after him!" They could see a large man running down through the field in the direction of the town's plaza. Within seconds, Daniel and Patrick were down the stairs and giving good pursuit. Elphinstone, heavier in stature led the rear, all of them brandishing long knives – swords.

"There he is," Alcorn called out.

"I see him," Daniel answered. "It looks like there are two more down there, holding horses."

"Hurry," Alcorn called out. "They're going to get away."

"We can't let that happen," Daniel snapped. "If we do, they could come back and try again!"

The two raced toward the plaza but paused and hit the ground when they saw one of them in the moonlight raise another musket aimed in their direction. They saw the flash of the musket. The ball passed over their heads followed by a loud BOOM. They both looked around in time to see Elphinstone ducking to the ground. "Another miss," Daniel panted. "Let's try to get them before they can spur those horses or reload. Do they only have one musket?" The man they were chasing finally reached the horses, leaped onto one of them and the three raced to the west.

"Too late!" Daniel plopped to the ground to catch his breath. Alcorn sat down beside him. Elphinstone came walking up to them, sliding his sword back into its sheath.

"It's no wonder that someone may be trying to kill you two. I heard what success you had for Great Britain in the campaign from Savannah to Charleston. There are probably a lot of people who would like to see you dead or worse." Elphinstone straightened his jacket as he talked.

"We're supposed to be safe in Florida. This is British territory." Alcorn's quivery voice revealed how shaken he felt. "Yes. There are probably many who would like to come after us, but the only one whose name comes to mind is one we met at Fort McIntosh, before it was built. We burned him out of house and home, confiscated his property and left him destitute, and justifiably so, in my opinion."

Daniel lifted himself back to his feet, dusting off his clothing. "You're thinking of John Barker, aren't you, Patrick?"

"None other," Alcorn answered. "He swore he'd hunt us down and kill us."

"Kill *me*, you mean," Daniel grunted.

○○ ○○

To thank and honor Daniel McGirtt and William Cunningham for their efforts in burning South Carolina and the spoils of war that they brought to East Florida, they were to be given grants of land. Daniel received what Tonyn named Maxton Island. For an inspection of the land, Tonyn provided for and paid Francisco Sanchez to use some of his sailing river craft to transport Cunningham to his land grant on the east side of the St. Johns River and Daniel to Maxton Island, farther north and on the west side. The boat, large enough to carry a small company of armed men, was fully loaded. Francisco, curious to see what these men were being awarded, captained one of the two vessels himself and obviously felt free to order the East Florida rangers about the vessel to act as crew. "Tighten that sail," he called out to two of them. "Steer more to port. We'll capture the wind better. We can tack to starboard later, when we start approaching the shallows on the other side of the river!" The shallow-draft vessel carried sideboards instead of a keel, making it easier to navigate the shallow waters and unexpected sand bars of the St. Johns River. As soon as they were well away from the land, Francisco ordered that the sideboards be lowered all the way. After half a day of sailing, Francisco altered the boat's course to put in at what was known as Cecilton's Plantation, near the Cow Ford ferry. Nosing the boat gently toward shore with partly luffing sails, the sideboards were raised halfway, still deep enough to afford steerage with less likelihood of scraping the bottom as they entered the shallow water.

"We need to send most of the men with Cunningham to find out the status of the property," Francisco explained. "Since the beginning of the war with the colonies up north, a great many who wished to remain loyal to the Crown have fled to British Florida. Tonyn estimates there to be at least ten thousand new British subjects, bringing with them around eleven thousand slaves. This has been very good for me since I sell meat, vegetables, eggs, chickens and numerous other things that these people need and have the money to pay for. They are making my fortune, but St. Augustine can't handle so many people. There is no housing and no means for them to continue to support themselves other than with the wealth they brought with them. It creates a problem sometimes, too, because the meat I am selling them was confiscated from their own farms in some cases."

"War is war," McGirtt interjected.

"The situation creates much anger," Francisco continued. "Many of these immigrants from the colonies have taken over farms abandoned by the Spanish when they left Florida in 1763. Many of these abandoned plantations have houses and barns, cooking sheds, smoking sheds. They had blacksmith equipment for the horses and other things made in such places. My people were very unhappy about having to go back to Spain and to Cuba and the other islands. Their land is still here, sometimes occupied by squatters. Those squatters are often hostile when the King gives the land to others. This land was owned by Lady Egmont. The Egmont family never developed the land and only used it once when they fled a rebel incursion on their plantation on the St. Mary's River. It had no buildings when it was last inspected, but it's never wise to assume the land is unoccupied."

With the remainder of the day spent exploring – wandering the thousand acre estate and finding the land vacant of human activity – it was unanimously decided to camp there for the night before proceeding to Maxton Island. Cunningham was well pleased. "There are large cedar trees and from what I've seen of the cedar trees in this area, it's superior to mahogany. The huge live oaks will be excellent for ship building. There is much sellable lumber on the site and when it's cleared the land will be excellent for indigo and cotton. The marsh areas can be used for rice. This is a rich site, indeed."

"Daniel," Francisco observed. "I think you will be equally pleased with Maxton Island. The land was formerly owned by one Colonel Elias Ball who developed the land and built numerous buildings. He fled the area when he saw that the war was going badly for Britain. News of the Preliminary Articles of Peace were no encouragement for him since in that document, La Florida is to be returned to Spain."

McGirtt frowned. "That'll never happen."

CB ⚜ BO

In the morning, most of the original party boarded the boats for the trip across the river and the miles of sailing north to Maxton Island, Daniel McGirtt's new home. From many miles distant, they could see smoke rising from among the trees. "Cooking fires," Daniel commented. "Someone's there."

Landing at the very northern extremity of Maxton Island, as far from the rising smoke as they could land and still approach the property without having to wade or swim, they secured the boats and prepared for a trek through the thick forest. Cunningham and the people he brought with him were still among them. "I'll stay with you in case you need help at Maxton," he explained as he boarded the boat that morning with his armed companions. "When we get back to St. Augustine, I'll load up a few wagons to carry supplies back to Cecilton. Then we can get started clearing, building and planting." Cunningham was clearly filled with thoughts and plans for his new plantation. As they hacked their way through the forest, Daniel was amused as he watched Cunningham's distracted expression. *He'll make a fine neighbor.*

Finally, they reached the edge of a cleared field, obviously fallow for at least the past year or two. "Nice of Elias Ball to not clear the entire island," McGirtt muttered. "If he had done that, we wouldn't have been able to get so close."

Across the field numerous slave laborers could be seen. Some of them drove fence posts into the ground while others were making boards using broad axes. A few cattle grazed in sight of an unpainted two story wooden house. At least eight horses stood tethered to a rail by the side of the house, apparently waiting for their corral to be finished. The cedar shake-shingled roof clearly needed repair. The front door to the house hung crooked to the doorframe with makeshift hinges rigged from worn out shoe leather. A veranda surrounded three sides of the first floor and McGirtt could see several men with muskets rocking there, half dazed with boredom.

McGirtt's small company nearly reached the house unseen when a tall, thin black man in a long apron emerged through the rickety door, apparently to call the men inside for a midday meal. It was the cook who raised the alarm. All three of the men stood at once and headed for the stairs from the porch to the ground. The one in front straightened his hat with one hand while he eyed his musket for readiness. The others followed him down the steps. "Who comes here?" he demanded, keeping his musket at the ready, but with the barrel carefully pointed down. "What are you doin' on my island?"

Daniel stepped forward, keeping his own musket pointed at the ground, but ready to fire. "I am Lieutenant Colonel Daniel McGirtt of the East Florida Rangers. If you check with the Governor of East Florida, Patrick Tonyn, you will learn that this is actually my island. The day is well worn, my friend, and I feel it would be unkind of me to evict you from my property on such short notice. So, I will give you until tomorrow at sunup to be off of my land. I have been awarded the land and all improvements, including the buildings, any standing crops and any other property that I find here. I want to point out to you that this will include these slaves I see on the property. I will make a gift to you of these horses and their tack that I see tethered to the rail yonder, so that your egression of the property will be expeditious."

"Exactly what the hell are you talkin' about? You want me to leave my island? I don't bleedin' think so. You're trespassin' and if you ain't gone or on your way in the next five minutes, me and my men are goin' to start shootin'."

Confident of the fifteen men behind him, all armed with loaded muskets, swords and other machines of war, Daniel smiled at the man's grit and bravado and replied. "I admire your bravery, my friend. If I had taken over an abandoned property and made it my home, I too would be most unhappy about having to leave. Perhaps you would like to consider staying and joining the East Florida Rangers? If you do that, you won't have to worry about where you're going to lay your head. You will have regular pay and the protection of the very King of England, Scotland and Wales. Come and make your fortune with us."

"Colonel McGirtt..."

"Lieutenant Colonel," McGirtt interrupted.

"Whatever the bleedin' hell... If I wanted to be a bloody soldier I would have joined the military in North Carolina. Now! You get off my land before I start shootin'!"

McGirtt gritted his teeth and called out, "Okay boys, shoulder your muskets, and don't forget the two men in the windows of the second floor pointing guns at us." With that, the man's face fell, he bent over and laid his musket on the ground, signaling his compatriots to do the same.

"All right, you son of a bitch. We'll leave."

McGirtt cut him off again. "I don't like your tone, sir. You will call your people out of the house right now, get on your horses and leave, right now."

The man just stood there, looking dumfounded. "You said we could leave in the morning. I think we'll take you up on that."

"I withdraw the offer. If you and your people are not on your horses and on your way off my land, immediately, I'll have you shot right here and now. The slaves, extra horses and the cattle you have grazing on my land will stay."

Mounted and about to leave, he turned to McGirtt and said, "How you think we're going to get across the water to the mainland?"

McGirtt's fit of charity had worn off. "Swim your horses, if you have to. On the south side of the island the water is shallow and you should be able to cross easily."

The man kicked his horse into a slow walk, headed south. As he began to leave, he turned to McGirtt again and said, "Lieutenant Colonel McGirtt. My name is Kermit Hoffman. These are my sons Rodney and Jeffrey. You will hear of us again, sir." Then he spurred his horse and headed south at a brisk pace with his two sons and three other men; two of them had women riding double with their men. One of the women held a baby in her arms.

Daniel turned to Patrick Alcorn, standing beside him and said, "I didn't know they had women and children with them. I hope they get across the river safely. I wonder where they'll go."

"Probably not far," Alcorn answered. "...and they'll probably be back."

"I'll post some guards."

10

1782

"No. She's hardly a ship of the line, ma'am." Rudolfo Hernandez's belly hung over his wide belt. Half his shirt tail was tucked in and the other half blew in the southeast breeze that kept the *La Conchita* heeled over on a tight East bound starboard reach, sailing as close to the wind as a ship of her nature was able. Rudolfo, the first mate, wore no shoes. A large kerchief was wrapped around his head, which he explained he used for wiping things up, polishing the fittings, blowing his nose and whatever else he wanted it for. Around his head was a good place to keep it, since he had no pockets.

Rudolfo's deeply tanned face and naked arms bore the scars of many fights. "No ma'am, I'm not a pirate, but I helped to fight off more than a few. The open sea is a dangerous place, ma'am. Hell, ma'am, the world is a dangerous place." He stood much taller than Mary. This and his coarseness made her uneasy, although, she chuckled inwardly, *my husband Daniel is also much taller than I am and I have no fear of him whatsoever.* She was grateful Rudolfo had adopted her as a friend.

"What is this kind of ship called?" Mary asked.

"She's called a brigantine, a cargo vessel. And just now, she's fully loaded. There's hardly room to twitch a whisker, forward." He pointed at the obvious. The deck was crowded with a mixture of negro slaves, cattle, pigs, crates of chickens. Below deck, as she could see through the open hatch near the center of the ship, more cattle mooed and bawled.

"Where did all this, uh, cargo come from, Rudolfo? And where is it all going?"

"Well ma'am, much of it came from confiscated goods in the plantation raids that the Johnny Bull boys conducted against the enemy. They're all going to Florida. Because so many British citizens left the colonies and went to Florida, they're having a hard time getting enough food. Some of it will pass on to other places, but most of it, like you, is headed for Florida."

Most of the cargo had been loaded onto the ship in Charleston Harbor, just as she had, with the crates of furniture and personal possessions that came with her. The first stop, at Cow Ford on the St. Johns River, gave Mary her first taste of the frontier ambience of North Florida. Sailing over the bar into the St. Johns River proved easier than Rudolfo thought it would be. "High tide is the best time," he told her, "but the problem then is we'll be sailing up the river against the falling tide, so it will take longer to get there."

Mary's first impression of Florida couldn't have been worse. "It's wilderness," she said to Rudolfo. "Beautiful, but wilderness. I see nothing but snakes and alligators in the river, dreadful things, but hiding among the beautiful water hyacinth and .... Is that a floating island?"

Rudolfo chuckled. "It's a big hunk of water hyacinth that broke off somewhere. We sometimes find them floating out at sea, even out of sight of land. It takes a long time for them to break up."

Mary James McGirtt watched the mud banks of the river slide slowly by as *La Conchita* struggled upstream. "At least, since we turned westerly, the wind is now more favorable."

"That it is, Mrs. McGirtt. By the time we get to Cow Ford, the tide will probably turn. Unloading won't take all that long, but we'll lay over for the night there and make way to Maxton Island in the morning."

Filled with curiosity, Mary tried to see into and through the thick undergrowth along the shore. "Are there Indians in there? Are they friendly?"

"I'll be back." Rudolfo and others of the crew made haste to make some minor adjustments to the sails to try to gather more breeze. Ropes were neatly tied to batons all over the ship, and Mary marveled at how they could know where they all went and what they did. The men at work on the ropes seemed to know instinctively. In just a few seconds, *La Conchita* heeled slightly more to starboard and she noticed a sudden increase in speed. Then Rudolfo was back.

"The Indians here are different than you might know up north," he began. "These are Creeks, Wakapuchasce's people. The local white people call him Ahaya, or Cow Keeper. Quite a few of the Andalusian Spanish cattle were wandering in the swamps when Ahaya came. He captured them and herds them. He really is a cow keeper and he's friendly to Great Britain. He hates the Spanish. You'll probably find quite a few of his people on Maxton Island."

Watching the cattle and slaves being driven off the boat at Cow Ford into the murky waters of the St. Johns River, Mary's surprise turned to horror as she watched the alligators staring from the banks with their eyes just above the water line. She anticipated the worst but the big toothy lizards kept their distance. All the cattle and slaves made it to the muddy bank in safety. There they were met by men who looked very Spanish to her. Mary turned to Rudolfo again and asked, "This is an English colony, is it not? Why are so many of those men Spanish?"

"There are lots of Spanish people here and in St. Augustine. The owner of the cargo is Francisco Sanchez. He bought these slaves and cattle free on board at the dock in Charleston. This ship belongs to Francisco. The rest of the cargo belongs to your husband. When we are offloaded at Maxton Island, we will go back to Charleston for more. That cargo will go elsewhere."

"Where?" Mary's question turned Rudolfo's face to stone.

"Elsewhere, ma'am. Please excuse me." He walked away, leaving Mary with an unanswered question that would continue to bother her.

The Maxton Island dock site boasted a larger pier where *La Conchita* could tie up, rather than riding at anchor to unload, as she had at Cow Ford. In the distance, beyond the tree line at the dock, she could see the roof of a house. On top of the roof, a balcony, or 'widow's walk' provided a place for a spotter to watch the river. *La Conchita* stood for the dock, still several miles off shore. The dull smack of musket shots echoed across the water and thick smoke arose above the tree line not far from the house that was visible in the distance. Mary stood near the stern of the boat, near the helmsman, horror slowly rising into her throat. "What's going on?" she asked loudly enough that the helmsman, Fernando Torres, could hear her.

The helmsman did not understand her English and loudly called out, "Rudolfo. Rudolfo. *Venga aqui, por favor. ¡La Mujer tiene una pregunta!*"

Rudolfo was at her side almost immediately. "Yes, ma'am?"

Mary was beginning to feel fearful about the rising smoke and the gunfire she thought she could hear. "I can see most of the crew is Spanish" she told Rudolfo, "but I had no idea some of them can't speak English."

"Florida was Spanish for almost two hundred years before the British came to us. Four hundred more Spanish people just joined the community at St. Augustine from the Island of Minorca. I'm afraid there are more people in Florida who cannot speak English than who can. Florida is in a turmoil of mixed cultures. It's quite interesting to watch. The British rule but most of the population is Indian of various traditions and now there are many Spanish again. What was your question, ma'am?"

"Look." Mary pointed ahead of the ship. "That smoke doesn't look like it's from a cooking fire. And I thought I heard guns. What do you think of this?"

"I think there may be some trouble." Rudolfo scratched his head and then an armpit. "Because of the rebellion, many colonists have fled the colonies up north. They fled by the thousands. Here, they raid plantations, steal for their food, kill as it pleases them. But I think they picked the wrong plantation, this time. Daniel McGirtt's Maxton Island is home to many of his troops. At least seventy five of Ahaya's people ride with Colonel McGirtt. This is a home to many of the East Florida Rangers. If *banditti* have attacked Maxton Island, I feel sorry for them."

Before the brigantine sailed within another mile of Maxton Island's docks, the smoke had mostly disappeared. Mary could still hear muskets from time to time, but the sound was much fainter, as though it had moved farther away. When the boat finally reached the dock, it had all but faded.

As the boat approached the dock, a great many negro slaves began congregating to help with unloading. The first thing to be unloaded was Mary James McGirtt. After the boat was secured to the dock, Rudolfo Hernandez, with the help of two others, ceremoniously lowered a wide gangplank for her. At the bottom of the plank stood a tall, muscular, very dark-skinned man of indeterminate age who introduced himself as Jonas.

"Welcome to Maxton Island Plantation," he said with a nod of his head that could almost be interpreted as a slight bow. "You must be the Mrs. Mary McGirtt I've heard so much about?"

Mary nodded in thanks and replied, "Where is my husband and why has he sent a slave to greet me?" She continued down the gangplank to the dock as Jonas stepped back to make way for her.

Jonas retreated another step and with his hands in the air denied the charge. "Oh, ma'am, Jonas is no slave. Master Daniel... Oh excuse me, ma'am, Lieutenant Colonel McGirtt doesn't want us to call him 'Master.' He rescued us from a plantation way up north and gave us our freedom. Me and forty five others of my friends and family live here under Colonel McGirtt's protection. We work for him. He pays us.

We're free to come and go as we please, marry who we choose and he leaves our women alone. He's good to us, your husband."

"I understand, Jonas. So, where is my husband?"

෫ ෭

Earlier that morning, at first light, Daniel had climbed to the roof balcony – *the widow's walk, or captain's walk,* he thought smugly, *depending on one's perspective* – to watch to the north, wondering if today would be the day when Mary would arrive on Francisco's brigantine. In the distance, beyond the tree line, where the river turned east toward the sea, he thought he saw, or hoped he saw, the top of a mast, moving west, above the tree line. *Just my damned imagination,* he scolded himself. *Maybe it'll be tomorrow.*

Daniel had given his workmen the weekend off to tend to their own gardens and spend time with their families, so the grounds were quiet. Even the fires in the cookhouse and the blacksmithing building were out. He turned to the grounds around the house to admire the crop of indigo that was maturing to the south and the west. *It's a peaceful life here. Mary will like it.* He glanced again to the north, straining his eyes for movement of a mast above the distant tree line. Suddenly he saw it. The bow of *La Conchita* appeared as a mere speck in the miles between them, thrusting into view from the bend in the river. Its headsails, even at this distance, appeared taut before the wind. He continued watching for a few minutes as the foremast became visible, square sails full of the southeasterly breeze, followed by the mainmast and spanker. *Here she comes, finally. I guess it'll take three or four hours to make the dock.*

Fate! The Universal Intelligence! God! Lady Luck! The only entities known to humankind that can smile and frown at the same time, wanted its moment in this happy time. Like a dog, snarling and barking while wagging its tail, fate took this moment to intervene. With a sound like a heavy oak limb falling on a large flat rock, a musket ball slammed into the railing beside Daniel's right hand, shattering the wood and spraying him with splinters. Daniel's head snapped to the smoke house where he could see a thin line of smoke curling from its southern wall. A tall man lowered his musket and two others raised theirs. Daniel could hear the big man shout at his two comrades, "Shoot the son of a bitch. I bleedin' missed again!" Daniel dropped flat to the deck, inching his way toward the stairway, back into the house. In the distance, he could hear the shouts of his people calling each other together to come to the house.

John Barker! Daniel's rage rose like bile in his throat. *John Barker. I will hunt you down and kill you and your sons, this time, if I have to track you all the way to Philadelphia!* Two more musket balls spun past him as he reached the stair. One of them struck the railing near where the other had made its mark, shattering more wood and again sprinkling Daniel with splinters. *Damn! How did they slip in here unseen?*

As Daniel reached the stairs, he could hear the shouts of his soldiers, who had been bivouacked nearer the river, running toward the house, calling out to one another. Then he heard horses. He stuck his head up far enough to see three southbound horses, two at a gallop, the third snorting in surprise as John Barker leaped on its back pointed his musket at Daniel. Just as Daniel ducked out of sight again Barker pulled the trigger, then spurred his horse southward.

When Daniel reached the ground in front of his veranda, he called to the soldiers to get their horses. He sent a runner to the west side of the island to fetch some of Wakapuchasce's people to come along and help with tracking. Before riding south after Barker and his party, Daniel stopped at the cottage Jonas had built for his family near the great river, to ask them to greet Mary when she arrived and explain his absence.

Patrick Alcorn rode beside Daniel. Observing the widely spaced tracks of the horses, Alcorn recognized they were still at a full gallop, several miles south of McGirtt's main buildings. "It looks like Barker thought you were alone on this island. He's apparently learned his mistake. They're riding hard. I don't think they'll keep up this pace for very long. It'll kill the horses."

McGirtt still rode Gray Goose, his favorite mount, but he recognized that the mare was growing old and he would soon have to replace her. Just now, though, the Goose kept up with the others very well and, thought Daniel, *she could still take the lead if she wants to or if I ask her to do it.* "He won't get away this time," Daniel told Alcorn. "He can't know the territory very well and even if he does, he doesn't have Red Stick Creeks to wipe out his tracks or help him evade us. They are an amazing people."

Alcorn kept his peace for a few minutes, then asked, "Are you going to kill him or turn him in to Tonyn?"

Daniel's lips pulled to a thin, downturned line. "I can't blame him for hating me. We burned him out of his home and left him destitute, unable to care for his family. If I were him, I'd hate me too. But it was war. I was under orders. I did my job, and if I don't mind saying so myself, I did it rather well. We left the rebels between Savannah and Charleston unable to fight. We left them too consumed with the need to survive and feed their families to have time left to go to war against King and Country. Though I would hate Barker if the roles were reversed, I would understand that a good military officer does what he has to do to accomplish the needs of his country. Just so, a man living in the wilderness like this must do what he has to do to survive and protect his family. Barker is obviously going to keep coming back as long as he's able. And as long as he's able, my life and the lives of my family won't be safe. I'm going to kill him ... and his sons.

"The track leads far to the south," Daniel went on. "If we cut across Pablo's Ford to the west, we can cut them off and maybe catch up that much sooner. I sent a couple of the Creeks to see if the ford is low enough to do that. It probably is. Barker won't know about the ford. He'll run all the seven miles south before he turns west, then north for Georgia. When he takes the trail north, he'll find us waiting for him. We'll leave twenty men at the bend in the river to the north and the rest of them will come with me. He won't get away this time."

"I feel sorry for him." Alcorn said, uncomfortable with the idea of virtually executing Barker and his family for the attacks, with no trial at law, no formal judge. It would be simple execution. "Maybe it would be better if we take him to Tonyn?"

"So – what would Tonyn do? He'd lock Barker with his sons in that damp dungeon where he would lose his health and die anyway. A simple shooting is far more merciful and it will give me the satisfaction of knowing that neither Barker nor his sons will come back. Tonyn might even release him on the promise he'll return to South Carolina and never come back. I would make such an agreement myself, but I would not honor it."

Pablo's Ford was deep in mud and muck, but the snakes and alligators kept their distance as Daniel and his party waded across on horseback. One of the horses got stuck in the mud and several of the Florida rangers riding with McGirtt argued about whether to shoot it and leave it for the alligators or get covered in mud themselves trying to rescue it. They decided on rescue and managed to get the horse out of the muck after lightening its load of rider and equipment. When they reached the north/south trail beyond the north branch of McGirt's Creek, they took up posts behind trees with the horses tethered well to the north and out of earshot. It was clear that they had outflanked Barker and his people: there were no fresh tracks on the trail.

Not much over an hour later, Daniel could hear voices approaching. Barker and his sons were on foot, leading their horses, trying to help the creatures cool down after the hard ride. As the sounds grew closer, Barker's voice could be heard above the others: "I wish we scouted that out better than we did. We didn't know he had troops on the island with him. It would have been a clean kill, but poor scouting turned the tables on us. We'll get him next time. Third time's a charm."

Daniel stepped out from behind the trees in full view of Barker and his sons and called out, "This *is* your third time, Barker. It's the third and last time you will attack me." Half turning without taking his eyes off Barker, he called out, "Fire, boys!"

A barrage of musket fire deafened even the squirrels in the trees around them. Birds lifted off in clouds, squawking with fright. The thunder of so many muskets being fired at once startled even Daniel, who had called for it. Barker and both his sons dropped, each struck with multiple musket balls.

"Reload and be ready," McGirtt called out. "There may be more of them." Daniel carefully approached the men on the ground. Barker's sons were both dead, already turning the ghastly pale of corpses. Their blue lips were silent, but John Barker lived. As Daniel approached, Barker struggled to get his musket lifted and pointed, but Daniel stepped up quickly and kicked it out of his hands. "You're a tough old son of a bitch, aren't you, Barker? How many times were you hit? And you're still breathing. I think I'll stand here and watch you die."

Barker rolled onto his back. His eyes flashed with rage but his breath was choked with the blood pouring from his mouth. He tried to speak, obviously to curse Daniel, but he was unable to get any words formed. In just a few minutes, his eyes glazed over and he stopped choking. Daniel remained there, watching impassively. "Goodbye, Captain Barker."

☙ ❧

The ride home to Daniel's plantation house and his waiting Mary took longer than usual, because Daniel's party, instead of heading east and back across Pablo's Ford, headed south to find the Rangers they had left to cut off Barker's retreat. Together, rounding the south bend of McGirt's Creek and leisurely walking the horses, they spent an extra two hours, so by the time they arrived at the plantation, the sun was low in the west. McGirtt rode in the lead. When he reached the edge of his cultivated fields, he could see the figure of a lone woman, sitting on his front veranda, rocking comfortably and watching his approach. It reminded him of their courtin' days. Mary often came to visit in the Camden area. She had family there. When she visited, she always stayed with the Chesnut family on the Mulberry plantation, next to the Cantey Plantation. When he came to see her, he would dismount as soon as he was in sight and walk his horse to the front gate. "To keep from raising dust," he would tell her, but the real reason was to savor the anticipation of seeing her again. *I wonder if she's thinking of that?*

The distance was not as great as in the older days, only a few hundred yards. He watched her as he closed the distance. It had been more than a year since his last stolen visit to Camden where she was staying with his sister's family, the John Canteys. She was distressed, then, about his siding with the British against the American patriots, but even the Canteys, who were on the side of the Patriots, rationalized his decision. "A man's gotta do what he's gotta do," John Cantey said when Daniel tried to make a sort of indirect apology. "You and I aren't at war," Cantey continued. "My wife's brother will always be welcome in my home." Then he slapped Daniel on the back and invited him in for a snort of brandy.

Mary had stopped rocking.   Daniel was close enough to see her watching with a half-smile as he tantalized her with his deliberate approach. That, in fact, is what she said about his not raising the dust. "You just do that to tease me. You know I can't wait to feel your arms around me, yet you drag out the moment for as long as possible. You are a devilish rogue, Daniel McGirtt!"

This time it was different. As he drew near enough for voice communication at normal tones, she rose from the rocking chair and descended the porch steps. She stopped three feet away and look at him from head to toe. "You're a muddy mess, Daniel McGirtt? What have you been doing, chasing alligators?"

"No point in that," Daniel retorted.   "They're as chewy as overcooked clams. The Creeks seem to like them, though."

"I'd hug you, but not until you've bathed and changed clothes. You smell about as good as you look."

Daniel enjoyed the banter. "I'll do that immediately."

"You can't," Mary stated flatly. "There is a messenger waiting here to speak with you. He says he's from Governor Tonyn. There's trouble over toward St. Marys. I'm afraid you will have to go there and see to it."

11

1782 ... Nearing the end of the year.

Mary James McGirtt, half awake, was torn between enjoying the cozy warmth of her bed and drifting back to sleep. She rested in her near-dream-state, under a quilt comforter. The warmth of her husband next to her felt good after the long cold of loneliness while Daniel fought his wars away from home.

Their north-facing window, closed against the late November chill, admitted just a glimpse at the top of the star-filled cloudless sky. The lower part of the window, now in darkness, in daylight would show off the thick growth of live oak trees, Spanish moss and a growth of vines which Daniel called wisteria and Gabrielle's trumpets, after the shape of the flower they produce in the late spring.

When he was gone, she filled her time with friends and family. Her children were near. Her brother John James and his family welcomed her, even though Daniel had 'gone over to the dark side,' fighting for the Crown against American freedom. "A man's gotta do what a man's gotta do," her brother James said. "Daniel was always a man of principle – good as his word, for the most part. They don't come any better than him. I don't understand why he didn't stay with the Patriot cause. Maybe he'll explain it to me, one fine day. I'm sure he had his reasons."

Mary dismissed the memory, trying to clear her mind in pursuit of those last precious hours of sleep, the sweetest sleep that comes just before dawn. That was not to be. She could hear footsteps coming up the stairs, quietly, but nevertheless, audibly. Then the knock came at their bedroom door, prying her from the security of her dreams. The knock sounded respectful – not loud enough to startle but enough to awaken. She nudged Daniel who eventually roused himself enough to answer the door. She heard whispers that took no more than a moment. When Daniel turned back to her, he said, "There's something I've been saving for you to see, but we can only see it when conditions are just right. We have the conditions now. I left word for someone to waken us when this happened again. It's happening now."

She rolled over and buried her head under a pillow with a low groan. Daniel continued, "Come, Mary. This is something you will only see once or twice in lifetime, and then only if you're lucky enough to be in the right place at the right time."

Chitto, one of Wakapuchasce's people, held horses for them, saddled and ready. At the north end of Maxton Island, McGirtt's holdings, a long, thin peninsula reached northeast into the St. Johns River. Near the end of the peninsula stood a tall observation platform. Daniel had had it built to spot ships approaching as early as possible. "Surprises out here in this wilderness are usually not pleasant ones," he explained. The platform reached about thirty feet into the starry sky. Daniel and Mary dismounted at the foot of the observation tower, handing their reins to another Indian man who appeared to be waiting for them.

"What's this, Daniel?" Mary looked at the tower with concern. "You know I really don't like heights," she reminded him.

"It's dark. You won't be able to see the ground. Come." Taking her by the hand, he led her to the foot of the stairs and they climbed the tower. Mary watched her feet as well as she could, considering the low light of the night sky. "Keep your eyes lowered till I tell you. I want this to be a surprise."

"Daniel," Mary muttered in near exasperation. "You got me out of a nice cozy bed where I was in a beautiful state of dozing and sleep, with no explanation other than 'trust me' and 'you'll like this.' We've had no tea. No breakfast. We're met in the dark by one of your savages who hands us these horses without saying a single word. And now you have me climbing a tower, more or less against my will, with still no explanation."

They reached the top of the observation platform. Putting his arm around her waist, he softly said, "Now look."

Mary raised her eyes. If Daniel's arm had not been around her, she would gotten dizzy. She thought for a brief moment that she was standing in the sky, except there were two full moons. One hung in the sky in front of her, in a downward direction from where she stood watching. The other stood in a direction that was more upward. The world glowed, filled with stars both above and below. Gradually, she realized that the St. Johns River was in a state of glassy calm. Not a breath of air moved over its surface. The result was a perfect mirror image of the sky. The mirror rested silently in front of them, stretching three miles to the north east, two miles to the east and nearly eight miles to the southeast. Daniel faced her to the southeast before asking her to raise her eyes, the farthest view of the mirror effect. She could not tell where the sky ended and the Earth began. "Daniel, are we standing in the sky?"

"I thought so, too," Daniel said softly, "the first time I came up here and it was like this. Even now, when I come up here and it's like this, I have to check my feet to see what they are standing on. There's another piece to the puzzle," he said, pointing. "There and there and there, it looks like there are clouds below us, but if you look at the mirror image of the sky, above, there are no clouds to be reflected in this way. Do you see it?"

Looking where he pointed and squinting for a moment, she said, "Yes. My God! There are clouds on the river? How could that be, unless, we really are way up in the sky and the sky is all around us just as it appears? What could that be, Daniel?"

"It could be clouds and we actually are standing in the sky, looking at stars all around us. What do you think it is?"

Mary knew she was on an observation platform Daniel had had built so that watchmen could spot boats approaching, but her senses told her otherwise. She looked straight down at her feet and could see they were standing on the platform. She glanced behind them and could see the shadows of trees and the earth as it should appear at night. Then she looked back at the river and the reflected sky. "This must be what God sees when He looks out from wherever He's hiding."

"Yes," Daniel remarked. "It sometimes seems that He's hiding, but what do you make of the clouds on the river?"

"You tell me."

Daniel gripped her a little tighter and said, "There are places in the river where the air is moving slightly. Where it touches the water as it moves, it makes tiny ripples and from here, under these conditions, it looks like clouds. It's an amazing effect. No?"

"I can see why you came to love Florida so much," she answered. "Do you think we will ever return to South Carolina?"

"We will go there to visit, unless the rest of the family comes here. I think we will be here for a long time."

Mary disagreed. "Great Britain seems to be losing this war. Most of Europe is against her. The Dutch, the French, the Spanish have all sided with the Americans. There are even forces from Eastern Europe – Germans, Polish... There is talk in the peace discussions of giving Florida back to Spain. What will we do if that happens?"

"That's not going to happen," Daniel's voice became sterner. "The King's no fool. Florida is rich in agricultural resources. We have been here nineteen years. Many loyal subjects have built homes, ranches, successful businesses. They are raising indigo, rice, cattle. There is even a profitable turpentine trade coming out of Florida. Why would Britain be willing to give all that away? ...not to mention the incredible source of lumber, hardwoods, pine... Florida is a rich place. Great Britain needs Florida. And she's vast. This could even be a New Britannia. The climate is perfect, the forest rich in game. Why would Great Britain give up Florida"? That will never happen."

ଔ ଓ

Daniel sailed north just after noon on one of Francisco Sanchez's brigantines, accompanied by seventy five East Florida Rangers and twenty five Creek Indians. These were the Red Stick Creeks, the fiercer of Wakapuchasce's people. They were loyal to Daniel. He would be safe among them. Daniel had taken precautions for Mary's safety as well. "We never know when raiders from Georgia will show up," he fretted. "We have scouts watching for them constantly. When they do show up, it's either by boat or they come in over the land bridge from the south." Daniel had introduced her to Chitto on her first day on the site. "His name means 'Brave.' Chitto is charged with watching over you while I'm away – and I will have to be away quite a lot, I'm afraid. Governor Tonyn uses The East Florida Rangers to protect Florida's borders. With the Colonies evicting Loyalists and confiscating their properties, many of them are fleeing to British Florida. In the last couple of years, Tonyn estimates ten thousand white people have come to Florida from the colonies and they brought somewhere around eleven thousand negro slaves with them. Dealing with those large numbers of people has been a real problem. Food and housing is a real problem. St. Augustine is a small town. It can't handle those numbers. Tonyn has spread them all over the area, given some of them land, broken up larger, abandoned plantations so they have somewhere to go. It's amazing how he's coping with the problems."

Mary felt safe on Maxton Island, as long as Daniel was there, but among of the things that made her very nervous was the fact that Daniel had nearly fifty negroes on the property who were armed with muskets and swords. Several times she had seen them practicing at targets, and when she asked Daniel about it, he smiled and said, "Those people are not slaves. Remember what Jonas told you the day you arrived? They're free people, from a plantation in South Carolina. I promised them their freedom in exchange for helping us subdue the plantation. They have chosen to stay here for the time being and help me protect Maxton Island, and my family – you. We supplied them with the weapons as soon as we were able to capture enough muskets and powder. We make the balls here. Ahaya has said he will welcome them to his villages any time they wish to join him."

"And Ahaya is...?" Mary was a little overwhelmed with all the foreign names, all the new people and places.

"Ahaya is a Red Stick Creek Chief. His real name is Chief Wakapuchasce, but everyone calls him Ahaya, which means 'Cow Keeper.' He has a village about ninety miles west of here at a place he calls Cuscowilla. He rounded up the wild Andalusian cattle left by the Spanish, domesticated them, and now has a nice business selling cattle to the British, and I suppose to the Americans. Chitto is one of Wakapuchasce's people. He's very fierce and very reliable."

Mary wasn't about to let the subject go. "Why is Ahaya fighting on the side of Great Britain? I thought most of the Indians hated the English."

Daniel smiled. "Ahaya hates the Spanish. They treated his family shamefully, he says. He has vowed to kill one hundred Spanish and I think he sides with Great Britain because Spain is a common enemy. Maybe he has other reasons. If he does, he has not told me."

"So," Mary asked, "if there is trouble while you're gone, what will happen here?"

"You should be quite safe. Jonas' people, the armed negroes you were worrying about, will protect the hacienda. I am keeping twenty five Rangers here all the time to back them up. If Chitto feels that there is any danger, he will come for you. If he asks, go with him. He won't ask unless there is real danger and if you go with his people you can be assured you will be safe."

ಖ ಖಾ

Patrick Alcorn loved riding right up front when he was sailing. He liked to watch the water approaching, then sliding under the bow of the vessel silently, as the wind-driven water vehicle made its way through ripple and wave. Now and then he would turn to admire the tight stretched canvas high overhead and marvel at how the crew seemed to always know exactly which of the amazing bundle of ropes secured to batons on the deck, did what – what it was tied to on the other end. Patrick couldn't figure it out. He followed one rope or another, time after time, with his eyes, trying to see where the rope went, but the maze of hemp overhead always baffled him. "Believe it or not, there's a system to it," one of the sailors answered when Patrick raised the question to him.

With a very satisfying southeast wind, the brigantine approached within a mile of Cow Ford in just a few hours. Patrick was delighted with the marvels of modern science. A sailing ship saved them better than a day on horseback. It gave him the chance to study the ropes again and enjoy his amazement at how those incredible people kept track of the endless miles of rope that controlled the ship. Before he could satisfy himself that he had admired the ropes to their fullest extent, a shot rang out from shore. The musket ball went high and whistled through the rigging, tearing a small hole in the fore, upper top gallant, head sail. Patrick ducked below the forward port bulkhead. Just as he popped his head back up to take a look, the sound of many more muskets and a cannon – about a four pounder, he reckoned – sent more lead whistling through the rigging. After the first ball, the captain ordered the ship hard to starboard to try to sail out of range of the fire arms, but that would take a while, provided they didn't lose all their rigging from the bombardment. The next round of shots came in lower. The ambushers were lowering their aim. Most of the crew had taken shelter behind the bulkheads, but some of them were still adjusting the sails. Fortunately, no one got shot and only the sails were damaged.

Captain's orders: everyone kept their heads below the bulkhead rail until the ship was out of range. It didn't take very long. The shot dropped lower and lower with each volley, until the balls all hit the water farther and farther aft of the ship. At Cow Ford, the river was too narrow to get out of range by simply sailing across the river, so the ship had to turn south the way it had come. Daniel reconnoitered with the captain, suggesting a landing at the next plantation to the south. "Doubtful they have the whole west side of the river covered. We can disembark there and sweep down on them from the west. Lord Loughborough, my neighbor to the north, has a pier we can use for unloading."

The voyage almost all the way back to Maxton Island took the rest of the day since the wind was wrong for sailing in that direction. By the time they landed, the sun was low on the horizon and the wind was calming. Another day lost... In the morning, at first light, McGirtt mustered his men and they began skirting the river, inland so they could arrive unnoticed by those trying to hold the north side of the river. "So," Alcorn asked Daniel, "are they Patriots or Loyalists? Seems to me they'd be rebels from the colonies trying to encroach on Florida. What do you think?"

Daniel shook his head. "Who knows? I think it's colonists trying to take part of Florida and hold it. It's interesting that they tried that a couple of times before and couldn't accomplish the deed. The first time – what were those men's names? Button Gwinnett and Lachlan MacIntosh, I think. They both led sizable armies and together they might have succeeded, but they couldn't get along well enough. What did they argue about? Was it a woman? Probably... In their duel, Button Gwinnet died of his wounds and MacIntosh had to go home to heal."

"I heard the story," Alcorn chuckled. "They were both wounded on the first round. Then they both got up and decided to have a second go at it, but their seconds pulled them off of each other."

"Fools," Daniel snorted. "Now what are they going to do, try it again with much smaller forces? If there were any sizeable forces approaching, we would have heard about it long ago. I think this is another ragtag bunch of sorry ragamuffins set out to make their fortune. I'm afraid they're going to learn a hard lesson!"

Alcorn swept his hair out of his eyes, reset his hat and glanced out toward the river. "It won't even matter if they outnumber us. They'll have their backs to the water. They'll be trapped."

Daniel had his men skirt widely to the west and the north so that the approach toward Cow Ford could be as much of a surprise as possible. "As rumor has it," Daniel told Alcorn, "Cunningham is somewhere just south of St. Marys. Send a runner and ask him for help if it's possible. A little reinforcement would make sure these raiders don't escape."

಄ ಄

Mary McGirtt remained on the veranda of the plantation house, watching Daniel ride off into the morning mist with his seventy five men and assorted Indians. She felt suddenly very alone. She knew no one here. Friends and family were all in South Carolina. She knew Daniel's brother James and his family kept a house in St. Augustine, but that was pretty far away with the wide St. Johns River representing the first barrier. She could hear the sounds of the house slaves cleaning up the breakfast dishes and moving around inside the house. Then everything grew quiet. Gradually, Mary became aware of the presence of a young woman standing not far to her right and somewhat behind her. Miranda's skin was so dark she would have been invisible, had it been night time. Her slender figure seemed almost inadequate to contain her fierce eyes. Not far behind Miranda stood Jonas, the former slave. In the distance, Mary could see some of the Indians who had remained behind. "They'll watch over you," Daniel had told her. "If Chitto comes for you, go with him. Trust him. I asked him to get you out of here if any trouble is coming. He may take you as far as Cuscowilla, but if he does that it's to protect you. You will be safe with him and Wakapuchasce's people. I'll come for you, if that happens." She recognized Chitto at the edge of the field. Some of his compatriots walked through the field as though checking on the progress of the crops.

Just then, Mary heard Miranda clearing her throat as though she wanted some attention. Mary turned to her and said, "Good morning, Miranda. You too, Jonas. Is there something I can do for you?"

"Good morning to you too, Miss Mary. We was just wonderin' if you know how to read?"

Somewhat taken aback, she smiled and said, "I do."

Jonas stepped a little closer and Miranda continued, "We was wonderin' if you would teach some of us how to read?"

Mary turned her chair to face them better. "You are some of the people who Daniel freed are you not?"

"We are, ma'am," Jonas answered. "There are forty-six of us."

"If you are free to go," Mary answered, "why are you still here?"

"Master Daniel said we could stay if we wanted to, that we could work here, for him and he would pay us."

"Is he paying you?" Mary queried.

"He is, ma'am," Jonas smiled. "We stayed with Master Daniel because we really don't know where to go. Daniel says it's dangerous for us to stay here, that any white man might claim us and we might be stuck again in slavery. He says we should join the Indians, that Wakapuchasce is a good man and he will protect us and help us to live with his people."

"How do you feel about that?" Mary was uncertain about the wisdom of such a choice, but she knew what Daniel told them to be true.

"Master Daniel has never given us reason to distrust him, ma'am. If says it's true, then we believe it is. If you teach us to read and write, if we ever do decide to work as freemen, then we will be better able to survive."

"I will teach you," Mary answered. "We'll begin tomorrow morning. I need a little time to gather my thoughts about how to get started. Meet me here after breakfast and we'll get started. Will you bring more of your people to join us?"

"Yes, ma'am," Jonas and Miranda said almost together.

☙ ❧

Daniel's attack upon those trying to hold the north side of the landing at Cow Ford began taking shape. His people slipped through the forest as quietly as possible and spread out as they got nearer. "We'll try to take them without any gunfire," Daniel told his troops. "Tonyn can probably use them for free labor and house them in the old Spanish fort." Daniel was disappointed to learn the rebels had watchers posted at both the north and south ends of their encampment and that guards also watched the western approaches. Daniel's Creek Indians sighted the spotters first and silenced them with hardly a sound. "I never imagined those Indians could move so quietly though the woods," he told Mary later. "They came up on the guards from behind and they were dead before they knew what hit them. We crept up on the encampment and had them under control before they were all out of bed. They did somehow manage to get the four pound cannon swiveled around to face us, loaded it and had it ready to fire, but they never got off a shot."

Daniel sent for the brigantine, still tied up at Lord Loughborough's home, to transport the captured rebels to St. Augustine. He waited for the ship to make sure the captives were loaded safely and secured for the short voyage. He had not lost a single companion in taking the small rebel stronghold. When the brigantine hoisted its sails and headed toward the open sea, Daniel signaled his men to move out. They were tasked with guarding the Florida border, keeping out raiders who were constantly attacking plantations west of St. Augustine and even, from time to time, threatening the town itself. Tonyn was taciturn when he had remarked to Daniel on their last meeting, "The rebels seem to think that Florida is open game for them, and maybe it is. Great Britain is at war with the United States and this is British territory. I think they'd do better to focus their efforts on thwarting our troops that are actually in their colonies than seeking out British territory elsewhere. I think they're opportunists, set on enriching themselves at Florida's expense. But we have our defenses. Thank you for that, Daniel."

Daniel sent a runner ahead to inform Cunningham that his help was no longer needed, then set course for St. Marys, Georgia, just over the Florida border. The plan included that as a starting point. He was to sweep west as far as the Suwannee River then start working his way south, crisscrossing North Florida, looking for raiders' encampments. It was a 'cleanup' action. Tonyn's message said raiders had been seen as far south as Tomoka and that they were all to be removed. "Find all of them. Bring what you can to the fort for slave labor and kill the ones you can't capture. Hunt them down and kill them!"

"Grim orders," Daniel remarked to Alcorn. "And what about Maxton Island? That's just about right in the middle of all this. I hope Mary is safe. She should have stayed with her brother in Stateburg!"

༃ ༄

Mary McGirtt watched as all forty six of her husband's freed people assembled at the foot of her porch. The Indians, about twenty of them, all men, watched from the edge of the field, seemingly amused at the sight. Mary could see the hope in the freedmen's eyes. 'Would such a time come?' they seemed to be thinking and expressing in every movement – hope. And now, Mary could see this in their eyes, too: Mrs. McGirtt was going to give them the tools they needed to compete, successfully, in a white man's world.

"There are twenty six letters," Mary began.

"What's a letter?" someone asked.

"How many is twenty six?" from another.

"I can see," Mary said softly. "I am also going to have to teach you to count and maybe some basic arithmetic. Then we'll get back to the letters." Before long, she had all forty-six people counting to twenty-six, then to one hundred. Once she was satisfied they all had the idea, she asked, "How many is twenty-six?" Some could retain the information more quickly than others and she took extra time with each one to make sure they were all keeping up. "Maybe I should have been a teacher?" She chuckled at herself. Not only was she pulling off the task at hand rather easily, she was teaching negroes to read and write – AND count. That was strictly forbidden in some places where she used to live.

She quickly ran through the twenty six letters of the alphabet, "to give you an idea of what we have to cover," she commented. "Then we'll practice until everyone has it down pat. Then we'll start to read things."

Mary could see Chitto briskly approaching from the far side of one of the fields. She tried to ignore him, knowing full well that there could be only one reason why he had left the forest. When he was within earshot, he flatly stated, "We must go. People are coming. Many people."

"Let me just finish th..."

Chitto interrupted her. "We must go now. You must be safe. These others," he indicated the former slaves, "must come with us. All must be safe. Come *now*."

12

1782

November 30 – Preliminary Articles of Peace were signed in Paris. April 15, 1783, the Preliminary Articles of Peace were ratified by the Congress of the United States.

1783

The first sovereignty to declare war on the new United States of America was the Muslim Barbary States of North Africa.

The New Spanish Governor Vincente Manual Zespedes A.K.A Cespedes y Velasco of Valencia Spain was appointed Governor of East Florida by Bernardo de Galvez, Viceroy of New Spain.

The Russian Empire annexed the Crimean Khanate

November 25 – British Troops leave New York City

December 23 – George Washington resigned as Commander of the Continental Army.

   A chilling northeaster howled through the trees as McGirtt's East Florida Rangers worked their way along the trail toward the St. Mary's River. Dead branches, high among the live oak trees that had rotted through during the last few years, crashed to the ground around them, the sound nearly overwhelmed by the howl of the wind. Large clumps of Spanish Moss fell from the trees, flying sideways. The occasional chilling gusts, reaching probably thirty five knots, took Daniel's breath away. The hundred men following him shivered under their heavy wraps, glad there was no rain today, yet.

"Winter weather in North Florida isn't much more pleasing than winter weather in South Carolina," Patrick Alcorn observed through pale, shivering lips.

"Tomorrow it'll be eighty degrees," Daniel snapped back. "Or maybe the next day... If we keep moving, at least, we may be able to keep a little warmer than if we sit back and huddle over campfires. It's just another northeaster."

"The horses don't seem to mind it." Alcorn pulled his wrap a little tighter around his throat to keep the wind from entering. "They're friskier than ever. I remember watching them in the fields near Camden. When it got cold like this, they'd practically dance with joy."

"They're practically dancing with joy, now," McGirtt grunted. "If we turned them loose, I bet we'd see some rearing up and general prancing."

Since word had come out about the Preliminary Articles of Peace, the influx of Loyalist refugees from the colonies subsided. But those who had already fled to Florida were still present. "It's too bad about all these people from up north," Daniel commented.

Daniel likes to hear himself talk, Alcorn observed inwardly. *How many times has he said this before? He's right, though. They have nowhere to go and no means of self-support other than brigandry.*

Daniel held a nostril shut with one finger then cleared the other, then reversed the procedure. "No one could have foreseen the way St. Augustine and the surrounding area would be overwhelmed with refugees. How many camps have we passed today?"

"Seven or eight, I guess," Alcorn replied. "Two to three hundred people in each camp."

"They seemed peaceful enough while we were there, but I wonder where they're going next? How will they earn their next meal? They can't survive on game and fishing."

"The Indians do," Alcorn retorted.

"But the Indians started farming on a limited basis and trading for food stuffs with others farther inland. Wildlife isn't a reliable source of food for a large population." Daniel wiped his lip and pulled his muffler tighter around his throat. "I hope Sanchez has his Diego Plantation well guarded. That herd of cattle he keeps there will be very tempting to these hungry people."

The St. Mary's River appeared in front of them suddenly. The undergrowth had concealed its presence until they were nearly right on top of it. McGirtt's horse stopped suddenly, as one of its front feet slipped at the edge of the riverbank. "Well, there's Georgia," Daniel remarked, pointing across the river. "Now we need to start working our way westward. Send some of the Indians to find us a westward trail. No – ASK some of the Indians. They hate being ordered around but they seem friendly enough if we treat them like equals."

After riding the rest of the day, shivering through another night, Alcorn was pleased to see a clear sky full of stars at first light. "There will be sunshine today," he smiled as he handed Daniel a hot cup of tea.

"I told you. Near freezing yesterday and sweat all day today. Welcome to Florida." Daniel held his tea with both hands, warming them around the hot mug. "No southbound tracks yesterday," he remarked. "I doubt we'll be so lucky today. We're nearing the headwaters of the St. Mary's. There'll be shallow crossing places up ahead. Remember that family we routed west of the big swamp? I bet they've gathered some friends and will be back looking for us soon. And they weren't the only back country settlers in that area. We could even be facing a small army. We'll see."

Alcorn shivered against the cold. He too held his tea with both hands, grateful for the warmth. "I seem to remember that James Oglethorpe thought the American Colonies would be a good place to move some of the people from London debtors' prisons, to give them a chance to be industrious. I read it was a disaster. He said the ne'er-do-well there would be ne'er-do-well wherever they went."

"Many of them left Savannah, where Oglethorpe brought them and sought their fortunes in the wild country where they didn't have to pay taxes or bow to highbred gentry that splattered them with mud as they sped by in their carriages." Daniel snorted. "The high pride of the lowbred condemned them to living in the wilderness. But their inclinations remain unchanged – taking advantage of any opportunity at the expense of those who are momentarily weak. That's who's raiding North Florida right now. I say we'll find tracks headed south today."

Later that day, as the sun neared its zenith, Patrick Alcorn stopped his horse right beside Daniel and announced, "Well, Daniel, you're a prophet. There are your tracks, fairly fresh too."

"A few days old, I think. Maybe a week. If there had been rain these last few days, we might not even have seen them. Let's find out where they're going." Daniel sent the word back through the troops and turned his horse to follow the trail. "It looks like quite a few horses and quite a few more on foot. Is Payne still with us? Let's see, and if he is let's get his opinion."

With Payne, the son of Wakapuchasce, riding beside them, keeping a watch on the tracks they followed, the East Florida Rangers picked up speed. "Payne will tell us when the tracks are getting fresh enough that we might be catching up. The last thing we want is to ride into an ambush." Those on foot were unable to keep up with the horsemen, but they would make a good surprise of reinforcements when they caught up, if needed. The trail led south, but kept veering to the east until it finally led nearly due east. "Feels like I'm headed for home," Daniel remarked with a very stern look in his eye. "Maybe we better hurry up a little more."

Payne finally raised a hand, pointing out that they were overtaking their prey. "These tracks are only a day old," he said with a grim smile. "This trail ends at Welaka."

"Maybe we better get a move on," Daniel spurred his horse.

"What's Welaka?" Alcorn wanted to know.

"It means 'River of Lakes,' Daniel called over his shoulder. "That's what Wakapuchasce's people call the St. Johns River."

The eastward trail ended just as Payne said it would, at the St. Johns River, south of Maxton Island, at the entrance to the Padamaran Plantation where Daniel had routed the raiding party before. From there, they followed the trail north toward Maxton Island. As they turned north, Daniel picked the pace up to a trot, leaving those on foot far behind. Where the trail split, with the branch to the right going to Maxton Island and the branch to the left heading for Cow Ford and St. Marys, the tracks headed for Maxton Island, then returned, veering west and north toward Cow Ford. "They've been and gone." Daniel spurred his horse for home with fifty mounted men behind him.

The house and grounds were empty of people, cattle, horses, slaves. The house appeared abandoned with the front door swinging in the morning breeze. Smoke still rose from the cookhouse, but the fire was nearly out. No horses stood in the coral or the barn. No cattle grazed in the nearby pasture. No Mary stood on the porch waiting for him. Daniel frantically ran through the house looking for signs of anything he could find – a struggle, blood. The house had been ransacked but there was no sign of foul play. Back outside at the cookhouse, it was the same. All valuables had been taken – tools, finished horseshoes, saddles, bridles and all tack was gone. Alcorn stayed by Daniel's side through the searching, thinking of his own family who waited for him in South Carolina. "There's no sign of them, Daniel." Daniel strode toward the barn. Alcorn stopped suddenly, almost running into Daniel who had stopped by the fence. He was studying an odd fixture of twigs, tied hurriedly and suspended from the upper rail of the fence, not far from the barn. One long stick, bent like an archer's bow and tied with a string, hung from the rail with the ends of the stick pointed upward. Suspended in the middle of the bow, hanging below, a slice of a branch, cut with a saw or the single blow of a heavy ax swung slightly in the breeze. "What are you looking at?" The thing held no meaning for him.

Daniel removed the bow from the fence rail and held it up so Alcorn could see it more clearly. "It's a message from Chitto. It's an image of the bull's horn. He has taken Mary and the others to Cuscowilla, to Cow Keeper. They are safe. Let's go after these raiders."

The hundred mounted men charged north along the trail toward Georgia. In Alcorn's memory, he had never seen Daniel in such a rage. Tight-lipped and silent, he pressed north, refusing to stop even to rest the horses. As the early darkness of winter began to settle in, they were forced to stop for the night on the Florida side of the St. Mary's River. At dawn they pressed on again, wading the shallow western reaches of the river and into Georgia. When Daniel's men overtook them, all the raiders were slaughtered in a sudden, deadly battle. The raiders' cattle and horses recovered, Daniel sent his men farther north in search of more potential Georgia raiders. Those of the raiders who were slaves were taken with the cattle and horses back toward Daniel's Maxton Island to be sold to Francisco Sanchez. Francisco found a ready market for such booty in the Windward Islands and the Caribbean Islands, so not only was Daniel's desire for revenge sated, but his pockets would be lined as well.

೦ಽ ಏಂ

Francisco Sanchez's brigantine, *La Santa Lucia*, rode at anchor in La Bahia De Matanzas on the north side of the island of Cuba. La Bahia de Matanzas was chosen as anchorage over the La Bahia de Habana because of easier access and better protection from the sea. The donkey cart that carried Francisco from Matanzas to Havana frustrated Francisco with its perpetual stops, bumps and speed. "I could have walked it faster than this!" His complaint to the driver was answered with a grunt, a spit over the side of the wagon and a snarled, "Then walk."

"I'm sorry for complaining," Francisco answered. "I wonder if I could rent a horse somewhere for a few days. The horse would probably be faster."

"Few of the people you see in these squalid huts around us own horses. If they did, they would not trust you to return it, if they were even willing to part with the horse for any time. They use these animals in their farms. They only own a horse if it's needed for their work."

"There is unrest in North Florida. I need to return as soon as I can." Francisco's concern for the safety of his people and haciendas was well warranted, as Daniel McGirtt could attest to, in view of his own recent troubles.

"You should have anchored your ship at Havana."

"I agree," Francisco tried to be polite.

The Governor of Cuba, Luis de Umzaga y Amezaga appeared to Francisco as an aging Bureaucrat. *Short! Even for an hombre de España. Fat! Too many frijoles! Bald! Maybe he wears hats too much!* Luis's pencil-thin mustache accented his pencil-thin eyebrows and the thin tuft of whiskers he cultivated, reaching in a pencil-thin line straight downward from his upper lip. "Francisco Sanchez?" He snorted at the introduction. "Who the hell are YOU? North Florida? What's that to me?" *Pencil-thinness!* The thought forced itself into Francisco's mind. *Maybe he does this as a clue and warning to his visitors that his perception is as pencil-thin as his manners!*

"I am the owner of several haciendas in North Florida, your honor," Francisco answered with a friendly smile. "I raise many thousands of cattle. I own much freestanding lumber ready to be harvested. I have access to many slaves that come to me from the war to the north of Florida. Does Cuba have need of such things?"

"Indeed it does. Indeed it does. Have a seat, my friend."

Francisco was not taken in by the sudden change in Umzaga's demeanor. *This man will accept my products and may not pay me. I will keep my shipments small until I am sure he is a man of honor.* After the small talk, Francisco presented his problem and solution. "For the last twenty years, Great Britain has been the master of the lands where I live and farm. Now, thanks to God, sweet Spain has come back to us. Now, at last, I am free to serve the people of my father's birthplace again. I can provide food, building materials and labor..."

"I am surprised that our interim governor Vincent Zespedes, did not tell me about you. Maybe he didn't know?"

"It was dangerous for me to communicate with Spanish dignitaries during the British rule of Florida," Francisco answered. "During Zespedes time in Cuba, though, I did send some shipments here, secretly, so he did know of me."

Luis Umzaga coughed a short 'ha' of derision. "Zespedes is such a fool! He's a social climber! He's from Valencia but he lisps like a Castillano; even spells his name with a 'C' so he can justify the lisp. ME? I'm from Málaga where we speak Spanish as it's meant to be spoken. None of this effeminate lisping!"

"Why do the people of Castile lisp, sir? Do you know?"

"Some say the lisp originated in Roman times but others blame it on King Phillip II. It is said that the English Queen Elizabeth rejected his marriage proposal because of it, but we suspect she had heard from her sister Queen Mary that Phillip had unique preferences that Mary did not approve of."

"Who can say," Francisco demurred. "It is probably wrong of us to speak of our sovereigns in this way, even the dead ones." His chuckle brought a smile to Umzaga's eyes and Umzaga quickly changed the subject.

"So then, shall we make a contract?"

◊ ◊

The Diego Plantation, lying between St. Augustine and the mouth of the St. Johns River, experienced the same chilly weather Daniel McGirtt and his men complained of on their raid into Georgia. Francisco's seven hundred cattle seemed not to mind it. They grazed peacefully in the plush meadows left by Francisco Sanchez's lumbering operation, which had clear-cut nearly the full thousand acres. Francisco Sanchez grew gradually wealthy on his sales of lumber and cattle. When Francisco's own land was clear-cut, he felt no compunction about cutting farther into the plantations of the Spanish who had abandoned their land to go back to Spain and into the plantations of the British absentee owners who never even inspected their holdings. On the surface those sales went to St. Augustine and provided food and building materials for the British troops during the American War for Independence, but other, less than out-in-the-open shipments went to Cuba and the Spanish forces at war with Great Britain during the war with the colonies. Most of the cattle grazing in Francisco's plush meadows came from South Carolina plantations where Daniel McGirtt, William Cunningham and Stephen Mayfield had so dramatically conducted their raids for Brigadier General Augustine Prevost. He disposed of the slaves first because they brought so much more money than cattle. Many of the slaves had also been shipped to Cuba and Spain's other holdings in the area. With most of the slaves gone and sold, he still had large herds of cattle to dispose of, now grazing on not only his land but the land he had cleared on neighboring properties.

Jorge Espinosa, growing stocky with his advancing age, stood taller than most of Spanish descent. His mother, he liked to say, was from Dresden in Germany and was responsible for his height and muscular build, but his father had also been a big man. Now, as chief overseer of the Diego Plantation for Francisco Sanchez, Jorge allowed himself to grow comfortable. It was in comfort, dining on roast beef from the South Carolina plantations that his second in command, Felipe Edimborough found him. Jorge was eating in relaxed delight when Felipe Edimborough came bursting through the door, gasping for breath. Felipe, a trusted slave and skilled butcher, had held his position of leadership through many years of service to Francisco. Jorge resented that his second-in-command was a slave, vaguely suspected that Felipe knew of Jorge's dislike for him and was subsequently slow to take advice from him.

"Many are coming ... from the north," Felipe exclaimed, waving his hands. "I don't know how so many got over the big river without us hearing about it, but they did. There are hundreds. If we don't get out of here, I think we'll certainly be slaughtered like hogs! Quickly, get your wife and let's go!"

Jorge swallowed his bite. "We have enough men on the hacienda to fight them off, don't we? What? We must have sixty men, all with arms. All can shoot. All are loyal? Why flee?"

"There are hundreds!" Felipe repeated. "They outnumber our people six or seven to one, maybe ten to one and they are armed and the scouts say they are coming fast. We barely have time to get out alive. I'm leaving now. Goodbye!"

03 80

Francisco Sanchez, stuck again on a donkey cart, headed back to the Bahia de Matanzas and his ship, groaned again with boredom and frustration at the loss of so much time. *A full day to ride such a short distance is outrageous. Have they no horses on this God-forsaken island?* Finally, boarding *La Santa Lucia*, he gave the order to unfurl the sails, hoist the anchor and head for the *Bahia de Habana*. There they would unload the cargo Francisco had loaded secretly aboard the ship – the other reason for not landing at Havana. Had he landed at Havana, Umzaga would have known he had livestock on board and driven a much harder bargain. At Havana, he off-loaded fifty horses and a hundred head of cattle, the once-wild Andalusian cattle whose ancestors arrived in La Florida with Pedro Menendez de Aviles. Mixed with the Andalusians were Sussex and cattle of North Devon captured from the plantations of South Carolina. The British cattle were heavier and brought a better price but the Andalusians were nearly free to Francisco so they brought a higher profit. He was very satisfied with the bargain he had cut with Umzaga and satisfied that Umzaga was very likely to pay in gold.

The voyage home followed the Gulf Stream, heading into the northeaster that was howling across North Florida. Sailors knew that when the wind blows against the stream, the normally high seas of the stream obey the commands of the north wind, rising higher than ever. Ships beating their way north against such weather frequently failed to come home. Francisco and his captain were no strangers to Florida weather and the Gulf Stream. They traced their course far west of the Stream but there too, the northerly drift of the sea opposed the wind, providing a rough passage for the mariners. Tacking north against the wind and sea made the voyage longer than Francisco had anticipated. He was no stranger to the sea but the combination of the cold wind and the six to ten foot seas way over matched his resistance to seasickness. By the time *La Santa Lucia* entered the mouth of the St. Johns River, Francisco and half the crew were weak with exhaustion and ready for rest in beds that did not rise and fall, toss and roll. As soon as the ship crossed the bar and began skimming the calmer water of the St. Johns River in the heavy northeaster, the captain ordered the ship to come about, furl the sails and drop anchor to give the crew and his passengers time for a hot meal and some badly needed rest. The next day, they planned to anchor at Cow Ford, just north of the Diego Plantation.

03 80

Governor Patrick Tonyn, the last British Governor of East Florida, relaxed on his high balcony, overlooking the Matanzas Bay at St. Augustine. His tea was hot. His crumpets, also sometimes known as English muffins, were warm and freshly baked by Juan Andreu, just a few blocks south. The northeaster that had plagued St. Augustine with abnormally high tides, minor flooding and generally uncharacteristic chilly weather was gone. The balmy breeze from the southeast carried the smell of the sea. Packs of white spots, which Tonyn knew were ring billed gulls, floated on the Matanzas river, dreaming, or so Tonyn thought with a smile, of the fishing boats that might come in soon, where they could steal a few bites. The only guest on his agenda this morning owned a thousand-acre plantation eighteen miles north of town and a few other sizable chunks of land along the St. Johns River, west of St. Augustine. Tonyn knew Francisco Xavier Sanchez to be smart, aggressive and skilled in not only raising cattle, harvesting lumber, expropriating slaves and other goods from nefarious sources but in negotiating agreements with government officials such as himself. Tonyn sort of trusted Francisco Sanchez, but then... sort of not.

There was the matter of the ship full of Spanish soldiers sent by the interim governor of Cuba, Vincent Zespedes, to capture the Bahama Islands from the British. The ship was taken and wrecked. The soldiers were brought to St. Augustine and imprisoned in the Old Fort. Sanchez provided them with food and clothing – an act, nearly, of treason, by a British Citizen, aiding the enemy. It came to Tonyn's attention that on Francisco's recent trip to Cuba, he gave those men passage and freed them on Cuban soil to the present governor, Luis de Umzaga y Amezaga. *I have to consider the man is descended from Spaniards. His father, Joseph, was born in Ronda. It's natural, I suppose, that he would feel some kinship to these men, and after all, the war is, for the most part, over... Still...*

Tonyn had just taken a bite of one of his warm butter-smothered crumpets when his confidential secretary, Bill McLendon, interrupted him. "Your boy's here, Governor. Shall I send him in?"

Tonyn dabbed the butter from his lips with his cotton napkin and answered, "Yes. Please."

In the years Tonyn had known Francisco, he had watched him age and mature from the wise-for-his-age youth he met when he became the Governor of East Florida in 1774. Francisco was thirty-eight years old then, and had been managing the Diego Plantation on his own for eleven years. Tonyn had not seen Francisco in nearly a year. "Good morning, my friend." Tonyn rose from his seat and offered Francisco his hand. "So, how is Maria Piedra and the many children this fine morning?"

"She's fine and pregnant with another," Francisco smiled as a cup appeared in front of him with a small tray of crumpets and butter. "You know, of course, why I am here?"

"Yes." Tonyn wished Francisco would spend a little more time being sociable. *He always jumps right to the point. No small talk here.* "You went to Cuba to negotiate a trade deal with the new governor. On the trip you took the Spanish prisoners I had entrusted to your care and released them on Cuban soil. I ought to have you hanged for treason."

"The war is over, your honor. What harm is there? They won't come back to fight. Most of them are in poor health because of the accommodations at El Castillo de San Marco, or Fort St. Mark, as you call it. Many of them have what the doctors call 'consumption.' They won't live long, either in Florida or with their families in Cuba."

"I'm not going to forgive you for that, Francisco. Neither am I going to punish you for it. Personally, I agree with what you did, but you are still a British subject and I am still the British Governor. If you give me any more reason to distrust you, I WILL have you hanged. Is that clear?"

"Yes sir." Francisco lowered his head slightly, keeping his eyes on Tonyn's. "You are aware that while I was away, the Diego Plantation was raided?"

"Yes," Tonyn sighed. "How bad was it?"

"My overseer, Jorge Espinosa is dead. His family is missing. The raiders slaughtered over four hundred of my cattle. They stole sixty-three slaves, thirty-seven horses and anything they could find in my house that they thought they could sell. My Diego Plantation was raped! Where were your Florida Rangers? Where was Daniel McGirtt? Cunningham? Mayfield? Brown? Are planters in North Florida to be left vulnerable while the Florida Rangers are pillaging in Georgia and South Carolina? Are they not here to protect us from such atrocities? The raiders didn't steal four hundred head of cattle! They slaughtered them right there on my property. I came home to find rotting carcasses. They took the choicest pieces of meat and left the rest to rot!"

☙ ❧

Daniel McGirtt, unhappy about being summoned to St. Augustine when he was eager to ride to Cuscowilla to fetch his wife, sipped a beer in Maria's Taberna, across from the British military barracks on St. Francis Street. His only companion, Francisco Sanchez, fidgeted as he complained about the raiders from the north. Daniel, although well-meaning, failed to placate Francisco with the stories of his own land being raided. "I can't bring back your old friend, Jorge, Francisco, but on the last raid, in addition to recovering my own cattle, I captured another fifteen hundred head, three hundred slaves, several hundred horses and three cartloads of sellable chattel. Out of that, you can have four hundred head to replace what you lost. Take your pick of the slaves. I didn't go into the colonies to enrich myself, but to recover what was stolen and to pay back what they did to us. They have been adequately paid back. Take what you want and give the rest to Tonyn. I've already recovered my cattle, horses and slaves."

"How can these raids be stopped?" Francisco's eagerness and his coming to McGirtt for advice gave Daniel a feeling of responsibility that he didn't want.

"Francisco, my hundred Rangers and myself are a single gun in a wilderness. We can hit hard, here and there, but to stop what's happening will take more power than you and I can wield. As you know, for the last few years, people have been flooding into North Florida as though it's raining people up north. They're bringing their slaves, their property, as well as they can and they're bringing their anger. They're displaced. They're armed and they're angry. Tonyn doesn't have the resources to placate all of them. He's giving away land like it grows on trees. He's offering tax incentives to new planters and now all that he's done to solve the problems has been undone by the negotiators in Paris.

Florida is going back to Spain. The British, all those people who have come here and made their lives here, will have to leave. Their property will be given to Spanish people who have the courage to come to the new land. I wonder how many there will be."

"What did Tonyn want of you?"

Daniel smiled wryly. "He wanted to tell me what I already know – how hopeless the situation is, until the war is finally over. He wants me to stay in Florida and guard planters like you, instead of raiding in the Rebel Colonies. But we didn't go raiding this time. We went to recover what was stolen in Florida and to return it to its rightful owners. We succeeded."

☙ ❧

After Francisco left for his house on St. Charles Street, Daniel took a stroll toward Juan Andreu's bakery, La Panederia. He was surprised to find it no longer had a second floor. The roof was new. He passed the building and found Juan Andreu seated on a bench in the western yard, beside the well. Juan's gray hair hung down around his lowered face. He held a cup of café Cubana in his hand, super rich, super sweet and very hot. "Would you like a cup?"

Daniel declined, saying, "It looks and smells delicious but it would keep me up all night and tomorrow I have hard riding to do. What happened to your second floor?"

Juan shook his head sadly. "Fire."

"Sorry to hear it," Daniel replied. "Accidents happen sometimes. We never know when."

"What really puzzles me," Juan continued, "is this well."

"What about it?" Daniel asked.

"This sounds odd to me. Maybe I shouldn't say anything, but I dug the well. I built the stonework around it. I put that little roof over it and built the crank people use to draw water."

"So?"

"What's odd is that I didn't dig the well, there." He pointed at the well. "I dug it ten feet to the west, and now it's over here."

Daniel shook his head, turned to walk away and said, "Juan, maybe you need to get some sleep."

13

1784

Daniel McGirtt's path through the thick Florida wilderness wove through towering cedars, ancient live oaks and across many streams. There he and his two companions, Patrick Alcorn and Isaac Bournoff, avoided alligators, low hanging branches, thorny vines and snakes. The mosquitoes, easily fended off with the salve whose secret Daniel learned from Wakapuchasce's people, stank, but the mosquitoes stayed away.

"Hold!" Patrick Alcorn alerted the three. "Look ahead. There's smoke. Can't you smell it?"

The three men dismounted. Slowly, watching carefully ahead for any movement or sign of a camp, they worked their way west. At Cuscowilla, another fifty miles at least, Daniel's wife and the others waited with his friend Chitto, where they were, Daniel hoped, safe. Suddenly, those watching for intruders to their camping site revealed themselves. Some had bows, bent in readiness. Others had muskets, all pointed at Daniel's oncoming party.

"It's me!" Daniel called out. "It's Daniel McGirtt. We're friends, on our way to see Wakapuchasce at Cuscowilla."

A curt command could be heard but the speaker remained unseen. The fierce expressions on the faces of the numerous Indian men who had been bent on bloodshed relaxed into expressions of disappointment. "They are not Spanish," one of them called over his shoulder.

Just then, Daniel was relieved to see, Payne stepped out of the bushes. Beside him came his brother, Bolek. Payne made some more comments in his native Creek tongue and the men lowered their weapons altogether. "Welcome, Daniel McGirtt," he said. "Come. We have food."

The camp, Daniel was surprised to see, had over a hundred men, all armed. One small tent stood near the fire. "My father has fallen ill," Payne explained. "He told us that we must go to St. Augustine and attack the city. He feels he is dying and he has only killed eighty six Spanish men. For him to rest well in the next life, he must kill fourteen more, but his illness advanced while we were on the trail. I fear his sons will have to kill the remaining fourteen Spanish in his name."

The remaining distance to Cuscowilla took several days longer than Daniel expected because they brought the ailing Wakapuchasce with them, taking many rests to ease the Chief's discomfort. "We could pick up and just go," Alcorn pointed out after listening to Daniel's constant griping. "We'd be there much sooner."

"I'm sure Mary has been worrying about me more than I've been concerned about her. At least I know where she is and that she's among friends, however strange they may seem to her. I need to get to her as soon as possible, but we owe Wakapuchasce and his people our lives many times over. We'll take the slower pace and help as much as we can."

Alcorn and Daniel scavenged wood for the cooking fire, as did Isaac Bournoff. The Creek men seemed to find it amusing that the famed Daniel McGirtt and his party were hunting firewood. While they did not openly smile, from time to time one would point out a piece of dried oak lying on the ground that either Daniel or Patrick would pick up, after brushing off the spiders and dirt. "I think this is their way of telling us this is woman's work," Patrick sniggered as he added a medium-sized log to the pile that he intended to carry back to camp.

"It may be so," Daniel answered with a smile. "I don't know what else we can do for them and there are no women in the party do the firewood collecting. Maybe we should just leave. I doubt they'd miss us, but if we do that we may find that Wakapuchasce has died on the trail and there may have been some service we could have rendered. I think I'd rather stay with them, even if it's just out of respect."

The fifty miles remaining to Cuscowilla took four days. When they arrived, Daniel found Mary shucking corn with three other women, all Creeks. He stood back and watched for a few minutes as the women chattered while they shucked. Mary seemed to be joining right in, speaking the Creek tongue, as though, Daniel thought, she had been born to it. When he approached her, it was from behind. When he was within about six feet, he took a seat on a nearby stump, cleared his throat and said, "I never realized you had such a gift for languages."

It occurred to McGirtt, as he watched Mary rise and the look in her eye, that she had learned that Indian women don't leap on their men when they come home after being gone for a while. He did notice that she had dropped the ear of corn she had been pealing, and that her hands were trembling. "I was beginning to wonder if you were still alive, Daniel McGirtt. I'm sure you will tell me where you have been, as soon as there's time."

"I surely will," Daniel answered. "As soon as there's time. Feel like a walk in the forest?"

Mary agreed, after Daniel explained the situation, that the best place for her to stay for the time being, was in Stateburg, South Carolina, at the home of her brother, Johns James. The best way to get there lay through the forest, across hill and dale, where they would not likely be seen, and if seen, not identified.

03 80

While McGirtt vacationed in South Carolina's sweet, early summer weather, a hurricane filled the St. Augustine inlet with silt and sand to a shallower depth, forcing the ship carrying Don Vincente Manual de Zespedes to seek deeper water for port. The former Governor of Cuba landed in the St. Mary's River instead of St. Augustine. Finally arriving in St. Augustine, nearly a month later than expected and depleted of money and supplies, Zespedes's exasperation expressed itself with hurried and snapped orders, issued so rapidly and impatiently that his subordinates could barely keep up. "It's as though he's been memorizing them ever since he left Cuba and now he's reciting them as fast as he can," one complained.

"And angry when we can't keep up," another chimed in. Among those orders, there was one that would cause difficulty for Daniel, still in South Carolina, who would not hear of it until it was too late. That order mandated that all English and non-Spanish who owned land in East Florida and wished to remain and keep their land must register their intent within twenty days and become Roman Catholic if they were not already.

Finally, established in the mansion of the Government of East Florida, Zespedes took a seat at his new desk for the first time. His first guest, Francisco Xavier Sanchez, was introduced by his Sergeant at Arms as an 'influential citizen.' Francisco was flushed with pleasure to be meeting a Spanish governor. "After twenty years of the British tongue in this house, it is splendid to once again be speaking Spanish and to hear the accent of Castile." Francisco was alluding to the Castillian lisp. Zespedes didn't pronounce his name with a 'Z' as pronounced in English but as though the name were spelled Thespedes. Although Zespedes came from Valencia where the lisp was not part of the local dialect, he imitated the sound of the Spanish Royalty for his own purposes. Francisco's greeting to Zespedes did not go unwelcomed.

Zespedes smiled, called to his guard, "Bring us *café negra, por favor.*" Turning to Francisco, his smile continued to widen. "The pleasure is all mine," he began, "to greet what I expect is a representative of the kind of people I will grow to know in this place. Of course, not everyone is as careful in business as you, to grow so strong at such a young age. How old are you, if you don't mind my asking such a personal question?"

"Forty seven," Francisco answered. "When the British acquired our land, here, I was twenty seven. Most of my family returned to Spain and Cuba then. Two of my brothers and I remained to operate the haciendas and watch over our property here, in hopes that one day Spain would once again rule in its rightful place in La Florida."

After the café and the small talk, Zespedes turned to more serious matters. "I have some dire situations to deal with here. Maybe you can offer some insights as to the best ways would be appropriate to do that. The British are leaving, most of them. This leaves us with a sparse population, a vacuum that is quickly being filled with Indians from the north and the west, American rabble from the north who move into our territory and claim it as their own by squatters' rights. Most of the land between the St. Johns River to the north, and the St. Mary's River, is now being settled by such people and they are loyal neither to the United States nor to Spain. They raid to the south, farther into Spanish territory, stealing cattle and slaves, crops. Some of these people are no more civilized than the native peoples. The only way they can be distinguished from Indians is by the color of their skin…and they interbreed like dogs, taking no pride in the appearance of their children. I, for one, want my children to look like me and my family, not like some inferior race of some other color. Don't you agree?"

Zespedes was clearly confused by the hardening of Francisco's expression following this remark. He did not know that Francisco's mate of many years, Maria Piedra, and the mother of his eight children was a mulatto, half negro, and that Francisco's children by her had every appearance of negroes. The word mulatto came from the Portuguese word for mule because of the mule's mixed breeding between a donkey and a horse. A human mulatto, however, is able to reproduce with other humans while a mule cannot reproduce.

Francisco, a wise man for his youth, nodded his head and said, simply, "Certainly, sir."

◦₃ ₈◦

Governor Patrick Tonyn, just as unhappy as Zespedes, reclined in the subordinate office he had taken in the governor's mansion, having given up his former plush surroundings to the lisping, strutting, Spanish peacock, as he liked to call him. "I will obey the King's mandate. I will make this transition as painless as possible for Great Britain."

Lord Peter Edwards, grandson of Keith Edwards who was brother of Queen Mary's third cousin, had fallen on hard times and, thankful to be appointed a secretary of Governor Patrick Tonyn, listened patiently to Tonyn's meandering. "You certainly have a full plate, sir."

"Many of our people are resisting this change from enlightened British rule to the darkness of Spain. They will refuse to become Catholic, I'm afraid. Those who stay will pay lip service to the Church of Rome to keep their land but they will never submit. The Americans encroaching from the north present problems enough for Spain and for Britain, but the real danger, I believe, right now is the growing movement in West Florida under William Bowles. No one knows, yet what is to become of that. Then there are problems with our own Florida Rangers. I've ordered Cunningham, Mayfield and McGirtt to stop raiding in Georgia. McGirtt says he only goes there in pursuit of raiders who came here and he goes there to recover stolen goods. But look at the repercussions! The people of Georgia would have his head on a pike if they could catch him! But he continues to go there! I even have correspondence from the governor of South Carolina asking for his extradition!"

Edwards took a bite of his crumpet, a sip from the café negra he had beside him. He had taken a liking to Cuban coffee, much to the dismay of his wife, Margaret. "McGirtt has been very loyal to you, sir. He does what he thinks is best for all of us in Florida."

"But he blatantly disobeys my orders about going into the American territory. He's becoming a problem. Another aspect of that is this: King George III ordered that all stolen slaves, cattle and what-not be returned to the rightful owners in the United States. It's my belief that McGirtt still has close to a hundred slaves that came as spoils of war from South Carolina. They must be returned. That he ignores my orders to do so is infamous. He says he has no slaves that he did not acquire legally; some forty-six of them he has freed, but they chose, or so he says, to remain with him. If he does not comply with Zespedes' order in a timely manner, I will look into this and see that the so-called spoils of war are removed from his possession."

"I'm sure he can be reasoned with, sir. Perhaps he is just too zealous on your behalf. Zespedes says he wants McGirtt, Cunningham and Mayfield to be unmolested by government restriction, except, of course, for obeying the law of the land. Zespedes is hoping that such large landholders as these men will become assets to Spain's new community and that real peace will result, in time."

Tonyn practically coughed with vexation. "Those men have created their own local economy, independent of any national rule. When they go into American territory to recover stolen goods, they don't just take the stolen goods, they take everything they can get their hands on. I don't know how Cunningham and Mayfield dispose of the ill-gotten gain, but I'm pretty sure McGirtt sells his plunder to Francisco Sanchez and Sanchez sells it in the West Indies and in Cuba, far away from wandering British observation."

Edwards set down his empty cup and glanced at the door for a guard or servant, hoping to get his cup refilled. "Sanchez seems like such a forthright gentleman, well spoken, well dressed and very mannerly. Do you really think he would risk his life and property by such overt smuggling?"

Tonyn leaned back in his chair, crossed his arms and glared at Edwards. "Yes."

଼ ଽ

Three weeks later...

Zespedes decided to take a break from the formal atmosphere of Tonyn's former office and to have his mid-day meal at Maria's Taberna, which was still open for business. Word on the street was that Maria was considering retiring to a farm she had purchased on the east shore of the St. Johns River, north and west of St. Augustine. "I hope she doesn't do that, but I'd like to take advantage of this wonderful food and the beer she makes while she's still here." Maria took pleasure in serving him personally. She set a hot plate in front of him loaded with tamales and waited with her hands on her hips to watch him take his first bite. He chewed, then sat back and demanded, "Where did you get such a recipe? These are delicious! I've never tasted such a thing before today. Tamales indeed!"

Maria smiled triumphantly and said, "It's an Aztec recipe. It's said that Aztec warriors would carry these for a quick meal when they were on the march. The Spanish brought it here a hundred years ago. I'm glad you like it." ...and she was gone.

Mario Oquendo de Raquena was Zespedes' lunch partner on this warm day in late June. Mario's thin black hair and tanned bald head accentuated his portly build. Zespedes had chosen him from the office staff today because he thought Oquendo made him look handsome by comparison. Zespedes liked feeling superior. Oquendo was enough of a social climber, too, that Zespedes knew he would flatter anything and everything Zespedes said. Vincent Zespedes, slightly overwhelmed by the unsolvable problems of his rule as gvernor, needed some uplifting and even though he knew what he was getting from Oquendo was nonsense, he decided to allow himself to bask in it for a while. Maybe it would make him feel better.

Mario didn't let Zespedes down. "I'm glad I ordered the same thing," he commented. "Your choice was a wise one, Your Honor."

"The Aztecs may be a conquered people, but they had many things worthy of our attention, other than their gold, I mean. Chocolate, for example. I wonder if we can get chocolate here."

"I could inquire, if you like, sir."

"That'll be all right," Zespedes answered. "When Maria comes back, I'll ask her."

Despite his best efforts, Zespedes was unable to leave the problems of his office at his office. After small talk, chewing and burping, Zespedes began meandering. "Most of the English, I suppose, who want to remain in Spanish Florida have responded to my request that they register. Some, however, have not yet answered. Daniel McGirtt is one of those. I sent a messenger to Maxton Island last week, asking his intentions. The custodian he left in charge of the hacienda answered that McGirtt is out of the area on personal business but that he does indeed intend to remain in Florida. He said he would relay the necessity of coming to St. Augustine to register to Daniel as soon as he gets back. I left word for McGirtt that I would extend the requirement for another thirty days on his behalf. But I've received a petition signed by most English who have land on the St. Johns River to extend the deadline even further. I've decided to give them a year. I think that's very fair. Don't you, Mario?"

Mario swallowed the current bite, not quite chewed, so that he could answer promptly. "Very understanding of you, sir. McGirtt will be a real asset to us. He's a natural leader with a talent for business and commerce."

"Some of them have requested permission to immigrate as far as Louisiana, now under Spanish rule. I've granted passports. Not all that many have expressed a desire to remain. I've issued an order that all vacant and undeveloped land be confiscated by the crown to be disseminated to those who wish to come to our fair colony. Are you familiar with the terms I'm offering? Maybe you have some family remaining in España who would like to come here and own their own farms?"

Mario smiled and said, "I do, Your Honor. I believe the terms you offer are very generous. Was it not one hundred acres for every head of household, fifty acres for the spouse and each child and another fifty acres for each slave?"

"You're very astute, Mario. That is absolutely correct, but you missed one thing. No taxes for ten years!"

"With such gifts available, Your Honor, I think Florida will be overflowing with immigrants in a very short time."

"I hope so," Zespedes muttered. "The problem is that the land I am giving them is confiscated from former British residents who still hope to sell the holdings they once owned in La Florida. Some of them are resisting and some are resisting violently. They even started a petition to King George III to stop the transfer of sovereignty. They want La Florida to remain British, and well they might. They are losing a lot!"

Mario gulped. "Do you think King George will pay them any heed, sir?"

"No," Zespedes chortled. "Great Britain lost the war at great expense and is now in heavy debt. They will be looking for ways to recover their lost investment, any way they can. I wouldn't be surprised if they don't resort to piracy on the high seas as they have done in the past."

☙ ❧

Patrick Tonyn, coincidentally, decided to try Maria's tamales also, but he was taking advantage of a new service she had offered that she called, "Home Delivery." He smiled as he watched Peter Edwards struggle through the doorway, lugging a bucket of beer and a basket loaded with, not only tamales, but also plates and mugs. The down side of this new service was the deposit he had to pay to guarantee he would return the equipment. "I have a table set up, over there by the window," he gestured. Edwards obediently carried his cargo to the table and laid it out for Tonyn's convenience. As Edwards turned to leave Tonyn to his lunch, he called to Edwards, "While you're out, Peter, please send a message to Colonel William Young that I would like to see him. McGirtt has still not come to town to register and I think it may be time consider arresting him."

Edwards's eyebrows shot upward, but he kept his peace, except to say, "Yes, sir."

☙ ❧

Daniel McGirtt and his two companions, Patrick Alcorn and Isaac Bournoff, rode hard in their eagerness get back to the fray. They made it from Stateburg, South Carolina, to Maxton Island in just three days. Daniel was immediately apprised of the communications from Governor Vincent Zespedes and, taking note of the date of the order and the current date, he remounted his horse without even taking time for a meal. He called forth a company of fifty of the Rangers he kept guarding his ranch and set out for St. Augustine, taking the northerly route to take the ferry at Cow Ford. The sun had set before their arrival and the city gates were closed for the night. At first light, Daniel entered the city and went directly to Government House where he registered his intention to remain in Florida, citing his ownership of Maxton Island and his business interests with Francisco Sanchez and others. After that, he was escorted directly to Father Thomas Hassett. McGirtt found it amusing that Spanish St. Augustine had an Irish priest and said so when he met him. "I was afraid I'd have to speak Spanish to deal with you, Father, but now I find I have to understand the Irish brogue."

Hassett laughed heartily and retorted, "At least the Irish brogue is part of the English language. I wish I could say as much for the Scottish brogue!" McGirtt got on famously with the middle-aged Irishman. After reluctantly promising to favor the Roman Catholic Church in all things and to be obedient to its Pope, McGirtt thankfully headed back to Maxton Island.

McGirtt laughed as he rode out of town. "Now that I'm a Catholic, I don't have to suffer guilt for anything. All I have to do is go and see Father Hassett, give him a bottle of Drambuie, and ask him to forgive me. I'm sure he will."

The path McGirtt chose for the ride home took him to Tocoi, on the eastern bank of the St. Johns River, where he knew Francisco had at least one boat waiting. "Francisco misses no opportunity," Daniel quipped. "He runs ferries, cattle and firewood as far as Cuba. He's in the slave trade taking his merchandise from wherever he can get it and selling it far enough away that no one can ever make a just claim against him."

Daniel had been on the trail, at this point, for a solid week without meaningful rest or refreshment. His fifty Rangers, though, were fresh. As they picked their way along the trail west from St. Augustine, they joked and chatted as though they had little care for what was going on in the world. From time to time, the conversation would turn to Spain's take-over of Florida. "The change has some rough edges, aye?" Patrick Alcorn had insisted on coming along even though he had been on the trail as long as McGirtt.

"Zespedes is doing the best he can, considering," McGirtt answered. "He's a bit like a turkey gobbler, the way he ruffles his feathers and shakes his tail, but he's been in government service for a long time. That means he knows how to take a little gold with his left hand while he smiles politely at the king, from four thousand miles distance. Tonyn knows too, but he's more careful than a Spaniard would be. Bribery isn't as well accepted by the British, but for the Spanish, it's a way of life. I expect no trouble from him. Besides that, I think he wants people like us to stay. We're good for business and for the economy. We can also help him if there's trouble, or so he may think..."

Just then, the lead man stopped and held up a hand, signaling, "someone's coming." In just moments, Daniel had his men fanned out through the bushes, nearly out of sight. Their muskets were loaded and at the ready and Daniel was very tense. *Are they raiders from Georgia? Creek Indians attempting another raid on St. Augustine? Friends? Who?*

The first of the oncoming party appeared. It was Jonas and his forty-six freed slaves. Jonas immediately saw Daniel standing in the shadows with his finger over his lip, indicating, "Keep quiet and keep coming." When the former slaves had filed past, the first of the soldiers appeared. The first one was Colonel William Young himself, and young he was not. McGirtt took him to be around forty-five years of age. His trimness spoke of an active physical nature, his particular neatness, of an anal disposition and the grim look in his eye of a "black and white only" outlook on life. McGirtt stepped out of the shadows, musket pointed at Young and ordered, "Stop where you are. Drop your weapons to the ground and dismount. Any man pointing a weapon will be shot."

Young, either stupidly or defiantly, raised his musket, and McGirtt shot him. The wound in Young's upper arm was enough to knock him off his horse. Young's troops hastened to obey McGirtt's command and dropped their weapons and dismounted. McGirtt ordered them to return to town, except for Young, who was to be transported with McGirtt's troops so that his wound could be properly treated. McGirtt collected the people Young had taken from Maxton Island, along with his friend Jonas, and they continued toward home.

It didn't take McGirtt long to realize there were only thirty eight of Jonas' people with them. "Where are the other eight?"

Jonas, mounted on one of the horses they captured from Colonel Young's Light Horse Troops, frowned, scratched and said, "Colonel Young – he had a man with him – Sam Farley who said he'd buy eight of us. He give money to Colonel Young and rode off driving eight people in front of him."

"Samuel Farley! Thank you, Jonas."

ര ഇ

Preparations for a party to take place at the Castillo De San Marcos kept the town busy. Juan Andreu baked his heart out on St. Francis Street. When he finished, he had a cartload of biscuits, cakes and loaves of uncut bread ready to bring to the fort. Mary Peavett's staff at Maria's Taberna had been cooking for days. They wrapped hundreds of tamales, roasted pork and beef. Zespedes was sparing no cost for the celebration of his installation as governor of East Florida, on July 12, 1784. The high point of the celebration was the transfer of the Castillo San Marcos from British to Spanish rule under Governor Vincent Manual de Zespedes. The people of St. Augustine were preparing their finest clothing for the biggest event since the loss of St. Augustine to Spain in 1763. The whole town would be there, except for the slaves. On this night, even the city gates would not be guarded. Everyone was to attend the celebration.

Three of McGirtt's Florida Rangers waited on the west side of the San Sebastian River for nightfall. They were William Mangum, Daniel Cargan and John Linder. Daniel McGirtt entered the town that afternoon, with all his plans in place. He intended to join the party so that Zespedes, Tonyn and all others could see where he was, without argument, at the time his behind-the-scenes event would take place. A small dock accommodated three skiffs that could be easily rowed and were enough to carry Daniel's company of Rangers and Indians. Daniel called them Florida Rangers, but they were not really. Those white men came to Florida as refugees and were among the thousands who came to Florida to flee the uprising of the Patriots to free the continent of British rule. They were the men who Tonyn liked to refer to as "the Banditti." That, in Tonyn's mind, lumped all refugees who were not landed gentlemen or related to one in some way, into one group. That group was to be feared and hunted and punished and controlled, by the East Florida Rangers.

"They're not criminals," Daniel smirked. "They're lost souls who thought they had a life in Britain's colonies until the colonies evicted them. Some were tortured. Their goods were confiscated. Their lands were taken and they were cast upon the sea of life in the wilderness to fend for themselves." Colonel Brown of the Florida Rangers was one of those so treated. "I wonder where Brown is today. I haven't seen him since we laid siege to Charleston. What was that, six years ago? With the injuries he had from colonists, he'll never be the same! They even scalped him."

Night arrived and the boats were loaded with their cargo of warriors, both red and white. The home of Samuel Farley stood not far from Maria's Taberna. The affluent neighborhood was empty of inhabitants. Everyone partied at the fort. The two-story house, guarded by a coquina wall and wrought iron, gate stood exposed and undefended. The slaves were delighted to hear Daniel McGirtt's name spoken at their door and came willingly to the rescue he provided. Linder carefully closed the door and the gate so as to raise no alarm until the last possible moment. Their escape ship rode at anchor in the harbor, not half a mile south of the Castillo de San Marcos. As Daniel's banditti, Indians and freed slaves boarded *La Santa Lucia*, they could hear the music and revelry at the fort. It was the biggest party of the century. Daniel danced with nearly every woman at the party. He made sure that he offered toasts that all could hear to make sure he was seen by all. He greeted Tonyn and Zespedes personally, wishing Zespedes congratulations and the best of luck in the most charming tones he could muster. After the party he made it a point to go nowhere near the Farley residence or *La Santa Lucia* in the harbor.

No one had seen anything amiss yet. No one had seen the slaves departing. All disappeared below the main deck. They spent the night riding at anchor. The slaves were not missed until morning, but at first light, the anchor was hoisted and *La Santa Lucia* set sail for the open sea. Her destination was Maxton Island where they would board the other thirty-eight freed people. From there, they went to Pilotaikita (Palatka), and from there the freed people would make their way to Cuscowilla with the guidance of Wakapuchasce's people.

ଓ ଃ

"McGirtt did this!" Tonyn was outraged.

"There is no evidence," Zespedes countered. "He was in full view at the celebration last night. He couldn't have done it."

"I know he did this. It was bleeding Daniel McGirtt. He found out where the eight slaves were taken and he went and got them back. Not only did McGirtt do this he also killed Colonel Young when Young went to get the slaves."

"Wait a minute. Why did Young go after McGirtt in the first place?" Zespedes incredulity was complete.

Tonyn paced as he ranted. "McGirtt failed to come to town to register as required under the new Spanish Law. He failed to come in. I sent Young after him."

Zespedes' exasperation grew as reflected in the ruddy depth of color that was filling his face. "I gave McGirtt an extra thirty days to come in to register. He was here a week ago! He IS registered. He is not in violation of the law. The slaves were his. You had no right to confiscate them!"

Tonyn continued to fume. "He did this in direct defiance of me, personally. He knows I ordered the visit to his lands by Colonel Young and whether he was in agreement with that fact or not, Colonel Young is dead, murdered by McGirtt himself. The slaves confiscated from his property are all stolen back and McGirtt is at large and no doubt laughing at me!"

Tonyn glared into the sky, then at Zespedes. In silence he turned and walked away, but was stopped at the door, nearly colliding with Colonel William Young, smiling and in good cheer.

"I fear," he said, "the information leading you to believe I am dead may be skewed in some way."

14

1785

The first of the Indian Wars, known as Little Turtle's War, began in the northwestern United States over the Ohio territory. This conflict assisted and supported by the British and British held fortifications in that territory, lasted until 1795.

1785 – 1791

Imam Sheikh Mansur, a Chechen Warrior and Muslim mystic, led a coalition of Muslim Caucasian tribes from throughout the Caucasus in a Holy War against the Russian Settlers and military bases in the Caucasus as well as against local traditionalists who followed the common law of Adat rather than the Theocratic Sharia.

Autumn of 1784

Breakfast at Maria's Taberna today included roast pork sausage, potatoes sautéed in locally grown onions and garlic, topped off with fresh butter on piping hot rolls from Juan Andreu's Panederia. Earlier, Daniel had stood on the bayfront watching the departure of *La Santa Lucia* and its secret cargo of newly freed slaves. Its large square sails, filled from the gentle southeast breeze coming in earlier than usual, helped the falling tide carry the boat toward the open sea. The adventure had succeeded. No one but Daniel watched the departure, but there were Spanish soldiers searching the neighborhoods and asking questions. Daniel could hear them as he walked toward his breakfast.

A tall, thin private with two companions in ragged coats and sabers at their sides were questioning a slave they called "Jack."

"Did you hear or see anything unusual during the party last night?"

"No suh. We was sleepin'. We didn't see nothin'." The man turned his head to glance at McGirtt as he walked past, then turned his attention back to the private. "Massa was at the shindig. All'a us took the time for a good rest."

Daniel pretended to not hear or even be aware of the exchange as he passed. The Spanish private was not satisfied with the answer, but their voices faded with the distance that Daniel put between himself and the ongoing questioning. His breakfast delighted him, as he knew it would. Alcorn joined him just as he was beginning to eat. "Looks like all's well," Patrick opined. "I saw the tide and noted the wind. It's going to be a beautiful day."

"Will be for some," Daniel retorted. "We'll save that subject for later, shall we?"

Pedro Edwards, Tonyn's secretary, sitting two tables away, listened quietly. Edwards, fresh from listening to Zespedes ranting about McGirtt, made no move to draw attention to himself. Neither Alcorn nor McGirtt knew him. McGirtt knew when to keep his mouth shut. Pedro Edwards, however, was not the type of person who necessarily relied on observed facts to formulate his reports. His desire to please Tonyn, in hopes of an improvement in his employment situation, overrode his concerns about less important things, like honor. "You should have heard him bragging about stealing attorney Farley's slaves," he told Tonyn, later. Then he watched in satisfaction while Tonyn's lips grew into a thin, tight line of determination.

ଔ ଃ

Maxton Island, all business as usual, bustled with activity. Fences needed mending to keep the cattle and horses corralled; the feral hogs that came after McGirtt's vegetable fields must be driven out, killed and butchered; the other cash crops must be watched over and tended. Some of the marsh on the west side of the island was mounded off for rice. At the south end of the island, the area he was able to watch the least, McGirtt raised indigo, that valuable dye that took up hundreds of acres but would yield a small, very valuable block of the actual dye. The horses and cattle were corralled at the northern end of the island, better protected from thieves that might slip in over the land bridge at the south end of the island. Not as many raiders came slipping across the border from Georgia as before the end of the war, but occasionally they still came.

McGirtt's plantation house consisted of two stories of wood frame with hand hewn clapboard sides. The roof covering of short cedar boards and the clapboard covering of the exterior walls came from the trees on his own land. The veranda, wrapping all the way around the house, three feet above ground level, took its shade from an overhanging roof, trimmed with lattice work that McGirtt had protested, but the carpenters working on the project insisted. "If we're going to build a plantation house for Colonel Daniel McGirtt, it's going to be nice." Daniel quit arguing with them and watched it happen.

I'm glad I allowed them to do it, Daniel thought frequently when he was enjoying the end result. His guests, Bloody Bill Cunningham, Stephen Mayfield, John Linder and William Mangum apparently agreed as they sipped their hot tea and consumed their crumpets (English muffins) under the shade of the latticed porch roof.

The group had remained silent for quite some time as they enjoyed their afternoon refreshments, watching the field hands at their work. Cunningham broke the silence with, "Daniel, I still don't understand why you helped those slaves get away. They would have brought you a good price anywhere. Sanchez sells them at a premium in the Indies. You could have made a lot of money if you'd sold them, but not only did you just let them go, you helped them get away. Why?"

Daniel leaned back in his chair, setting down his tea cup. He brushed some crumbs off his shirt, lifted an eyebrow and turned to Cunningham. "I took those people from a plantation in South Carolina during the war. They were spoils of war. I took thousands of slaves off those plantations and turned most of them over to Prevost and Tonyn. I was allowed to keep a share –a portion of the slaves I took as booty, like the privateers that Great Britain turns loose on the high seas. They get a healthy percentage of what they capture, in return for the larger percentage they turn over to the King. Those particular slaves agreed to help me loot the place. They told me who and where the owners were and if and when they would come back. I promised them their freedom if they would do that. I can't always keep my word, Bill. But I do my best to keep it when I can. I gave Jonas and his people my word."

"But they were just slaves," Cunningham persisted. "Why would YOU care?"

Daniel leaned forward and took another sip of his tea. "They are human beings, the same as you and me. They eat the same food, die of the same diseases. It's not their fault or mine that they were born in a world where the rich can buy anything, including human beings. Oglethorpe had the right idea, in Georgia, when he outlawed slavery in – what – 1728? When Oglethorpe left Georgia, his wisdom left with him. His act gave hope to the world that the institution would someday die. But it hasn't."

Mayfield joined the fray. "Daniel, if you feel that way about slavery why do you still own, buy and sell slaves? You're as guilty as anyone, as me, as Cunningham and the rest of us here. Don't you feel a little hypocritical, sometimes?"

"Yup." Daniel yawned and stood, stretching. "But if I don't own them, someone else will. I can't collect all of them and send to Wakapuchasce. He'd be overwhelmed and he'd stop welcoming them."

"What are we going to do about Tonyn?" William Mangum changed the subject. Mangum had just finished a crumpet. He took the last sip of his tea and leaned back in his chair, crossing his legs comfortably. With his hands clasped behind his head he continued, "Tonyn sent Young out here to arrest you. Tonyn is not a friend."

"Neither is Zespedes," Daniel answered. "He's creating a nasty situation. I know it's not his fault that most of the British planters are leaving. Most of them don't want to live under Spanish rule, but their plantations are abandoned. Zespedes is confiscating all vacant land for the king and he's giving it out in smaller parcels to people we used to call raiders from Georgia. These people are criminals and the children of criminals. Oglethorpe thought he was killing two birds with one stone when he brought debtors' prison inmates to Georgia. He did what Zespedes is now doing here. He gave them parcels of land to farm, but he didn't give them any conditioning involving a work ethic. He thought he was populating Georgia with an agrarian society that would produce an economy for that colony, but he angered the Indians whose land he was giving away – without their consent, by the way – and he created a new class of criminals here in the New World. Those are the raiders we fought to keep in Georgia and keep them from looting and plundering farms here in Florida. Now Zespedes is giving land to these same people and enticing them to come here. They're all around us."

Mayfield, leaning against a porch post and staring out over Daniel's fields, interjected, "Another problem Zespedes is creating is the fact that, in the past, all these plantations consisted of thousands of acres each. Daniel here owns over two thousand acres of Maxton Island and all the new homesteads are only a few hundred acres, maybe five hundred if the homesteader owns enough slaves. There is going to be envy. The larger landowners like Daniel will be at their mercy."

As though as an echo to Mayfield's words, Daniel Cargan came running toward the house crying, "LOOK! LOOK!" A large company of horsemen could be seen approaching from the south, still a good mile away. The land, still moist from the recent rains raised no dust. The horsemen appeared as hardly more than shadows at this distance.

"Quick!" Daniel ordered. "Get your muskets. Make sure they're loaded and ready to fire."

By the time the horsemen arrived at the front gate to Daniel's yard, the five men stood ready. The man who appeared to be in the lead sat tall in the saddle with long sandy hair hanging out from under his planter's hat. His homespun cotton shirt hung over his belt and in his belt, Daniel could see two pistols. Daniel's greeting was an attempt at friendliness. "Well, if it isn't my good neighbor, Billy Mitchell – and who are all these others? Oh yes. You are also my neighbors from way down south, up through the old Padamaran Plantation and some from the north as well. How many people now own the old Padamaran, Billy my friend?"

"About sixty people," Mitchell laughed. "We raided it before and now we own it! And there's plenty more land yet to be divided, but that's not why we're here, Daniel." Mitchell smiled and continued. "We remember you coming to Georgia, not so long ago, Daniel. We remember burned homes, stolen cattle and slaves. Stolen horses. Do you remember that, Daniel?"

Daniel shuffled a foot in the sand before answering. "When a man raids the farms of his neighboring country he shouldn't be surprised when that neighboring country sends Rangers to recover the stolen property and pay back the thieves for the damaged property they left behind. That was then. This is now, Billy. You folks are all now citizens of Spanish Florida. Now you would be protected in the same way."

Billy Mitchell spat in the sand at Daniel's feet. "The hell with then and now, you son of a bitch. This is payback. We're going to run you right out of Florida. Ain't we boys?" He raised his voice on the question. A cheer went up behind him.

William "Billy" Mitchell straightened himself in the saddle. "Daniel, we're going to take all your cattle, your horses and your slaves. If you follow us, we'll skin you alive and stretch your hide in a tree so you can watch it start to dry, while you die."

Outnumbered more than ten to one, Daniel watched with his friends, Stephen Mayfield, Bloody Bill Cunningham, John Linder, William Mangum and Daniel Cargan, as the company of around sixty men rounded up Daniel's horses, cattle and slaves and herded them to the south, off the property. Not a shot was fired. Not a cutlass was raised.

Daniel watched in stunned amazement while these former raiders from Georgia stripped him of most of his property.

As the last of the raiders disappeared into the south, Daniel smiled. "They missed the north pasture," he said. "Our personal horses and several hundred head of cattle still graze along the north shore of the island."

"How long do you want to wait before we start paying them back, again?" Cunningham ventured.

"Let's give it a week," Daniel suggested. "That will give them time to separate and go to their individual homes. Then we can start taking them one at a time. I need to contact Francisco and arrange for a couple of his brigantines to meet us. If we take the cattle back, they'll say we stole them and if we have the cattle, they can prove it. Francisco will be brazen enough to sell some of the cattle in St. Augustine, right under Zespedes' nose. The rest he'll no doubt sell in Cuba and the other Islands."

"Zespedes will send troops after us, you know," Cunningham stated offhandedly.

"I know," Daniel answered. "Our time is over as we knew it here in Florida. I wonder what the future holds for us now."

The first of McGirtt's eight payback raids took place on the former lands of the old Padamaran Plantation. Daniel returned the compliment by not burning their homes, but he left no cattle, slave or horse, anywhere. The only resistance he ran into was about as weak as his own resistance had been. When totally and vastly overwhelmed and outnumbered, one just tries to pacify the robber and survive the incident. They did the same as Daniel. They stood by and watched as Daniel McGirtt and his company herded the cattle, horses and slaves off the property. As was Daniel's practice when punishing raiders in Georgia, he took not only what was stolen but everything. "Paybacks are hell, buddy," He said to William Mitchell as he turned to ride south after the large herd of cattle he had collected. The slaves tended to the cattle and to their own families as they trekked toward Pilotaikita to meet Francisco's first ship.

"Do you think you can make the sea without any problems from this far south?" Daniel was concerned that the ship may be taken by Spanish military before escaping the St. Johns River.

"No problemo," the ship's captain smiled. "Señor Francisco say the first stop is St. Marys, Georgia. Very funny, no? The second stop is Savannah. Then we go to Charleston and from there we go to Bermuda. If we have any cargo left, we will go to St. Augustine, then return for more."

"It's unlikely there will be more from us," Daniel sighed. "I thought since Spain had taken over and that the war was over we would be able to settle down and just be farmers. I guess that isn't going to happen."

"Asi es la vida, mi amigo. Asi es la vida." The captain laughed and walked away, shouting orders to his seamen about the rigging.

Daniel stood on the wharf as the square-rigger caught the southerly breeze and headed east toward the great bend in the St. Johns River. He watched silently until the course changed to the north, rounding the bend, disappearing beyond the trees.

In the morning, Daniel and his troop set out on a northerly tack, through forest trails and rutted cart paths, sweeping more farms farther west of the St. Johns River, making another clean sweep of all cattle, horses and slaves. He avoided farms and plantations that were not owned by any of the men who had raided his home. William Mangum's land stretched just west of the St. Johns and as a token of good will to William, who was riding with him that day, he dropped off fifty head of cattle and twenty five slaves. "Think anyone will notice?"

"Mangum laughed and said, "Probably. These people are angry. We haven't heard the last of this, Daniel."

"William, you were there at my home when these people stripped me of everything I had in the form of cattle, horses and slaves. I'm surprised they didn't burn the indigo crop and if they could, they might have tried to burn the rice. They're criminals. Zespedes government can't do anything about it. You saw how weak the Spanish Government is now. Zespedes can barely govern one city – St. Augustine. They have no control out here in the western lands and Zespedes seems to have no interest in taking control. Tonyn always relied on me and you to do that – and Cunningham and Mayfield. We were the police out here during the British reign. Would the Spanish rather allow outlaws to run wild? What should we do? Should I ignore being robbed when I know the robber and have the means of redress? I don't think so."

Daniel met the next boat at Maxton Island. This was *La Santa Lucia*, a boat he felt he knew. It managed to handle most of the cattle, horses and slaves he had collected, but not all of them. He and two of the others decided to drive the remaining cattle to St. Marys and sell them there. The drive took longer than he anticipated. The weather posed a problem. Heavy rain made the paths muddy and swelled the creeks that were usually quite shallow. Daniel knew the paths, so the drive avoided the main routes that were likely to be guarded by the Spanish, requiring identification, passports and other inconveniences that could forestall their journey. He had taken this path so many times that he was known along the way and greeted with warmth and friendship at most places – until he crossed into Georgia. There, Daniel McGirtt was remembered differently. He was the vengeance of Great Britain to many. To some he was a liberator but most people in Georgia, at least those away from the coast feared him.

The sale took place amiably enough. The traders who knew McGirtt, Cunningham and Mayfield were always eager to see them because they knew some favorable transactions were about to take place. So it went. Mangum and Linder were still present, so they were a party of five.

In the morning, the blue sky promised fair weather for traveling but the air, much cooler than before the rain, induced the five to pull out heavier clothing for the ride south. "So where are we going?" Cunningham, brutal in battle, a cunning planner and remorseless in action, was often teased about his name because he was known as a cunning pig to his enemies. All he would say to such taunts was, "I accept this high praise."

"I think we should go to St. Augustine, to Governor Zespedes and tell him what happened out here. We should tell him that Maxton Island was robbed, who did it and what we did about it. What do you think?"

"I don't trust Zespedes," Mangum answered. "If the raiders got to him first, he's likely to believe what he hears first and what the majority tells him. He may well be looking for us!"

"William is right," Linder contributed. "Zespedes is probably still angry at McGirtt because of the William Young Episode. He thinks McGirtt stole the slaves from Samuel Farley and the fact that McGirtt had a legal right to those slaves is irrelevant. That the Young incident was a miscommunication is irrelevant. Politicians never admit to miscommunications. Whether Daniel was involved with that or not doesn't matter. Zespedes *thinks* Daniel was involved and if he thinks Daniel was involved, Zespedes is likely to blame all of us for being part of it."

"He'd be right if he thinks that," Mayfield added. "But he can't prove it. His opinion that we were involved is pure conjecture. Zespedes is a politician. He knows how to survive on public opinion and if we come across his sights, he's very likely to pull the trigger."

"So," Daniel asked, "if we can't go to St. Augustine, where can we go? Maxton Island is the first place Zespedes would send soldiers looking for me. I can't go back there. I can't go home to South Carolina. I think they'd hang me, there. The work I did for Brigadier General Prevost put the nails in my coffin, if I'm found back there."

Daniel Cargan who had been silent during most of this exchange offered, "Louisiana is an option. Cunningham, here, requested permission to immigrate to New Orleans and was given permission."

"I even went," said Cunningham. "They speak such a bastardized version of French there that I couldn't understand much of what they said. The food they eat is horrendous."

"What do they eat?" asked Daniel with a smile. "Snails?"

"Yes. Snails," said Cunningham. "But not only that. They eat crayfish."

"I used crayfish for bait, fishing in the Wateree sometimes," chuckled Daniel. "But I never considered eating them myself."

"They eat crayfish," repeated Cunningham. "The worst part is that they smother everything in hot peppers. Take a bite of literally anything and you're likely to have to drink a quart of beer to wash the fire out of your mouth."

"So you came back because you didn't like the food and you didn't like the language. Is there anything you did like about it?"

"You would not believe the women!" Cunningham grinned. "They have a breed of woman there that's tall, with long, red hair and green eyes. They are living banshees! They call them Cajuns."

In the distance, Daniel could see a lone man approaching on horseback. He was dressed as a middle-ranking soldier of the Spanish nation. He had a long sword dangling at his belt. Daniel watched with some concern as the man grew closer. The thick forest around them would prevent flanking him, if there were more. The only path of escape was the way they had just come. When the man reached a distance of about fifty feet, he stopped, blocking the path. He put his fingers to his lips and gave a shrill whistle. When he did, more soldiers appeared behind McGirtt and his friends. Almost simultaneously, a small company of Spanish soldiers appeared at a trot, approaching their position from behind the first soldier.

"We're surrounded, gentlemen," William Cunningham announced. "We are thoroughly outnumbered. There is no escape."

"Bill! You're quite good at announcing the obvious," Linder snapped. "Now what?"

When the soldier was finally satisfied that McGirtt and his friends were not going to try to escape or to fight, he came a little close and announced, "*Buenos tardes, caballeros.* You are under arrest. You will surrender your firearms and your swords to the gentlemen who are about to come to you to collect them."

☙ ❧

"I have never been inside this place, before." Daniel surrendered his horse at the drawbridge to the Castillo De San Marcos in St. Augustine. "Except for the party Zespedes threw when he was about to take over the city back in July, last year."

"I've never been in here before, either," Cunningham said.

The others groaned in agreement. But Daniel Cargan added, "I was in here a while back to do some work on the draw span. It seemed they didn't have anyone handy who could work with the gearing mechanism. It was fun. But I don't think I ever wanted to do an overnight visit. I wonder how long we're going to be in this place."

"It could be a long time," Cunningham answered.

Their accommodation consisted of a single room they were to share, on the fort's ground floor, near the southeast corner of the building. The room was furnished with a bale of straw scattered on the floor. "Well, this is quite nice," Daniel said to the jailer, Sebastian Esteve. Sebastian, tall and rather thin, spoke English with a French accent. They learned later that his English was better than his Spanish. He was born in Brest on Rue de Kerraros to which he made reference every time he spoke, or so it seemed. "When I was a boy on Rue de Kerraros...." I met my wife one block north of Rue de Kerraros, where I was born." My children will never see Rue de Kerraros where I was born..."

To McGirtt's sarcastic statement of appreciation about the sparse, straw-strewn cell where the five of them were to subsist for the time being, Esteve answered with appreciation. "It's nothing like where I was born on Rue de Kerraros, but it's better than sleeping on the top deck in the rain. Sometimes they make prisoners stay out in the weather like that! The Spanish are such bastards! But thank you, *monsieur*. It's sparse but it's the best I can do at the moment." And he was gone.

Daniel made the best of the situation. He bunched up some straw from the floor, making a cushion of sorts, and sat down. "I never particularly liked or disliked coquina," he said. "I never thought I'd get such a close up experience with it. They say these walls are fourteen feet thick at the bottom. I doubt we could dig our way out."

"We have no weapons," said Cunningham.

"We have no tools," added Mayfield.

"We're stuck," groaned Cargan.

"We have nothing and no hope." Linder hung his head as he said it.

Not about to be defeated by a situation in a present moment, McGirtt tried to encourage his friends: "Things change. We might be here a few minutes. We might be here a few years. We have hope. Let's not get too discouraged yet."

"What do we have? We can't dig out through fourteen feet of coquina. We can't get out through this door, especially with armed guards on the outside. We have nothing." Linder clung to defeat.

Daniel stood, looked around the room, not for the last time and said,

"We have guile."

Esteve the jailor returned in just under an hour, by McGirtt's estimate. He had two men with him whom he addressed as Etienne and Carlos. Between them they bore a pot of steaming hot food. Daniel couldn't determine exactly what it was, but the smell led him to believe that it was edible.

"You're a good man, Sebastian. I bet your children are proud to have such a father." McGirtt's compliment lit up the jailor's face.

"Thank you, monsieur. They are good children. I wish I could take them out of this forsaken Spanish community, but alas, the money I make here would beggar a church mouse. I am imprisoned here the same as you, by low wages, unappreciative management and the burden that moving back to France would place on my family. I would go back to Rue de Kerraros in a moment, if only I could afford the passage."

"We may be able to help you there, Sebastian. Money is not a problem for us. We even have friends with ships that could give you passage. Rue de Kerraros may yet see you again." McGirtt smiled at the man as he dipped a spoon into the porridge in the pot. "It's certainly enough for five men," McGirtt added. "We are all grateful for your hard work. If you would like to think about a loan from us that you would not have to pay back... a loan that would enable you to return to beautiful France, let us talk about it, when you have time. Perhaps Etienne and Carlos would like to enjoy some freedom as well. Do you think so?"

When Esteve and his helpers were out of hearing, Cunningham said, "McGirtt. I think I enjoy participating in this kind of skullduggery. Do you think he will help us?"

"We shall see. He hates the Spanish. He longs for his home in France. He wants his children to grow up on Rue de Kerraros just as he did and probably his family for hundreds of generations. The longing for home can be very strong." Daniel's smile faded at this thought. Shortly his brow furrowed and he seated himself again on the small bundle of straw the Spanish garrison had seen fit to provide for his bed, dining room table, chairs and – he eyed the wooden bucket in the corner of the cell from which came a strong odor – the elaborate toilet facilities...

As they forced themselves to eat the porridge provided by the jailor, a well-dressed man appeared at the door to the cell. He introduced himself as Lawyer Samuel Farley and he had with him a brief that he read with affected tones. Farley, tall, thin with long, black unkempt hair and a black beard, glanced at them from time to time as he read the brief, as though for emphasis.

The brief, signed by twenty nine of McGirtt's neighbors, described

Daniel as a cutthroat robber who had fleeced them of their property. It listed how many head of cattle, how many horses and how many slaves Daniel had recently taken from them at gun point. It petitioned Zespedes to have McGirtt, Cunningham, Mangum, Linder and Cargan arrested for these thefts. The brief went on to describe Daniel's alleged crimes against nature, humanity and especially against them over the past years, although none of the signers had been in Florida for a full year. When Farley read the names of the signers, Daniel was not surprised to have a full list of the names of the men who had recently raided Daniel's Maxton Island Plantation and stolen most of his cattle and horses. "A preemptive strike," Daniel muttered to Cunningham. They got to Zespedes first so that is who he will believe."

In the morning, just before first light, Daniel heard an articulated, "Ahem." The sound came from the door of their cell. It was Sebastian Esteve. "Shall we talk, monsieur?"

౮ ಐ

The five men spent another day in the cell subsisting on the gruel supplied them by their jailor. Conversation remained limited to the coarseness of the facilities, the limited imagination of the Spanish, their lack of any sense of decency and the unfairness of this incarceration. "We haven't even had a hearing. We haven't been informed as to why we were arrested. What are the charges? Who the hell is in charge here, anyway?" Linder, the most vocal of the five, paced the cell intermittently.

Cargan answered once, but on the repetition of the complaint, ignored Linder as did the rest of them. "The Spanish are a slow people," he said. "They like their wine, their pasta and their women. Those are the only things they hurry for. Zespedes is a career soldier. He's steeped in the school that teaches nothing matters enough to hurry for it. The comfort and well being of others is an afterthought. He'll get around to us when he's ready."

In the morning, the sound came again at the door to their cell, "Ahem."

Daniel was surprised to see Carlos and Etienne dressed as Spanish soldiers. They even had muskets. "Where did you get these things?" he asked Sebastian.

"*Shhh!*" came the reply. "Stolen."

First light arrived and as it did, the fort's drawbridge slowly and noisily came down. With the sun not quite up, heavy cloud cover and *even a little fog,* McGirtt was glad to observe, Sebastian, Carlos and Etienne marched McGirtt and his four companions across the draw bridge and into the city, in the general direction of Government House. As soon as they were on St. George Street, out of sight of the fort, they changed directions and entered the house of James McGirtt, Daniel's brother.

"Nice to see you, brother. Why are you taking such a risk? I thought you opted for the residential and civil way of life?" McGirtt sneered.

"Come, Daniel," James answered. "There's no time for chit chat. Change into these clothes so that you are not recognized. Sebastian, Carlos, Etienne – I have clothing here for you as well. You won't get far dressed as soldiers and accompanying these prisoners across the western city gate."

At the western entrance to the city, a rickety wooden bridge crossed the San Sebastian River. At the other side, there were horses and weapons. "Did you get word to Francisco?" McGirtt asked.

"I did," James answered. "He said he would have a boat waiting for you at Tocoi Landing tomorrow at first light. Where will you go?"

"James, my brother. I would love to tell you, but if I don't and you are questioned, you won't have to lie when you tell them you don't know where we are."

15

Late December, 1784

Excerpted from *The Boston Planet* by Guidi Peterson:

...The war goes on in the deep south. The lack of clarity in laying out the national border between the United States and Florida (which is Spanish once again) has resulted in violent ambiguity. A disputed no-man's-land over a hundred miles wide is confused not only about what language to use but which nation holds sovereignty: who is the enemy and who the friend. The East Florida Rangers, once agents of the British, now informally serve the Spanish and are tasked with defending the hundred mile wide border line – but the Rangers are personally conflicted: many want Florida to remain British and the subsequent inner rebellion they feel expresses itself in quaint misbehaviors. The former British governor, Patrick Tonyn, is still there, co-governing, in some odd fashion, with the new Spanish governor, Vincent Manual De Zespedes. Tonyn has the necessary soldiers to enforce the laws but can't use his troops in Spanish territory. Zespedes makes up the law as he goes along, but lacks the troops for enforcement.

Our sources tell us that, although the two governors despise each other, they interact with a stiff and formal respect. Many of those living on the hundred mile wide border line are the children of London's debtor prisoners brought to Georgia by James Oglethorpe many years ago. Even under the strict hand of British rule, they were a wild lot, living in the wilderness like Indians. Some farm and raise livestock while others – opportunism, it would appear, being their genetic gift – raid North Florida plantations as well as their own neighbors and as far north as Columbia, South Carolina.

Zespedes' latest maneuver to repopulate the colony is to offer free land. A head of household is allotted one hundred acres. If he has a wife, he is entitled to another fifty acres, plus fifty acres for each child and each slave. If the land is not developed, it will be forfeited back to the crown. This offering on the part of Spanish Florida is to be tax-free for ten years.

This seems to be a very enticing offer indeed, but considering the turmoil of the area, be advised not to go there unarmed.

Daniel's visit to Cuscowilla lasted about two weeks. "Wakapuchasce is dead," his son Payne told Daniel on his arrival. "He told us his kill of Spanish ended at only eighty six. My brother Bolek and I must kill fourteen more in his name before we can begin killing Spanish in our own names."

"Why must this be done? Why kill anyone? It only raises anger and the desire for revenge. The Spanish now own Florida again. If you kill too many of them, they will send soldiers." Daniel knew the answer but he wanted Payne to hear himself say it.

"Wakapuchasce vowed to kill one hundred Spanish so that he could rest in peace in the afterlife. He killed only eighty six. It is a matter of honor." As Payne finished, Bolek approached indicating food was ready.

"Do you want food?" he asked. A boy of about 6 years was with Bolek, gnawing on the leg of what seemed to have once been a squirrel. Noticing Daniel looking at the boy, Bolek volunteered, "This is my first son. His name is Hitchiti. I am proud of him. When he becomes a man, his name will be Micanopy."

Daniel accepted the offer of food. Cunningham and Mayfield, who had come to Cuscowilla with Daniel, joined him. The three ate silently, each with his own thoughts, but it would seem the thoughts were very similar. "Where can we go from here?" Mayfield's tone was so soft that Cunningham asked him to repeat it. "No matter where we go, we will be arrested," he pointed out.

Daniel poked at the fire with a long stick, sending up sparks. He shifted his feet before he spoke. "What Stephen says is true. Zespedes fears us because we represent, in his mind, the center of the many remaining British who want Florida to remain British. He thinks of us a rebels, and he's not that far off the mark. Tonyn hates us because we embarrassed him with the episode of the freed slaves we took back from Samuel Farley. West Florida is Spanish again, too. We can't go there. If we go to the United States, we'll be remembered for the scourge we put on South Carolina and Georgia. If we go the Bahamas we might be arrested there, too. That's British territory."

Cunningham just glared at the fire. Mayfield shifted again as though he was about to speak, but said nothing. "I'd like to go home," Daniel concluded.

"Do you mean South Carolina?" Cunningham asked him.

"Yes." Daniel remained silent for a moment then added, "My wife is there. I have aunts and uncles, cousins, nephews and nieces. I have brothers and sisters. My life, which I thought was going to be in Florida, is really in South Carolina, where I am hated. I can't go home."

Mayfield cleared his throat and changed the subject. "I'm surprised at how our neighbors turned on us and on Daniel. They came and robbed him of nearly everything, then claimed he robbed them when we took his property back. They petitioned Zespedes to have us arrested and Zespedes, people pleaser that he is, had us arrested. I think we have a debt to collect along the St. Johns River. When we finish that, we can take ship for the Bahamas and leave this mosquito-infested swamp of a peninsula forever."

"It's not surprising that they hate us." Cunningham half chuckled as he said it. "Most of them are from south Georgia and South Carolina. We turned eastern South Carolina to cinders and drove some of them off their plantations. We took their cattle, horses and slaves and left them destitute. Who would have thought they'd turn up on our doorsteps? It's no wonder that those neighbors are not eager friends."

"I've had enough of fighting and warring," Daniel replied. "But what you say is true. But we can't let this treachery go unpunished. Let's go back. What say you all?"

CB 80

The ride back to the St. Johns River area took two days. The trails were flooded in some areas and from time to time they stopped to build a fire to warm up. While the December weather didn't match the northern climes, it still grew cold enough that, with the wind and dampness, they were rubbing their palms together and shivering after a few hours on horseback. Since Wakapuchasce was dead, some of his sons, including Payne and Bolek, accompanied them. "We must kill fourteen Spanish," they told Daniel. "We must do it in the name of our father who cannot rest in peace until fourteen Spanish are killed in his name."

"If you have to slaughter more Spanish," Daniel told them, "Please do it when we are nowhere near. I understand Wakapuchasce's desire but none of us three wants to take credit for it in the eyes of the Spanish. They are angry enough."

As they traveled, they saw camps along the way consisting of refugees who had come to Florida during the Revolution but had not yet returned to their earlier homes. "We have nowhere to go," they told them. "Our lands in Georgia have been taken over by the Americans and we never had clear title to those lands, anyway. We just moved into the wilderness and cut down trees and started farming. It was free land. The Indians didn't much like it but if we gave them food or, sometimes, liquor, we hoped they would leave us alone."

"Some of us practically joined the Indians. We took Indian wives and some of our daughters married Indian men. But when the war came, we had to leave. The Spanish are after us too. We made free use of the access we had to poorly guarded farms and homes. Governor Tonyn started calling us banditti."

"Yes," McGirtt told them," and Tonyn thinks I'm the chief banditti." Quite of few of these dispossessed people joined Daniel and his crew, so that by the time they reached the ferry at Pilotaikita, their band had grown to nearly fifty armed men. The crossing took most of the morning since the ferry had to make several trips to accommodate all of them. Daniel found it surprising to find no guard on either side of the river, but as the ferry landed on the end of the first crossing, Daniel noticed a man on horseback, trotting off toward the east. *Zespedes will know we are back.* His thoughts turned dark. *He'll send someone after us.* "I wonder if the Spanish have enough troop strength to stand up to us," he said to Cunningham, who rode next to him.

"Hard to say, Daniel," he answered. "I wouldn't be surprised to find myself locked back up in that old stone fort, though. It could happen. Not a nice place."

"Well, as long as we don't kill anyone, we'll probably be able to work our way through it and maybe wind up in a situation where we don't have to fight anymore."

"Yah," Cunningham answered. "The path to paradise is through the valley of the shadow of death."

"Ride on with a grin," Daniel retorted, and turned his horse to watch the ferry head back west for the next load of passengers. "Pilotaikita. Crossing place. It's well named, I guess. It's the narrowest place on the river for quite a few miles that doesn't have swamp on one side or the other. The Indians swam across."

"I thought they used canoes," Mayfield interjected.

"Well, maybe some canoes to fend off the alligators," Daniel smiled. "I thought they mostly just swam across."

Francisco Sanchez's plantation, Diego Plain, the intended destination, still remained thirty some miles to the north and the east. When they were all gathered, they set off, keeping close to the river on the main trail, rather than taking the more easterly trail toward St. Augustine. Not far along, they encountered a small entourage accompanying a carriage pulled by a team of two horses. "What's this?" Cunningham asked.

"Let's find out," came from Daniel as the team of so-called banditti stopped the carriage by blocking its path.

"Stand off!" cried the driver. "Chief Justice John James Hume is on government business and must not be delayed."

"Well, I'll be!" Cunningham exclaimed softly to Daniel and Mayfield. "This is the guy who was arguing with Tonyn about the clear title to most of the slaves in St., Augustine. He insinuated that they were stolen or somehow illegally taken from others and smuggled to St. Augustine and North Florida. Tonyn insisted that there were no 'legal irregularities,' as he put it and was angry. Remember?"

"Yes," Daniel answered. "Tonyn hates this guy. Let's send Tonyn a gift to show him we remember him fondly and have a little fun at the same time."

"Hold!" Daniel commanded the driver. "Hold or be shot." Daniel raised his musket, pointing it at the driver. *It certainly won't hurt the driver to know the musket is not loaded or even primed.* Daniel smiled at the thought. None of them carried their muskets loaded unless they were expecting problems that would require fire power. Cunningham also raised his unloaded musket as did Mayfield. Their fifty companions, Indians and Englishmen, stood by silently, frowning. Some drew swords while others brandished knives. The coachman stopped the team. Hume leaped out of the carriage with a male secretary behind him.

"What is the meaning of this? How dare you brigands delay an official of the court on official business? Stand out of the path and allow us to proceed, this instant!"

"How can a former British judge claim to be on official British business in Spanish territory?" Daniel asked politely. "Do you carry a margin of British land that moves with you as you travel, beyond which it becomes Spanish again, after you pass?"

"Ah!" Former Chief Justice Hume seemed to be given to exclamation on this day. "It's Dirt McGirtt. You look clean enough today, Dirt. Have you taken up bathing?"

"So, you *were* at Fort MacIntosh that day. That you would stand idly by while a man of authority tries to steal a horse from a subordinate speaks clearly of your own integrity. It's no wonder Tonyn finds you disgusting. That you would address such a superior force with such lack of manners indicates that your education has been somewhat abbreviated. Stand off, yourself. I'll give you exactly one minute to remove your luggage from that carriage. We are taking it – and the horses. You can walk back to St. Augustine."

Hume fumed as he and his driver removed a chest from the back of the carriage. When the task was completed, Daniel called in one of the people traveling with his entourage and put him in charge of driving the team. They continued in their earlier direction. When Hume and his driver were out of sight, Daniel replaced the driver with another traveler who was not part of their company, asking him to deliver the carriage to Governor Tonyn with McGirtt's compliments. They cheered as the man drove away.

Soon the path to the northwest split, one branch heading toward St. Augustine and the other taking a more northerly direction. They felt that bypassing St. Augustine would be the wisest course, so they followed the more northerly path.

After spending the night a few miles south of Tocoi, well away from the path, the travelers set out again only to find another man on horseback, leading two more horses behind him. Francis Levett, a former rice planter from Georgia, had received lands at the hand of Vincent Zespedes as part of the new Spanish governor's attempt at resettling Florida with loyal Spanish citizens. Levett started laughing when he saw McGirtt. "Hello, McGirtt," he called out. "I heard you bribed your way out of prison. That was well played, but it won't be long until you are back there and in chains."

"Daniel," Cunningham spoke softly enough that Levett could not hear. "He was with the men who raided your Maxton Island plantation while we were there. Do you recognize him?"

"I do," Daniel replied. "He was the one that called out to the others, - 'Hey, don't forget the barn!' and they took my best horses. It's unlikely I'd forget him."

Levett did not yet realize his disadvantage so he continued laughing. "Your Maxton Island Plantation now belongs to over a dozen people.

Zespedes gave it away. Where will you call home now, you brigand?"

Daniel and his troop were blocking the path again, so Levett could not pass unless they permitted it. "You rob me, then call me the brigand?" Daniel snorted. "You rob me, then accuse me of thievery when I recover my property?" Daniel's smile had faded. "You can count yourself lucky that I don't filet you right here and now." McGirtt's anger grew, but Mayfield put a hand on his arm to calm him.

"We haven't killed anyone in Florida yet," Mayfield reminded him.

Daniel shook off the hand and shouted, "You would hand me the filth of your dishonor, then deride me and taunt me? I would ask if you are a fool but the answer is obvious. Dismount!"

Levett appeared uncertain and began turning his horse with the obvious intention of riding in the other direction at high speed. Daniel raised his unloaded musket again in Levett's full view. "Dismount right now or I will shoot you clean in half."

Levett paused, looked at the size of the opening at the end of McGirtt's musket barrel, then quietly dismounted. "What do you think you are going to do, McGirtt? You are on the east side of the St. Johns River. You can't get across it easily and Zespedes and Tonyn both have military forces not all that far away. You were probably seen when you returned from wherever you fled to when you escaped from the Castillo de San Marcos the last time. I would be surprised if Zespedes doesn't already know you are back. He probably has people coming after you right now."

"You might live longer if you shut your mouth, Levett." Daniel dismounted, holding his musket pointed at the man. Daniel took the reins from the man's hand and said, "Now walk."

"You can't have my horses, McGirtt. They're mine. You can't have them."

"For all I know," Daniel answered, "These are some of the ones you stole from me only a few months ago. What are you doing now? Do you think you found a buyer for two of them? I don't think so. Walk away, while you are able."

The crew watched in silence while Levett began walking north. "No." Daniel stopped him. "If you go north, we will be behind you all the way. Go to Pilotaikita. There you may find a ride back to St. Augustine, where you can tell the governor of our misdeeds."

As they watched Levett walk away, Mayfield shook his head. "We're stirring up more trouble, Daniel. If we have business in this section of Florida, we must finish it and be away as soon as possible. I'm growing very uncomfortable with this situation."

"So am I," Cunningham chimed in. "We aren't asking for trouble.

We're begging for it."

"You're both right, of course," Daniel answered. "I must see Francisco. As soon as I do, we can leave quickly for St. Marys. We haven't offended very many people there and besides that, we've enriched quite a few of them with the trade we've done there of cattle and slaves. We may even find some friends."

Daniel picked another of the travelers who had come with them but had nothing to do with their enterprise. This one called himself William Jamison. "William," Daniel addressed him. "Please take charge of these three horses. If you ride east on the trail we are about to come upon, you will arrive in St. Augustine in about three hours, maybe four. Please present these horses to Governor Vincent Zespedes as a token of my respect." Daniel started grinning. "We can't be herding horses and carriages to St. Marys today. We need to make haste."

William rode off with an equally broad grin calling over his shoulder, "Yes, sir."

CB ED

Former Governor Patrick Tonyn rocked on a comfortable chair on a small porch across the street from Government House. Since Vincent Zespedes' inauguration as governor of East Florida, Tonyn had taken another spot for office space. Peter Edwards and others remained inside the building hovering over desks and tables, executing documents from Tonyn's dictation. The headaches of the day continued to be the British people who had established lives in British Florida and had been given a choice to either leave for other British possessions or register as Spanish citizens. It grieved Tonyn to find so many deciding to remain and become citizens of Spain. "How can they hand over their citizenship so easily?" he muttered to himself. "Britain is a far better culture than Spain's ignorance and medievalism. The fools still use *rejas* instead of glass in their windows. Their houses are full of insects and rats. Even the squirrels that live here in such great profusion find free access. They try to keep the insects out with their bloody *brasseros* where they build a fire right in the middle of the room and keep everything smoky. It works for the bugs, but not the rats."

Tonyn was shaken out of his reverie by a carriage coming from the west. The horses seemed sweated up and tired. The man holding the reins looked equally disheveled. Having his break interrupted did not please the former governor. He tried to ignore it, but the carriage pulled up right in front of him and the driver called him by name. Tonyn gave the carriage his full attention. "My God, man! That is the carriage of Chief Justice John James Hume! What are you doing with it?"

The man seemed chagrined, but had his mission to fulfill. "I'm sorry, sir. Yes, sir, it is the carriage of Chief Justice Hume."

"How did you come by it? Where is Hume? Is he all right?" *Not that his demise would trouble me a whit.*

"I crossed the river at Pilotaikita," the man began. "I was traveling with a large group of men. Many were Indians, some ragamuffins from the swamps. We came upon this man traveling in the other direction with a driver and this team of horses. Some men in the large group stopped this man and made him dismount the carriage. They sent him walking back to St. Augustine. He should be here soon, I suppose. The man gave the reins to me and asked me to drive it into St. Augustine and turn it over to you personally, sir."

"What, exactly, is the meaning of this?" Tonyn demanded.

"The man told me his name and asked me to give you his highest regards."

"And his name? Good God, man. Tell me!"

"Daniel McGirtt, sir."

"God's blood!" Tonyn shouted. Tonyn, not usually given to such profanities, succeeded in getting the attention of Peter Edwards, who had been just inside the door transcribing correspondence. Edwards came outside quickly.

"What is it sir? What is it? Is everything all right, sir?"

"God's blood!" Tonyn shouted again. This time he got the attention of Vincent Zespedes, who was seated on his king's balcony on the upper floor of government house considering siesta. Zespedes leaned over his balcony to get a better view of the proceedings. "Where in hell," Tonyn continued shouting, "is Colonel William Young right now?"

"Let me get you a cup of tea, sir," Edwards suggested. "It might help you calm down a bit, sir. You are most agitated."

"You're damned right, I'm agitated," Tonyn's volume had diminished only slightly. "McGirtt is back. And look what he's done! He appropriated the carriage and horses of Chief Justice Hume! And the bleeding bastard had the cheek to turn them over to me!"

"Indeed, sir!"

"The most miserable part of this is," – Tonyn's voice was sinking almost, but not quite, to conversational tones – "I can't charge him with stealing them because he turned them in to me! His only sin this time was to inconvenience Hume, which I'm sure gave him great pleasure!"

"A prank, perhaps, sir, but he did indeed steal the horses and carriage and had possession of this stolen property until you received it from, not the hands of Daniel McGirtt, but this disheveled gentleman before us." Edwards turned to the driver of the carriage. "Your name, sir?"

"Daniel Evans," the man offered humbly. "I didn't have any part in this theft, your honor. I only delivered the carriage and horses to you as requested."

"Leave the rig here, sir," Edwards directed. "You have done nothing wrong that I know of. Please enjoy the rest of this beautiful day."

Tonyn grabbed Edwards' arm and repeated his question, "Where is Young? I sent him south toward the lake shaped like a crescent to check on some planters in that area. That's a few days' ride south and west. Has he reported in yet?"

"No, sir."

"Send a rider to retrieve him, immediately."

ଓ ଓ

Vincente Manual de Zespedes was finally enjoying the peace of his siesta after Tonyn that *bufón Englesa* had stopped his shouting. He had had his people slide *la sofá* out on the balcony so he could enjoy the cool December air. He found it very comfortable. The sounds of the mockingbirds chasing each other around disturbed him not in the least. He would reach his sixty-sixth birthday this year. His service of many years to Spain would soon be rewarded with peaceful retirement, at home in Valencia. *Aw, Valencia. That beautiful City. I can hardly wait to see her again.* The mockingbirds provided a sort of music for him to relax by. His sleep, however, was disturbed again by the sound of horses' hooves galloping down the street. *¡Por Diós! ¡Que inferno!* He stood and leaned over the balcony for a better look. Another man, even more disheveled than the one driving the carriage, appeared on the back of a sweating horse, leading two more on lengths of rope.

The man stopped at the foot of the balcony, having seen Zespedes leaning over the rail. When he got his horses stopped and calmed, the man shouted to him, "Governor Zespedes, Governor Zespedes!"

"It's Cespedes, if you don't mind, terribly. Cespedes. What can I do for you, young man? Zespedes always insisted on the Castilian lisp (Thespedes).

"Governor Thespedes! These horses belong to Francis Levett. He is a planter that now lives on some of the land that used to belong to Bill Cunningham. He encountered Daniel McGirtt on the trail and insulted him. McGirtt took his horses as punishment and asked me to deliver them to you."

ଓ ଓ

Patrick Tonyn, now seated comfortably, if irritably, in the office of Vincent Zespedes, listened patiently as Zespedes enumerated the reasons he wanted McGirtt arrested, incarcerated and sent to Cuba for interment, if not hanging. Tonyn had heard this liturgy many times. "McGirtt provided good service for me in the past," Tonyn pointed out. "He was always a little too zealous for his own good, but what he did for Britain and Florida cannot be denied. When our plantations were raided, he pursued the villains all the way to their homes in Georgia and sometimes even South Carolina, recovered the stolen property and returned it to the rightful owners. He's a good man, overall.

"This change from British to Spanish sovereignty has been very hard on many people," Tonyn went on. "A great many have been in Florida for twenty years, building homes, farms, lives, and now they are uprooted and sent packing. I certainly understand why it's hard to take. I want McGirtt arrested because he has defied my orders to cease and desist his actions as a representative of the East Florida Rangers, which no longer exist. But his position in the area, looked up to by his former neighbors and now down on by his present ones, is not good. His current neighbors are people from Georgia whom he punished for raiding and to whom you have given land. Is that their reward for formerly terrorizing the area? I'm suspicious of this petition we have from them asking for his arrest. I think it's just vindictive and has no merit. Yes, I want him arrested, but I want to deport him to British territory, not to a dungeon at the Castillo de San Marcos or in Cuba."

Zespedes used a translator whose name, Micael Verde de Ribera, reminded Tonyn of Isabel De Ribera, the wife of Pedro Menendez. While Tonyn waited for the translator to finish, he wondered if Micael came from the same place in Spain as Isabel. *Eventually, perhaps I will ask,* he mused. Finally Zespedes began to talk. The translator attempted to talk simultaneously.

"Daniel McGirtt," the translator began, "has been a thorn in my side ever since I came here. I wished to grant him amnesty at the beginning of my authority here, because I believed he would be a good man to have on my side. Unfortunately, I have been unable to win him over. He is one of many of your people who resent that Florida is once again Spanish, as it should be. We have held Florida since 1565 in uninterrupted sovereignty. It is only right that Florida remain Spanish. I have made it clear to him that he is welcome to remain, under certain circumstances, which he attempted to fulfill. His apparent theft of Samuel Farley's slaves on the very night of my inauguration was a slap in my face that I tried to ignore. That he was present at the proceedings seemed to indicate that he was not involved, but I am now convinced that he indeed was involved, based on the reports from your very own secretary, Pedro Edwards. That McGirtt is such a braggart, even when his own mouth betrays him, astonishes me. He seems to be a refined gentleman otherwise, except, of course, after he has been in chains in my dungeon for a few days. And that seems to be all the longer we can keep him – just a few days. If I get him again, things will be different!"

Tonyn listened carefully because Micael Verde's Spanish accent distorted some of his words. But Tonyn was satisfied that he got the general idea and that clearly. After giving respectful consideration to what he had been told that Zespedes had said, he answered, "These thefts of his that we learned of today were actually somewhat amusing. Daniel knows of the tensions that exist between myself and Chief Justice Hume. The argument Hume presented about most of the slaves in St. Augustine being illegally obtained, if proven, would cast a serious slur on my rule as governor. That he brought the charge at all was deeply insulting, even if it may be, in part, true. Daniel did this to him as a prank. He did not keep the horses and carriage. He delivered them directly to me, without holding them for a moment. The theft of the horses from Francis Levett, while another cruel prank, was nothing more than another prank. Levett owned a plantation in the colony of Georgia. He was one of those who routinely invaded British territory and stole livestock and slaves from the plantation owners here. Daniel's prank clearly states that the fact of your gift of land to Levett does not reduce the fact that he is a rascal, a thief and a robber in his own right. Daniel also did not keep Levett's property for a moment but immediately turned it over to the territorial governor – you. So, while the prank was cruel, forcing Hume and Levett to walk back to town, it was not theft. The matter of Farley's slaves is another matter but even in that instance, the *report* that he bragged is not proof that he bragged nor proof of his guilt in stealing Farley's slaves. I maintain that McGirtt should be deported to British territory, not imprisoned."

The argument continued for the rest of the afternoon. Zespedes served tea, offered Tonyn cigars and extended every hospitality he could think of. The meeting, though both men distrusted and disliked one another, ended on an affable note of agreeing to disagree, although Zespedes made it abundantly clear that he was now in charge and he would make the final decision.

A week later, in Tonyn's office, Colonel William Young was announced by Peter Edwards and shown into Tonyn's presence. Young stood over six feet. His fair hair and complexion matched, but his skin dotted with red bumps had him scratching almost constantly. In explanation to Tonyn's questions about his scratching, Young told him.

"The area south and west of St. Augustine is consistently as beautiful as it is here but consistently infested with fleas, ticks, mosquitoes and a species of gnat that is so small that they are nearly invisible. They only come out when the wind stops blowing, but when it does, they are a tempest in their own right. I doubt that I have much blood left. It was mostly sacrificed to the insect population in Florida's forests. How can I serve you, sir?"

Tonyn lowered his eyes to his desk top for a moment and cleared his throat for effect. "McGirtt is back."

"I wonder where he's been," Young retorted. "I certainly hunted for him. There was no sign. He just vanished."

"He probably went west and stayed among the Indians. They seem to be his friends. Every time I hear of him, it is said that he has Indians with him. Colonel Young, I want you to find him and bring him to St. Augustine. He, William Cunningham and Stephen Mayfield are to be confined at the Castillo de San Marcos. Zespedes is planning to send them to Havanna for a trial."

"What charges is he bringing? What has McGirtt done that can be proved? It seems to me that it's all accusations by people jealous of his success or angry because he victimized them as enemies during the war. THEN, he was doing the right thing. What's he done now?"

Tonyn raised his eyebrows. "You of all people shouldn't have to ask that question. It was from you that he stole some thirty eight slaves. He even shot you. Have you forgotten?"

"I have not forgotten," Young answered. "I have also not forgotten that the slaves were taken by me, illegally and that when he shot me, it was I who raised my weapon first. He shot in self-defense. I also remember that he took me to his home and nursed me back to health at his own expense. It was a grand act of hospitality. And when I was well enough to ride, he gave me one of his own horses to get me back to town. Daniel McGirtt is a good man and does not deserve to be incarcerated in a stone dungeon. But I will obey your order and do as I am told."

16

    Still dogged by chilly weather and threatening skies, the troop continued north, following the St. Johns River. Daniel McGirtt, William "Bloody Bill" Cunningham and Stephen Mayfield worked their way north, bearing eastward and inland from the river when they passed Cunningham's former plantation. They were accompanied by ragtag followers consisting of Indians, volunteer former slaves and a few diehard English who wanted to keep Florida British. "Look," Cunningham pointed. "There are cat faces on the pines as far east as here. We used them to tap the pines for their sap to make the turpentine."
    "You certainly made good use of it at Fort MacIntosh," McGirtt remarked wryly, cringing inwardly at the memory of the burning fort with the soldiers trapped inside. "I wonder who's tapping these trees now."
    "Alcorn would know," Mayfield chimed in. "Where is he, anyway?"
    "He's in South Carolina," Daniel answered. "I sent him to Stateburg with a message for my wife. He'll be back soon, probably, but I have no idea how he will find us."
    The soggy trail, with ruts deepened by passing wagons, horses and cattle, was an occasional quagmire that the horses splashed through as the party continued north. Those on foot skirted the deeper places, watching for snakes, although the chilly weather probably kept the cotton mouth moccasins hiding in deeper, dryer places. "It doesn't pay to be careless around here," Daniel heard one of them remarking. "Ya never know when yer gonna step on one of those damned things."

Heavy clumps of Spanish moss, blown from the trees by the high gusts, promised the presence of chiggers and tics, so they were avoided as well. The chilly weather and gusty winds made the horses frisky and eager for a dash or a short canter. Keeping control of them was a real challenge for Daniel and his companions. "Are we going to find Francisco home at the Diego Plantation?" Cunningham's nature kept him eager for movement. Waiting was not his pleasure, ever.

Daniel half turned toward him, understanding Cunningham's impatience because he, himself felt it as well. "In fine weather like this, Francisco is probably huddled in St. Augustine with his lady, Maria Piedra, warming his hands over a low oak fire. I envy him. We'll have to send for him and wait until he sees fit to come to see us. We can wait at his plantation."

"It might not be safe to do that," Mayfield interjected. "After teasing Hume and Levett as we did, Zespedes may have ordered our arrest, again."

"Or Tonyn may have," Cunningham added.

"Maybe we should have left well enough alone," Daniel mused. "It was just too tempting and they were so insolent. We couldn't let that go by."

"It was very satisfying to watch Chief Justice Hume walking down the trail in the direction of St. Augustine. I wonder how long it took him to get there, if he's even there yet," Mayfield chuckled.

"I have a feeling, we're going to pay for that. Tonyn hates him, but Zespedes might feel differently and Zespedes is the one in power now." Cunningham's chilling prophecy quieted them briefly.

"Let's get on with it." Daniel urged his horse to move a little faster, even though the trail was littered with fallen branches. "We need to get this over with. If Francisco isn't home, there's an abandoned Indian camp east of the plantation. We'll probably be safe waiting there."

Before the crew came within sight of Diego Plantation, while they still had several miles to go, they could smell the smoke from Francisco's plantation. Though they did not want to tire the horses by moving faster, or force those on foot to try to keep up, the involuntary increase in speed was inevitable. "It will be good to get out of this wind," Daniel remarked.

"You can say that again," Mayfield quipped. The promised warmth proved irresistible. Their speed increased, leaving those on foot far behind.

The plantation house stood as Daniel remembered it. Its unpainted wood frame, south facing porch and roughhewn board walls stood against the wind like a welcoming island in a sea of cold. Some cattle stood against the wind in a corralled area near the main house. The blacksmith's shop, it turned out, was the source of the smoke. The smith worked feverishly, hammering out wrought-iron fixtures. The only horses in sight grazed with the cattle in the nearby field. As the three tied their horses to the rail in front of the house, they were surprised to find Spanish soldiers quietly gathering around them from behind the house. The arrest took place quite civilly with the three soundly outnumbered. They were permitted to use their own horses on the ride to St. Augustine, up the path to the Old Fort and across the draw bridge. Those who had been following on foot saw from a distance what was taking place and disappeared into the forest.

The horses' hooves clattered on the wooden planks as the three crossed under heavy guard. Several of the dragoons, as McGirtt like to call them, held muskets pointed at them in the event they would try to bolt free. Stephen Mayfield, not to be undone by the grim situation, quoted, "Home again, home again, jiggety jig."

"So you've read John Florio," McGirtt remarked. "Where's the fat pig?"

"I suspect," Cunningham ventured, "He's in the governor's mansion."

"Watch what you say," McGirtt cautioned. "He's already angry with us. Calling him names won't help our cause." Inside the courtyard the three were ordered to dismount, then led to what would be their home for the next few months. The cell was a stone rectangle with a very high ceiling. It boasted one small table, one chair, and a couple of bales of straw strewn about the floor. When Daniel saw it, he turned to one of the guards who he learned could speak English. Daniel handed him a gold coin and asked the guard to "Please get word to my brother James that we are here. He lives just about across the street from the Castillo. He will provide us with food and blankets."

The guard sneered, took the gold coin and said, *"Si, Señor. Tal vez."* (Perhaps)

"My brother may well give you another coin," Daniel added. "I certainly wouldn't want to rely on the goodness of your heart to do such a kindness for such desperados as we must be."

James showed up at their locked door in just a few hours accompanied by several servants. Some carried blankets. Others hauled firewood to provide fuel for the small fireplace at one end of the dungeon. "You'll be quite lucky if Zespedes doesn't hang you this time, Daniel. You're charged with stealing horses from Chief Justice Hume and Francis Levett, and the murder of Colonel William Young."

"But Young isn't dead," Daniel answered in surprise. "How can I be accused of murdering a man who isn't dead?"

"Spanish rule is different than English rule," James retorted. "Why couldn't you have just stayed away? ...or gone back to South Carolina?"

"I think they'd hang me in South Carolina, too," Daniel shrugged. "I caused more harm there than I ever did here!"

"Mary says you can live with her family in Stateburg if you keep it quiet who you are. Our nephew Zach Cantey has also volunteered shelter for you, if you're not too proud to accept it."

"I'm not yet finished with Florida," Daniel answered sullenly.

"Well!" James struggled to keep his indignation and frustration from the ears of the guards. "Florida just might be finished with you. Zespedes wants to hang you – and well he might!"

The three were quiet after James' visit. Each kept to his own thoughts, shivering under the blankets James had brought. The dungeon's dampness as well as its essence of termination drove them into themselves. The low fire they kept burning at the end of the room was small comfort. Sleeping passed the time most quickly, "But we can't sleep all the time," Mayfield complained.

"There's no point in complaining," Cunningham snapped. "We will be here until Zespedes decides to do something else with us. We can't bribe our way out like we did the last time. There are two armed guards outside the dungeon entrance and they change guards every few hours, always different ones."

"And they can't speak English," Daniel grumbled.

Maria Piedra, Francisco Sanchez's concubine, began showing up every morning. A welcome sight, bearing bread and meat, she stood right at five feet tall with rich black hair, smiling brown eyes and full lips that assumed the shape of a smile more than any other expression. Although she had not a single word of English in her possession, she managed to convey the information that her husband Francisco and Daniel's brother James were providing the money for the food. James continued to keep them in firewood while the weather remained cool. Some days seemed warmer, but the fourteen feet of stone between the prisoners and the outside world kept that warmth outside.

Keeping track of time became their chief challenge. When Maria arrived some mornings, smiling as always, Cunningham tried out his Spanish on her. "*¿Que dia es?*"

"*Lunes*," she answered.

"What the hell does that mean?" Mayfield demanded of Daniel.

"Hell if I know."

Another day, Maria answered, "*Viernes.*" Cunningham quit asking. All they knew for sure was that the air was not as cold as it had been.

After an indeterminate period of time, some special guards appeared at the door to their dungeon and escorted them to an office near the drawbridge. Walking outside for the first time in weeks – or was it months? – they were blinded by the brightness of the sun. The breeze that found its way down inside the courtyard of the Castillo de San Marcos almost stung their skin with its freshness. The heat from the sun on their skin, unaccustomed to such sensations for so long, felt like fire, welcome but frightening.

Two guards, one on each side of each man, gripped their arms tightly as though they feared Daniel and his companions would take flight into the sky like the small flock of pelicans Daniel could see passing overhead. Inside the small office, seated at a sturdy looking wooden desk with a secretary to one side and guards behind him, the governor of East Florida, Vincente Manual Zespedes, sat smirking like a cat that had just eaten a brown Cuban anole. His superficial greeting struck Daniel as small. "You're a hard man to run down, Colonel McGirtt. And you as well Colonels Stephen Mayfield and William Cunningham. But now that we have run you down, how do you like your accommodations?"

Angered, Daniel failed to hold his tongue. "The bathwater is not warm enough and for the first time in my life I have no private place to shit. It's good that you don't charge much for these luxuries."

Zespedes' English was not good enough to follow what Daniel had said. His secretary, who never bothered to introduce himself, translated for Zespedes. The governor smiled and, through his translator, replied, "The words of a wise man are always gracious, Colonel McGirtt. But I appreciate your sense of humor. I'm glad to see you can maintain it considering your situation."

Cunningham shuffled his feet, struggling to keep his mouth shut. Mayfield listened stoically. Zespedes continued, through his interpreter. "I gave you a hearing in my private offices, last week. We heard testimony from your victims, including Chief Justice Hume, Francis Levett and former Governor Tonyn's assistant, Pedro Edwards, whose horses you stole. Also there is the matter of the murder of Colonel William Young. Have you anything to say for yourselves?"

Daniel's feelings of surprise gave him a moment of pause before answering. "The horses of Francis Levett and Hume were themselves stolen by them and returned to your majesty and former Governor Tonyn immediately. We did not steal them, but returned them. We had no interaction with Pedro Edwards and do not understand that charge. As for the murder of Colonel William Young, the last time I saw him, he was alive, well and on a horse I gave him so he could return to St.

Augustine and resume his duties. If I wanted to kill Colonel William Young, he would be dead." Daniel's eyes grew fierce for a moment. "I don't understand the charge of his murder if he is not dead. Can you assist me, please, with a more detailed explanation?"

Zespedes snorted with impatience. "Edwards alleged that you stole his horses and testified to that fact at the hearing. You attempted to murder Colonel Young and the attempt is the same as the act. You will be punished for it whether he is dead or not. There is also the matter of Samuel Farley's slaves that we believe you stole on the night of my inauguration. Yes, I know you attended the inauguration but I still believe that you were behind the theft. It is my decision that you will be sent to Havana for trial and hanged there."

03 80

"It's March first," John James said to his sister, the wife of Daniel McGirtt. Stateburg, South Carolina, was enduring a howling storm that had lasted, so far, almost two days. The family tried to remain indoors as much as possible to avoid the driving rain, the mud and the flying debris, but they could not remain indoors all the time. There were chores to be done, animals to be fed, cows to be milked. John James' slaves did most of the work so there was no real requirement that he venture outdoors, but he always felt compelled to "check on things," as he liked to say.

Mary satisfied herself on such days of bad weather by sitting near a window with a good book, when she was not overseeing the kitchen or watching the house slaves tend to cleaning and their assorted responsibilities. "If March comes in like a lion, so they say, it will go out like a lamb. I'm looking forward to the beautiful beginning of the month of April. March is always so windy, but that's nice for drying clothes out on the line. They always smell... John. There's a rider coming down the path. I wonder what he wants."

After reading the letter from Daniel's brother James, Mary sat staring out the window at the driving rain. *Daniel is in a dungeon.* She twisted her hands together. Wiping her nose on her pink handkerchief too much was making it sore, so she stopped. The book she had been reading rested, ignored now, on the windowsill. Streaks of rain running down the pane joined and ran faster. *Must be quite a wind that can blow the rain all the way under the porch roof to hit the window.* Then she noticed that the water was not blowing that far under the roof. It was dripping from the porch roof above, running down the side of the house above the window, then down the window. *Maybe I should tell John, there may be a leak up above.*

Her brother left her to think in private while he ventured out to the barn where his people were preparing to plant cotton for this year's crop. She was glad for the privacy. She hated it when her brother saw her crying over Daniel's latest exploits. *Why is he in prison?* The letter said he was to be shipped to Cuba to be hanged. *Oh dear Lord! How can this be?* The front door to the house opened and her brother returned.

"All's well out there, Mary. If the weather cooperates, it will be a good harvest this year. I wish we could produce the quality of cotton they produce down south. That sea island cotton brings a higher price than ours does. I wonder if it's the salt air."

Mary looked up at him and wiped her nose one more time. "John, I have to go to St. Augustine. I'll be leaving as soon as possible. I think I can take the stage in the morning down to Charleston and get a boat from there."

John just stood there, frowning for a moment before answering. "Why don't you leave him to stew in his own juices, Mary? He's got himself into this, let him get himself out of it. If he can."

Mary stood, her lap blanket falling on the floor at her feet. "John, he is my husband. I love him. He's a good man. He has always a been a good man. If he's in this kind of trouble there is more to it than meets the eye. Daniel doesn't steal horses and he doesn't kill people. He needs help and I am going. If you were any kind of a man, you would come with me. I sent that rider off with a message to Zachariah Cantey up in Camden. I wouldn't expect Dan's sister Beth to come along, but her husband bleeding well should." Once roused, the Highland ire does not subside easily, however distant from its source. The children of Scotland though demure, charming, hardworking and full of fun are not to be meddled with. Mary James McGirtt, assembled in America of Scottish parts, was just such a person. Beautiful, strong of mind and a fearsome chess player, Mary McGirtt was about to go to war, bringing in her arsenal all the strengths of her kind, coupled with the feminine guile she learned as a Southern belle.

03 80

Governor Zespedes, seated on his balcony with the view of the Matanzas Bay, sipped a cup of *café negra*, watching the seagulls dancing after a fishing boat that had just come into the bay. His morning, busy as usual, entailed overseeing the recording of the new residents who were accepting his gifts of land. Hundreds had arrived over the last few weeks, mostly from South Carolina and Georgia but there were also immigrants from Scandinavia, Great Britain, Portugal, even Italy and Greece. Free land was a powerful incentive. *Funny. They're going to have to brave the alligators, the mosquitoes the snakes. What a place this is, La Florida, indeed. I'll be glad to go home to Spain. I wonder when that will be? No alligators in Valencia!*

The argument with former Governor Tonyn seemed ongoing. He bore Tonyn a grudging respect but disagreed with him on most things. Tonyn thought the gifts of land would create anarchy. *There are too many, he says. They are too diverse, he says. They will create havoc, he says. They were the raiders, he says, who were robbing plantations during his term as governor, the people he fought to keep out for all those years, and now I am giving them land. Bah! What does HE know? I am Governor now.*

The correspondence from Tonyn that now rested on his desk pleaded the case for Daniel McGirtt and his friends. Tonyn wrote:

> *I think it possible, if these unhappy men were transplanted into another country, that there might be yet a ray of hope, that upon proper reflection upon their past wicked courses, a reformation might be effectuated... Motives of humanity and commiseration, passions that will creep into the human mind, have been impressed upon me by the very decent Mrs. McGirtt, praying to have her husband transported to a British government. A similar memorial has been presented me by the friends of Major Cunningham and I have engaged to address your Excellency upon these matters, and to solicit your compliance in gratifying their wishes contained in the prayer of the petition.*

Zespedes, after reading these words from former Governor Tonyn, practically shrieked, "If he had taken this tone six months ago, much of this trouble could have been avoided, but NO. He insisted that McGirtt and his cronies be coddled. 'He's a good man' Tonyn said. 'He can be swayed to becoming a good Spanish citizen,' he said. What the hell was Tonyn thinking? What the hell is he thinking NOW?"

A guard appeared in Zespedes doorway. "You have a visitor, your Excellency. Mrs. Mary McGirtt, the wife of Daniel McGirtt, has come to see you and she has brought an interpreter with her so you can communicate most easily. She says her appointment time for meeting you has arrived. Do you have such an appointment, sir?"

The governor took a seat behind his desk and tried to compose himself. "Admit her."

Governor Vincente Manual Zespedes, governor of all of East Florida, long time veteran of Spain's wars all over the world and dedicated servant to the King of Spain, didn't discover until much later that when Mary McGirtt walked in the door, he didn't know what hit him.

Mary James McGirtt stood five feet six inches without her riding heels. Her slender form had caught the eye of many as she walked from her brother-in-law's home on Marina Street to the governor's mansion at the west end of the plaza, arm in arm with her brother John James and followed close behind by Zachariah Cantey. Her ankle length riding habit sported eight widely stitched and very elaborate buttonholes matching the sterling silver buttons on the other side, all open but the top two. Underneath, a blouse matching her red wool ankle-length skirt was topped with a wide fluff of lace at the throat. Her modified tri-corner lady's bonnet was cocked to the right side. Its crocheted hatband displayed the tartan of Clan Gunn, one of the northern most families from the land of heather and thistle. Its hints of red matched the wool of her riding habit, topped off with a silk flower the color of the thistle when in perfect bloom, also matching the hint of red in the tartan. If her attire didn't snatch the attention of any healthy man within sight, her auburn hair, framing fierce eyes the color of the sky on a clear day, did. Zespedes, nearly breathless, stood and bowed.

After the interview, Zespedes dictated a letter to Viceroy Bernardo de Galvez, the sixty-first Viceroy of New Spain. The letter recommended, in the most urgent and pleasant tones, that leniency be shown to Daniel McGirtt, William Cunningham and Stephen Mayfield. The letter indicated that the three would be arriving in another month, about the same time as the letter arrived, all coming on the same ship. Whether Galvez would acquiesce remained to be seen. Zespedes knew him as a ruthless leader after the manner of Machiavelli who believed that opposition should be remorselessly exterminated. Daniel, William and Stephen represented opposition, but in view of the fact they were all born of good families, Zespedes believed the viceroy might be swayed.

The ship departed Matanzas Bay as soon as the weather seemed appropriate and, based on the Spanish experience in Florida, the time of year they could expect the best weather for sailing. It was the end of April. The prisoners were quartered in the hold and for Daniel, who had never been to sea in his life, the adventure seemed endless. The first few days, his seasickness was only matched by that of Cunningham and Mayfield. Stephen observed, "If we could be aloft, it wouldn't be so bad because from there we could see the cause of all this motion."

"How do people live with this?" Daniel wanted to know. "Men go to sea and take sometimes years to get home. They are in this all the time. How can a man survive?"

"Try not to eat too much," one of their guards told them. "Less in the stomach, less to come up."

"How could a man eat, when feeling like this?" Daniel retorted.

The sickness passed after a few days of misery. The trip, all of it against the prevailing currents and beating into a southeast wind, took two weeks. "The trip back," the guard told them, "takes less than half as much time. We do it with following currents and winds. If you get to come back, you will enjoy the trip. It's gorgeous sailing, as long as the weather holds."

The ship entered Havana Harbor in mid-May. The men guarding the three invited them to come above and view the landfall. Still at least ten miles at sea, not much of the island of Cuba was visible, but a large promontory clearly stood out against the skyline. "What is that?" Daniel asked the guard whose kindness allowed him this view. Daniel pointed at the promontory. "That building is enormous!"

"That, *mi amigo*," the guard answered, "Is El Castillo de Los Tres Reyes Magos del Morro. The Castle of The Three Magi. That will be your new home for a while." The guard smiled but Daniel could see the pity in his eyes. "The accommodations are not very luxurious."

※ ※

Viceroy Bernardo Galvez frowned as he glanced down at the buttons holding his waistcoat together. They stretched. That disgusted him. *Why am I so fat?* Otherwise, the outfit pleased him. He enjoyed his lavish costumes. This one sported gold brocades over a matching vest also brocaded with rich gold thread. *It's right that a man of my station should dress in this way, not too far short of a king in my own right. I am king in fact, of New Spain, subject, of course, to his Royal Highness in Madrid.*

Galvez had just arrived in La Ciudad de Mexico from Cuba. His first weeks were consumed with getting to know the staff of advisors, secretaries and head bureaucrats who survived the last viceroy's reign. He found his quarters lavish. The food, though basically the same as he had had in Cuba and Spain, had a Mexican ambience, something he wasn't sure he could get used to in a short time. There were peppers he had never heard of that could light a fire in his pallet, paling previous exposures to peppers. He determined that he would not be put off by it. *Sharp peppers are good for the soul, are they not? And they are certainly good for keeping away internal parasites. I will eat them. I will get used to them.*

He had failed to attend to his first items of business until nearly three weeks after his arrival. The communications were piling up on his desk, but he set them aside until he felt that he had grown accustomed to his surroundings and knew what to expect. *Why hurry? Am I not the king in this place?* When he finally saw fit to seat himself at his desk for business, he found communications from all over New Spain, including Louisiana, Pensacola and St. Augustine as well as Cuba. He systematically stacked them in order of their arrival. But before he could really get a start on the work, he was interrupted by one of his guards with a message from far to the south. Something about a rebellion of the local Indians. He welcomed one Captain Garcia Carcaba into his presence and asked, "Report, please."

By the time Galvez felt he had dealt with the problem correctly and efficiently, it was time for Siesta and the letter from Zespedes slept beneath the pile, about a third of the way down.

17

1785 – Late Summer

El Castillo de Los Tres Reyes Magos del Morro had loomed over the harbor entrance at the port of Havana since 1589. Don Pedro de Menendez de Aviles had been dead fifteen years when this building was completed. Remains of the harbor chain, stretching between El Morro and Fort La Punta to forestall the raids of Sir Frances Drake, could still be seen by passersby entering El Morro.

Daniel noticed it as the three were conducted into the castillo under heavy guard. "Take a look at that," he motioned to the other two. "That looks a little bit like the harbor chain the Spanish used in St. Augustine after James Moore burned the town."

"It does," answered Cunningham, "and the castle is built from the same stuff they used for the Castillo de San Marco. Coquina."

"Very observant," chimed in their Irish guard, John Hudson, who had introduced himself when they were removed from their ship.

"And how did an Irishman get to Cuba when Great Britain was at war with Spain?" Daniel's tone was challenging. *Who is this traitor? Why is he in Cuba?*

"We all have our stories, Colonel McGirtt. We all have our stories."

Hudson, tall for an Irishman, had nearly black hair sticking out from under his Spanish helmet, uncut and unkempt. Twenty-seven years old, Hudson's slender build spoke of energy and wiriness. Of the five guards escorting the prisoners to their stone suite, he did all the talking because he was the only one who had any English.

If you can call that Irish brogue English, Daniel couldn't keep from thinking. Hudson's constant chatter wearied Daniel. *I wonder if we can make him a friend.* On that thought, Daniel began trying to engage the man in more meaningful conversation than the monologue about Cuban women and *las tabernas Españas* that seemed to dominate Hudson's mind. *I think this man's neck may be a little too long.* Daniel was clearly aware that he did not like John Hudson, an Irish traitor who obviously made his passage to Cuba after spying for Spain during the war. "So, John Hudson, sir. You say the Cuban rum is outstanding, aye?"

"Indeed it is, Colonel McGirtt. The best in this part of the world."

"Do you think it might make a good trade item in the Americas? The Americans and even the Indians enjoy a good drink now and again. I bet you could make some large profits selling it there. Buy it here in quantity and sell it to the ship's captains heading for the Americas, or at least Spanish Florida. Now there's a place, Florida. Not nearly as hot there as it is here. I bet you miss the cooling breezes of the emerald isle, now don't you?"

McGirtt's effort failed. At about that moment, Hudson passed them off to five different guards whose bailiwick was evidently the inside of the castillo; Hudson and his men were apparently guards from the harbor. "Such regimentation!" Daniel remarked after Hudson explained that to him. "I thought we might even become friends."

"Friends with a renegade Brit?" Hudson laughed. "I'm no friend of the Brits," he announced through gritted teeth. "...much less renegades. You seem like a decent lot, though. I wish the three of you well, but if you ever need anything, don't call on me."

Their suite of stone, shaped like a bread oven with an arched ceiling, had no fire pit. There was a small opening in the floor at the end of the room hardly big enough to allow passage to a small Cuban rat. The guard, although he had no English at all, demonstrated with a bucket of water that this opening was a scupper for emptying their chamber pot which sat on the floor beside the opening. It appeared to be nearly equal in age to the building itself and it had not been cleaned from the use of its previous occupant. "Splendid accommodations," McGirtt quipped. "It's not cold and it probably never gets cold in Cuba, so we don't need a fire. The room is bigger than the one in St. Augustine and, all things considered, by the time we get out of here we may have had the chance to learn a little Spanish."

Cunningham and Mayfield both rounded on Daniel. Cunningham was the first to speak. "Any more positive attitude from you today and I'm going to hurt you. Is that clear, Daniel?"

Mayfield did not remain the silent observer. "If it's all the same to you, I'd like to sit down and sulk for a while. We have no clue as to how long we will be in this room. Maria Piedra is not going to bring us food here. Your brother James cannot arrange for blankets and food as he and Francisco did in St. Augustine. We are in dire straits. If the Cubans don't feel the need to feed us, we will quietly disappear in this bread oven of a cell."

Daniel took a seat in one of the months-old stacks of straw on the floor. He was barely able to see it in the dim light coming from the corridor. "The Spanish are not animals," he said. "As much as Wakapuchasce hates them for their brutality, they are not animals. They will feed us, not much, but we will not die of starvation here, unless we offend them in some other way. Right now, we are horse thieves and murderers, according to Zespedes. The Spanish hang such men. They don't starve them to death."

"So," muttered Bloody Bill. "We have at least weeks of quiet enjoyment of this stone suite and then we have the rope to look forward to."

Daniel chuckled. "You were blaming me for having a positive attitude. Weeks? Let it be such a short amount of time."

As before, the close, isolated confinement resulted in loss of the time sense. The four months the three men spent penned up in El Morro left them believing they would always be there, dining on pest-infested rice, sleeping on filthy straw mats, chasing off the rats that came up the scupper, exploring for a scrap of the food here or there, sometimes nearly becoming food themselves. Their caretaker Julio startled them with his first appearance. It was the day after their first night. They had been served no food until that time. Julio's hair, thankfully, concealed most of his thin, drawn face. He was bent almost double; the prisoners speculated it was the result of his bearing heavy loads for many years down narrow, dark corridors. He constantly leaned forward so his hair hung in his face, and when he shook it back to have a look at the three, they were shocked at the rotted teeth, the sores on his lips and the bruises that he tried to conceal. "They must beat him from time to time," observed Mayfield. But whatever Julio's problems, he was regular with the food, once daily.

Daniel pitied Julio. "We might think we have it bad in here," he observed. "Julio has it worse. At least, so far, no one has laid a lash to our backs. We have no loads to bear. It's an extended vacation, although a somewhat tedious one."

"Shut up, McGirtt," from Cunningham. "I think I'm going to kill the last fourteen Spanish Wakapuchasce wanted killed in his name. But I might lose count and kill all of them, if I ever get out of here. No wonder he hated them. It's despicable to treat a fellow human being in this way!"

After their first week, Julio surprised them again. After he shoved their single pot of rice under the door, the prisoners were turning way when he said, "*Señores. Uno momentito, por favor.*" He reached inside his shirt and pulled out three oranges, one at a time. He rolled the oranges under the door to them and said, "*Naranjos, Señores. Comelos. Por sus bien salud.*" (Oranges, Gentlemen. Eat them. For your good health.) Then he brought his finger to his lips, silently asking them to not tell what he had done. After that, Julio brought oranges about once each week and sometimes, other treats.

"He doesn't look like much, but he's a good man, aye?" Mayfield was the first one to speak about it.

"I bet he tries to do this for everyone," Daniel answered. "If we are rescued this time, let's see what we can do about rescuing him."

It seemed as if the three had been in captivity forever when their quiet was interrupted by the clatter of armor in the corridor. A flickering light approached, carried by John Hudson himself. With him were four guards armed with swords, daggers and three muskets, apparently all loaded. They swore to each other in Spanish about the smell of the place, obviously angry about having to enter El Morrow's dungeons at all. Julio accompanied them with a key in his hand, smiling through the rotted spikes of his front teeth. "The day has come," Hudson announced, "for your trial. After that, I fully expect to have the privilege and honor of watching you die on the end of a rope. In the meantime, I am to be your translator. It would seem that not many people in Havana, much less the rest of Cuba, can speak English as well as Spanish. I can. Unfortunately for you, you must depend on me."

The three were ushered none too gently into a large courtroom, very unlike the courtrooms they were used to. This courtroom was designed more along the lines of a king's court. Tall pillars lined the room with crowds of people vying for position, not only in the well-lighted main room, but also in the shadows of the lower ceilinged alcoves behind the pillars. Many were dressed as courtiers, wearing powdered wigs and elaborate, high fashioned clothing one might expect to see in a king's court. Others, like Daniel, William and Stephen sported filthy rags that had not been changed or laundered in many months and in some cases, years. The prisoners' hair, ratty, tangled and lice-infested, testified to the humanity of the typical Spanish prison.

Daniel could not take his eyes off of one fascinating elderly woman who had apparently come to watch the proceedings. She was less than five feet tall. Her short dyed hair was the color of an orange that had been left in the sun for about a week. Her skin matched the withered texture of the orange's skin with deep lines around her mouth. Her thin lips opened from time to time as she chewed some nearly black substance which Daniel could not identify. Every few minutes she gesticulated animatedly with one hand or the other as she shouted some expletive toward the front of the room. Daniel watched in quiet amusement for a few minutes wondering who she might be and what might be her issue. "What's she saying?" Daniel asked Hudson, indicating the woman.

"You don't want to know. She's very vulgar. She's calling for the execution of the British prisoners she heard were to be tried today. That would be you three, most likely."

Daniel pulled his attention away from the colorful old woman and scanned the crowd, more or less out of habit, looking for familiar faces. He saw none, but soon the sound of a trumpet pierced the air. The crowd quieted. When the fanfare was finished, a loud voice announced something in Spanish that Daniel did not understand. "What's he saying, Hudson?"

"He is announcing the arrival of the Governor of All Cuba, Luis de Umzaga y Amezaga. He will review the evidence against you then order you hanged this afternoon, in plain view of the harbor so that all may see what justice is done to English pigs who defy his Royal Highness, the King of Spain."

Daniel smiled at Hudson's unabashed fervor. He turned his attention back to scanning the crowd and as he did so, he muttered just loud enough for Hudson to hear him, "Hanging us, Mr. Hudson, will be important to you because it just might save your life." Just then, Daniel noticed a face on the other side of the room that seemed familiar. He felt a rush of hope deep down inside as his eyes flew wide open. The face of Francisco Xavier Sanchez was partly obscured by the pressing crowds, but for a moment, Daniel caught his eye. Francisco winked broadly, with a smile of reassurance. Then he turned and disappeared. Daniel said nothing but the thin trace of a smile was irrepressible. *What is that rascal up to? What's he doing here?* Whatever it is, I owe him for this moment of hope. God bless Francisco Sanchez!

The huge courtroom offered nowhere for the prisoners or visitors to sit. The masses of standing people shifted their feet erratically, making a soft undertone that filled the room. The smell of unwashed bodies, especially their own, nearly overwhelmed the three. Hudson kept his distance as much as he could while trying to maintain the appearance of being on guard against any attempt they might make to escape. Escaping, though, was out of the question. The room was lined with armed soldiers in full dress uniforms, eyeing the crowd suspiciously. Governor Umzaga began his deliberations systematically and disinterestedly, like a priest pronouncing the magic words in monotone with little interest in their meaning. One after another, prisoners were either ushered out of the room to some unknown fate or released amid cheering from friends who waited for them. The day wore on. In time, Umzaga took a break for lunch, leaving the crowd to stand waiting for his return.

"If he doesn't get to you soon," Hudson muttered, "He'll break for siesta and leave us standing while he sleeps for a few hours. Why don't they just hang you and get it over with? I have better things to do with my life than standing in this room of stinking, unwashed rabble and listen to the governor of Cuba bore himself to death."

Just as Hudson finished his grumbling, Umzaga called out the names of Colonels Daniel McGirtt, William Cunningham and Stephen Mayfield. The three practically held their breath while Hudson translated.

I have a letter in my hand from his Excellency, Viceroy Bernardo Galvez, Viceroy of all of New Spain including Florida, Cuba, Mexico, West Florida and Louisiana, dated two months ago. It is the order of his Excellency that these prisoners be released immediately upon their promise to leave all Spanish territory and return to British governed lands. If they will deliver this promise to me, right now, in writing, they are free to go immediately. I have the papers prepared. All they have to do is sign them. Are these three prisoners present?

"You three are god damned lucky," Hudson swore. "If I had my way, I'd shoot you myself right now."

As Daniel walked away, he smiled sweetly at Hudson said softly, "Watch your back, John."

☙ ❦

The Port City of Havana on the island of Cuba reminded Daniel of St. Augustine, only on a much larger scale and with some differences. British occupation of Havana did not last nearly as long as it did in St. Augustine, so the Florida city had far more development of industry and commercialism. Havana acted as a center for tobacco and cotton trade with Europe and the Americas. Other major cash crops included rice and indigo, as in Florida, but the real major industry, government, flourished on the *Situado*, the periodic allotment of money that came from Spain for the maintenance of the colony. Without the *Situado*, Cuba would have practically dried up and blown away.

Another difference was that the sand acting as pavement for Havana's streets had a coarser texture than the sand in St. Augustine and the darker color came from the rich soil of the surrounding area. One thing Cuba has that Florida does not is soil. Daniel kicked some of it gently as he examined the ground under his feet. The sun's shocking brilliance dazzled the three who had been kept in virtually darkness for the last four months.

"So what are we going to do now?" Cunningham, relieved to be free from the prison of El Castillo de Los Tres Reyes Mago del Morrow, now faced the reality that Julio was no longer going to bring them vermin-ridden rice daily. "We have no money and no friends here. What can we do to survive and find our way back to Florida?"

"We're not going back to Florida," Mayfield stated flatly. "At least I'm not. We were freed on our word that we would not go back. If we do go back we could well wind up back here in El Morro. Do you want that?"

"Not really," Cunningham grunted.

Mayfield went on. "I don't understand why Zespedes didn't hang us himself, right there at the old fort in St. Augustine."

"He didn't want to get his hands dirty," Cunningham answered. "He wanted someone else to make the decision that we were to be put to death. We have too many friends in Florida for him to put himself at such risk."

Daniel's thoughts raced back to the brief sight he had of Francisco Sanchez in the courtroom. "Something is going to happen," he said to the other two. "I saw Francisco Sanchez in the courtroom. He's probably still here, somewhere. Look around."

The three stood just outside El Morro Castle on the northeast side of the harbor. The rest of Havana stretched to the south and to the west. A small wagon drawn by a single donkey sat waiting some fifty yards away, in the direction of the city. Seated on the wagon, a man dressed as a seafaring man shielded his eyes from the sun and simply waited, staring toward the city and away from El Morro Castle.

"Let's see if that man can speak English," suggested Daniel.

The three approached the wagon. "If we were in Florida, I wouldn't hesitate to commandeer the wagon to take us to some shelter." Cunningham smiled at the thought. "But we are in Cuba and have no shelter so we will have to rely on the good will of those around us, if we can find any."

McGirtt, too intent on the driver of the wagon to comment, just raised a finger signaling patience. When they reached the side of the wagon, the driver was still gazing off into the distance, in a sort of waking siesta. "Excuse me sir," Daniel opened. "Do you speak English?"

The man turned his face toward them, raised his eyebrows and said, "I think so, Daniel. The question is, do you? You spent enough time in that place I would think it likely you might have forgotten."

"Gentlemen," Daniel began. "I think you probably are acquainted with my brother, James McGirtt. What on Earth are you doing here, brother? This is a dangerous place for people like us."

"Calm yourself, Daniel. I'm on a mission and I won't be in Cuba for long and neither will you, I hope. Get in the wagon. A house has been rented for you with hot baths, servants, food. Francisco and I decided it would be best for you to have some recovery time before traveling. There is clothing waiting for you, clean beds and money. Francisco would be here himself but we agreed it would be best for no one to recognize any connection between the two of you. Francisco does regular business with Governor Umzaga and he feels that anyone knowing there is a connection could hurt his relationship with the governor. So, you won't be seeing him, and after I drop you off and make sure you're all settled, you won't be seeing me again either." James smiled broadly. "But I'll visit you in the Bahamas. I promise."

"It's hurricane season, James, September! You surely aren't going to sail for Florida now, are you?" Daniel's incredulity made James smile again.

"Francisco says a sailor can tell a hurricane is coming by the timing of the seas. That will give him enough notice, he says, that we will have time to run for port if a big storm is approaching. I trust him, Daniel. I think you do, too. If he says we'll be safe, then we'll be safe. He's been sailing these waters all his life. He knows what he's doing."

Daniel furrowed his brows. "James, I need to speak with Francisco. That's where we were going when we were arrested the last time, almost at his hacienda. I still need to speak with him and the only way I know of that I can do that is to come back to Florida. If I do that, I could be arrested again. I hate to ask him to make a trip to Providence to see me. Please tell him I am coming to Florida to see him. When we have spoken, I will go to Providence in the Bahamas or back to South Carolina. I haven't decided."

James shook his head. "Coming back to Florida is a bad idea, Daniel. It's common knowledge that you were arrested and sent to Havana. You're well known in Florida. Most anyone who sees you will recognize you. You will be in constant danger. Can't you deal with Francisco by writing letters?"

"No." Daniel lowered his head a moment before looking back up at his brother. "This is confidential. Letters can be intercepted. Face to face communication is safer."

"I'm coming with him," Cunningham chimed in.

"Not me, Mayfield flatly announced. "I've had enough of stone dungeons."

03 80

English speaking people trying to hire passage on a ship in a community that speaks only Spanish encounter challenges. Havana, hardly a tourist center in 1785, boasted no currency exchange houses, no tours of the city, no restaurants that catered to English speaking people, or German either, for that matter. McGirtt, Cunningham and Mayfield, strangers in a strange land, had to rely on the good will of those around them. As they were strolling on the docks looking for English vessels, they found one called the H.M.S. *Harvey Dolittle*, a three-masted, gaff rigged schooner that brought standing cattle to Havana from Florida. The Captain, J. Richard Pons, agreed to give the three passage to Providence in the Bahamas for a fee and help in crewing the vessel. "We're a wee bit short handed, ya see." They agreed to Pons' terms and put out to sea just after high tide the following day.

Delighted with the ride, Daniel spent as much time as possible standing on the bow as it pitched up and down, watching the sea. What he had been told on the trip to Cuba proved true. With a brisk, quartering breeze from starboard and the north flowing sea, they made it to Providence in only a few days. "Where is the ship going next?" Daniel asked the captain, two days out."

"St. Marys, Georgia," came the reply.

"So, Captain. Is it your opinion that you will be able to sign on more crew in Providence or will you still need some extra help to get to St. Marys?"

Captain Pons shook his head and smiled. "Colonel McGirtt, I have strict orders directly from the Governor of Cuba, Luis Umzaga, himself, to make sure you do not return to any Spanish territory, such as Florida, right across the St. Mary's River from St. Marys, Georgia. What exactly do you have in mind?"

"Well, Captain, my friend William Cunningham and I have business that we need to conclude with one Francisco Sanchez of St. Augustine in Florida. That business should take not more than a few minutes to transact and we will be on our way back to Providence. I also want to collect my family to go to Providence with me. That could take a little time. I don't want my wonderful wife to have to cross the sea to the islands alone. She doesn't much like traveling at sea and doing so will make her very uneasy."

"Still, Colonel McGirtt, I have my orders from Umzaga. What will I tell him when I see him again if you show up in Florida and get arrested again? If Zespedes finds out you are there, he will most certainly return you to your room at the Castillo de San Marcos." Captain Pons walked away shaking his head.

"Wait a moment, Captain." Pons stopped and half turned toward McGirtt. "You still need additional crew, don't you?" Daniel continued. "We need a ride to St. Marys. I understand your reluctance to disappoint Governor Umzaga, but he will probably never find out. What if Cunningham and I sweetened the pot for you…"

A week later, Daniel McGirtt and William Cunningham disembarked the HMS *Harvey Dolittle* in St. Marys, Georgia. A friendly parting with Captain J. Richard Pons and the exchange of just a little coinage giving the captain an even friendlier smile, Daniel and Bloody Bill walked away from the wharf with packs of luggage in hand. "I wonder if Mangum still has that inn of his, just on the other side of the river. What do you think?"

"I think," began Bloody Bill Cunningham, "that like Mayfield, I have had enough of stone dungeons. Haven't you? Let's send a messenger to Francisco and see if we can get him to come up here. It really isn't all that far, and if he went to the trouble of coming to Cuba to bribe officials to get us out of prison, he'll surely be willing to come to St. Marys."

Daniel smiled grimly. "Do you remember that stout beer Mangum brewed right there in his inn? I sure would like a glass or two of that again before I go back to Providence. Wouldn't you?"

"I would indeed," Cunningham answered. "Let's send him a messenger too and see if he'll send a couple of glasses of that stuff to us here in St. Marys."

As they approached the guest house where they hoped to find quarters for the next few nights, a man approaching from the other direction accosted them. "Well well well. If it isn't Bloody Bill Cunningham and Dirt McGirtt. You boys have a lot of brass showing up here. We all thought you were dead in El Morro, but no. Here you are in Georgia. You don't remember me, do you, Dirt? I was at Fort MacIntosh, the night you got whipped for givin' lip to that Captain John Barker. It was him that started calling you Dirt. Now I hear he's dead. And I heard you killed him. Is that true, Dirt?"

Ignoring the dogged bumpkin, Cunningham and McGirtt turned off the road into the house where they had planned to spend the night. When they made it to the porch, Daniel turned to Bill and said, "You know we can't stay here. We have to move on. It's not safe."

They waited for the bumpkin to go away, then left the house, walking back toward the center of the community where a livery stable offered horses for sale or lease. As they turned the horses south, Cunningham groaned. "I was looking forward to a comfortable bed tonight. I don't think we can get to Mangum's before nightfall. We're going to have to sleep in the woods."

Before the sun had made it half way to its zenith the next morning, Daniel McGirtt and William Cunningham rode into the courtyard at what was once William Mangum's inn. The sign above the door now read, "O'Neill's House of Comfort."

"Let's see if we can get a room and send a message to Francisco." Daniel dismounted his horse and wrapped the reins over the hitching post in front of the building. "I sure don't want to get any closer to St. Augustine than this!" Just then, the new owner of the building emerged. When he saw them, he went straight back inside, then emerged again with a musket.

"Come out boys," he yelled over his shoulder. A moment later, three Spanish soldiers from the garrison at St. Augustine came out, brandishing swords. "You two are under arrest!"

Back in Zespedes' field office at the Castillo de San Marcos, the two stood, downcast, in front of Zespedes. "I don't accept your explanation," the governor's translator said in English. "If you weren't so well dressed and humble in your demeanor, I would send you back to Havana and El Morro Castle. Instead, I am going to send you where you are supposed to be, Providence, in the Bahamas. If I find you in Florida again, I will not send you to Havana. I will have you shot. Is that clear?"

"Yes sir," they both answered together, then thinking better of it, said, "Si, Señor."

Zespedes allowed them to take rooms in the town on the condition that they paid for the two armed guards outside each of their doors. It was several weeks before a ship came in that was heading for Providence next, so they both had their face to face interviews with Francisco Sanchez, who was more than happy to ship their collection of money and valuables that he had been keeping for them.

"Now," McGirtt told Francisco, "We will live well in Providence, such as it is."

18

1786

Mozart's comic opera about oppression, *The Marriage of Figaro*, appeared.

June 8 – Commercially made ice cream first advertised (Mr. Hall, New York City).

June 29 – Alexander MacDonell and over five hundred Roman Catholic Highlanders left Scotland to settle in Glengarry County, Ontario.

August 8 – The United States Congress adopted the silver dollar and the decimal system for money.

September 24 – African-American slave and poet Jupiter Hammon made his Address to the Negroes of the State of New York advocating emancipation at the meeting of the African Society in New York.

November 30 – Peter Leopold Joseph of Habsburg-Lorraine, Grand Duke of Tuscany, promulgated a penal reform making his country the first state to abolish the death penalty. November 30 is therefore commemorated by 300 cities around the world as Cities for Life Day.

December 29 – The Assembly of Notables was convoked during the French Revolution.

1787

New York became the eleventh state to ratify the U.S. Constitution. Congress elected George Washington as president. Congress added ten amendments to the constitution: the Bill of Rights.

France went deeply in debt from wartime borrowing. Much of the government's annual budget went to pay interest on the growing debt. The government spent little for maintaining public welfare but decided to start taxing those privileged who had been exempt from taxation; the privileged objected. Clergy, nobles and commoners wanted political change.

1788

Louis XVI created more dissatisfaction by abolishing the power of parliament to review royal edicts.

Because of insufficient government planning and storage of grain for emergency shortages, France had its worst harvests in forty years. A hailstorm destroyed crops. Winter food riots occurred.

Back from South Carolina, Patrick Alcorn stabled his horse with the Genovars. He took a room across from Juan Andreu's house on St. Francis Street and was looking forward to a late lunch at Maria's Taberna. He snorted dissatisfaction that he had to wait for a table, but good food is worth waiting for. Seated on a bench outside the dining room window, he could hear the clamor of voices inside calling for another beer, more roast, an extra slice of Juan Anreau's delicious bread. Every few seconds a word or two would pop up that caught his attention. At the moment he was half listening to an ongoing exchange about the interbreeding of the wild Andalusian cattle with the British breeds. The gist of the conversation leaned toward the hardier stamina of the Andalusians over the higher yield of meat from the other breeds. But he was mostly thinking about the fact that he had not arrived in time to go to the Bahamas with the McGirtt family. Their ship had departed a week before his arrival in St. Augustine. He tried to overcome his disappointment with plans of how he could catch up to them. Just then the word "McGirtt" popped up in a conversation inside, not far from the window. He glanced cautiously in the window to learn the identity of the speaker.

At a nearby table sat William Mitchell, Joseph Summerlin, Thomas Hall and Alex Ramey. All had plates in front of them, loaded with different quantities of food. Their stoneware beer mugs showed streaks of dried foam from the beer on their sides and there were mug rings on the table. All four appeared to be fresh from the forest and only one of them had taken off his hat before eating. Their motley appearance brought back to Alcorn the memory, in quick flash of anger, of these very men raiding McGirtt's Maxton Island Plantation; the theft of cattle, horses and slaves and the haughty manner of the thieves. It was Mitchell's voice he had heard utter McGirtt's name. Alcorn pulled his head back outside the window as to not be seen, but continued to listen.

"We sure flummoxed that son of a bitch, McGirtt, didn't we?" (Laughter) "I told you fellows that if we organized our friends from Georgia that we could force Zespedes to arrest him."

Another voice: "I'll never forget the look on ol' Daniel's face when we showed up in force and stripped him of everything. I thought he was going to have apoplexy right then and there." (More laughter)

Patrick Alcorn stifled an urge to rise and slay the lot of them. These were the very people who had been raiding plantations in North Florida before the British ceded Florida back to Spain. Now they were being given the land, completely free, that they once raided and that McGirtt, Cunningham and Mayfield had protected. Zespedes had imported a den of foxes and given them the hen house.

In the morning, Patrick walked down Hospital Street to the city plaza to the offices of Governor Vincente Zespedes, where he requested an audience. Communicating with the Spanish speaking staff proved challenging but they found a translator who helped Alcorn with his appointment. Patrick waited in an anteroom for his audience. Zespedes, self-absorbed as ever, indulged himself with portraits, wall hangings and a hardwood desk so highly polished that Patrick could see the Governor's reflection in it. The plush, elaborate floor coverings bore illustrations from legend and myth. Zespedes' clothing capped the pompous image nicely with a brilliantly embroidered red and white jacket with each buttonhole lined in gold thread, over a waistcoat of white, equally decorated. Standing behind the governor, a translator stood with his hands behind his back and a carefully distracted visage.

As instructed, Alcorn waited for the governor to speak first. After the introductions, Alcorn explained to the governor the injustice that had taken place against Daniel McGirtt, William Cunningham and Stephen Mayfield. "The accusers were the criminals against whom those three protected Florida during the British reign. They were the raiders who pillaged the plantations. The Florida Rangers' responsibility was to pursue the villains into Georgia or wherever else they went and to recover the stolen property. Now they are here and have organized to pay back the men who forced them to justice in the past."

Vincente Manual Zespedes listened to the translator grimly. As he did so, his brow slowly furrowed and by the time the translator was finished Zespedes lips had drawn to a thin straight line. He took a deep breath and rose to his feet. After slowly pacing a few steps, he stopped and turned to Alcorn. He spoke slowly in Spanish and paused after each sentence so the translator could convey to Patrick what he had said. "I am aware," he told Alcorn, "of this situation. It is necessary that I populate the vacated lands as quickly as I can to produce commerce and a stable, protectable society here in La Florida. As I'm sure you know, I offered land grants, small land grants, to families willing to come to Florida and improve the land with planting and cattle, harvesting the meager resources the land has to offer. These are the people who came. I know they are the old enemies who held out against McGirtt, Cunningham and Mayfield in the old days. I am aware that the charges they brought against these men may well be contrived, but they are now a near majority of the people I rule over in Florida and I must hear their voices. It is because I believe the three men you speak for to be mostly innocent of the charges brought against them that I allowed them to leave Florida without punishment. It is unfortunate that life has hard turns for some and that mischief can ultimately prevail. Such is life. My advice to you, Señor Alcorn, is that you put this behind you, join the refugee families in the Bahama Islands and be at peace."

Now Alcorn's lips drew into a thin, tight line. "Thank you, your Excellency, for the kindness of taking the time to put this matter in perspective for me. I will, indeed follow your advice and take ship for Providence Island."

☙ ❧

April, 1786

Alcorn's ship, *La Margarita Pequeña*, landed with a load of supplies from the mainland and put Patrick Alcorn off at the City of Nassau. It took him three days to find Daniel McGirtt. The McGirtt tribe had scattered over the island. Daniel and his wife settled just north of the village of Adelaide on the south side of the island. Their native stone house supported a pyramid hip roof extending far enough from the sides of the house to cover a wraparound balcony, completely trellised to keep out birds and iguanas. "The damned lizards are all over the place," Daniel complained as they sipped tea on that covered balcony. "Almost as big as alligators and they have no fear of us. They actually get aggressive if we sit outside to dine. But on the other hand, wait till you've tried iguana tail, fried in butter."

After Alcorn related to Daniel what Zespedes had said about Maxton Island's new neighbors, Daniel shook his head and said, "I thought he probably knew that but it didn't keep him from sending us to El Morro Castle in Cuba to stand trial for our lives."

"But it was Zespedes' pleading your cause with Bernardo Galvez that got you released and exiled to this place."

"The exile is not a bad thing." Daniel took a sip of the tea just delivered to them by one of Daniel's house slaves, Marlena. "There is no one shooting at us here. No one is robbing us and the play is just as much fun."

"What do you mean?" Alcorn's puzzlement amused Daniel

"Playing the governments," Daniel continued. "Spain has made it illegal for Florida to have trade relations with the United States but not with Great Britain. We here are a British possession so Florida can sell to us. Then we sell to the United States. The ban on trade doesn't stop trade, it just makes it more expensive. Francisco still ships his cattle to Baltimore but before it gets to Baltimore, I buy it. Then I sell it in Baltimore. It's the same with the slave trade and the horse trade. The Americans are still buying Florida oranges but now they think it comes from Providence Island in the Bahamas. Isn't that fun?"

Alcorn smiled with appreciation for the comfortable arrangement Daniel had found. "I thought Panton, Leslie and Company has a monopoly with the Indian trade and that they were handling all of it."

"That's true," Daniel smiled more broadly. "I have become an agent for Panton, Leslie and Company as well as agent for Francisco Sanchez. Most of the trade from the Creeks, Choctaws, Chickasaws and Cherokees goes through Panton, Leslie and Company, but here on Providence Island, that is Daniel McGirtt. Their contacts have also given me the ability to communicate easily with William Augustus Bowles. Ever heard of him?"

"No." Alcorn shook his head.

"Bowles has ingratiated himself so well with the Indians that they have made him a sort of executive officer representing dozens of tribes. It's his goal to overthrow the Spanish and establish his own Indian State. At least that's what he says. He isn't ready to do anything yet. He's still working on organizing."

"Spain has little power in Florida right now. It's about all Zespedes can do to control St. Augustine. The countryside is still in turmoil, especially with all the outlaws he's imported and given land. An organized effort to overthrow the Spanish hold on the area just might succeed, if they're determined enough." Alcorn set down his teacup and gazed out through the trellis. "What a thought... Florida going back to the Indians."

"Panton, Leslie and Company, generally speaking, hates the United States. They are doing everything they can in West Florida to strengthen the Indians and the Spanish to hold West Florida. Their agents carry information to Galvez and Zespedes, so I'm pretty sure that Spain knows what's going on with Bowles. If I know and I got the information through the company, then the company has passed on the information elsewhere. Bowles sounds to me like he's the Daniel McGirtt of West Florida except he has joined the Indians."

"You almost did that, yourself," Alcorn smirked. "In fact you did join the Indians for a while!"

"True. True." Daniel smiled again. "But just for a short time and it was most expedient to do that. Zespedes had everyone he could muster out looking for me. I had to disappear."

That afternoon, Daniel, Patrick and Isaac, Daniel's head overseer, headed out to check what Daniel called "The Project."

"We got the land cheap," McGirtt began. "But what we got is swamp. The high land has soil too shallow for serious agriculture and there isn't as much rain as Florida gets so farming here will be challenging. I'm filling in a large part of the swamp by dredging the deeper sections to fill in the shallower sections. In time, I will have some fields with good soil. I'm going to try growing some indigo. Vegetables would be nice but the iguanas will eat most everything. I have some people working at training some dogs to keep off the iguanas. I don't know if that will work or not, but I intend to find out."

"Daniel," Alcorn began, "don't you miss Florida?"

"No. But I do miss South Carolina."

03 80

March 1788

Vincente Manuel Zespedes liked taking his after-siesta-stroll down St. Charles Street. The strong west wind that St. Augustine seemed to get every March for a week or two caused havoc here and there, blowing huge clumps of Spanish Moss from the trees. Occasional rotted limbs from the huge live oak trees, unnoticed before the wind arrived, provided free firewood for those quick enough to pick them up. Few paid much attention to pruning the big trees because the limbs seldom landed on anyone and they provided food for brief conversations and of course, the free firewood. Zespedes held onto his hat as he turned the corner onto Hypolita Street. Greeting the merchants and sometimes his neighbors gave him the feeling that he radiated goodwill and that this would help the people of the community learn to like him better. Even the English who still had shops in the town seemed to him to be glad to see him. He soon turned another corner and his steps carried him south on St. George Street and back toward the governor's mansion at the west end of the plaza.

Carlos Howard, Zespedes' secretary did not take siesta. *Englesa estupida*, Zespedes frequently mused about the man. On the other hand, while Zespedes slept, Carlos Howard worked and this provided Zespedes with his afternoon activities much of the time. *Mixed blessing. After siesta, I have to work. On the other hand, without Howard, the work might never get done.* And so it happened today. When he entered his office, he found a stack of correspondence waiting for his attention. On top of the stack, a letter from Galvez's office requested that he report on the progress of Panton, Leslie and Company for the first quarter of the year. Any taxes due? When will they be sent...? Zespedes gradually worked his way through the pile. Less than half way, he found a letter from John Murray, the Fourth Earl of Dunmore and the last royal governor of the State of Virginia. Lord Dunmore now presided as Governor of the Bahama Islands. *What does HE want?"*

Among other things, like the formal greeting, Dunmore's letter said:

"The bearer, Mr. McGirtt, goes from hence to St. Augustine in a sloop named the *Mayflower*, to settle his private affairs. He is a British subject and as such, I beg leave to recommend him to your excellency's protection."

Mrs. Mattie Gumble, of the Westmoreland Gumbles, straightened her hat which had been blown askew by the March winds. She intended her relaxed stride east on Picalata Road to bring her to the haberdashery a block away on Aviles Street. She wanted to buy buttons. Her ankle-length skirt gave her more wind resistance than she had anticipated and each gust of wind moved her along, for a moment a little faster than she intended. In spite of her ill use by the wind, she held her head high, looking neither to the right nor to the left and carried on with every bit of the dignity her family would expect of her, that is until the silence of the afternoon, other than the wind noise, of course, was shattered by a scream that seemed to be coming from Government House. She stopped abruptly and turned her head in the direction of the sound. She muttered to herself, "What is that Spanish man screaming about now?" Then she picked up her pace and scurried out of sight onto Aviles Street, lest she find out.

Zespedes' frustration drew the attention of half the town that resided within earshot. It especially drew the attention of Carlos Howard, seated at his desk in an anteroom to Zespedes' office. The next thing out of Zespedes' mouth came at slightly reduced volume. "Señor Howard! Señor Howard!"

Carlos Howard came as quickly as he could, practically stumbling into Zespedes' presence. "Yes sir? Yes sir? What is it, sir?"

Zespedes stood behind his desk, too agitated to remain seated. "Daniel McGirtt is back in Florida! He's BACK! Where exactly is he? Do you know?"

"When he dropped off the note, he said he would be staying at the home of his friend and business associate, Francisco Sanchez. That would be at 110 St. Charles Street, sir. Would you like me to check to see that he is there?"

"NO!" Zespedes' rage, although restrained as well as he could manage, still increased. "Summon my guards. We will all go together and find out. I want you to prepare a most gracious letter to John Murray, the Fourth Earl of Dunmore, Governor of the Bahama Islands and request that he issue no more passports to Daniel McGirtt for Florida!"

"Yes, sir." Carlos Howard scurried back to his anteroom.

03 80

Daniel McGirtt sipped a glass of dark red wine from a long stemmed glass he had received from the hand of Maria Piedra, Francisco's common-law wife. The courtyard, left deliberately open at the east end, provided a most satisfying view of the Matanzas Bay. A flock of six pelicans coasted easily north on the gusty afternoon winds, twenty feet or so above the water's edge. "I wonder why they always fly in a line formation," Daniel wondered aloud. "I mean, most birds, when they fly in a small flock like that don't keep a particular formation. They're just in a bunch, like a school of fish."

Francisco smiled and said, "I don't know, Daniel. If I ever get a chance to speak with one of them, I will ask him and pass on to you what he tells me."

Daniel took a final sip of wine and set the glass on a small table beside him. "I'm surprised that Zespedes has allowed us to have this conversation in peace. I thought he would have me arrested immediately. After all, he said if he ever sees me again he'll have me shot. That's what he said on parting, when I last saw him."

"Don't underestimate him. He was probably having siesta when you arrived. His secretary took the message and it's under a stack of other correspondence. He may not even get to it today." Thundering knocks on Francisco's front door, on the other side of the house ended their conversation, testifying to the fact that Zespedes *did* get to that day.

Zespedes' face was crimson. Daniel was concerned that the man's anger would result in a heart attack. The only words the governor spoke in Daniel's presence were, "Arrest him." With a guard on each arm, they ushered Daniel back to the dock where the *Mayflower* was tied up. They walked him up the gangplank and nearly threw him to the deck. One of Francisco's servants followed them with Daniel's luggage on his back. The guard who pushed Daniel off the gangplank gave one order. "Don't leave the ship while it's in port if you know what's good for you. You should know you are very fortunate that this ship's next port of call is Providence Island. Otherwise you would be in the Castillo de San Marcos – again." Then he went back down the gangplank and took up a position guarding the passage to make sure Daniel did not come back down.

CB EO

About one month later...

Vincente Manuel Zespedes liked April in St. Augustine. The chill of winter faded under the brilliance of the longer days, but drought often plagued April. The resurrection ferns that decorated the limbs of the live oaks looked dead. Vincente, however, knew that as soon as the first drops of rain arrived, they would spring to life again. With harder rain, the Spanish moss would lose its gray color and become green as well. *Everything here loves rain, especially the mosquitoes.* Zespedes' after-siesta stroll down the avenues made his afternoons; however, as he passed the home of Francisco Sanchez, he gave an involuntary shudder. *I hope I've seen the last of Daniel McGirtt. When he is in Florida, I am guaranteed problems. I must not think of that. My very thoughts may bring him back. He's gone.*

Back at his desk, the ever faithful Carlos Howard had a nice, medium sized stack of correspondence for Vincente to go through. This time, a letter from his aunt in Valencia rested on the top of the pile. Zespedes smiled as he picked it up. Tia Maria used a perfume that she ordered special, all the way from Constantinople and the Ottoman Empire. It held a faint hint of cloves. *Ah, The Black Rose.* The thought always came to him when he smelled it. Tia Maria doused her correspondence to him with that perfume to remind him of her and it proved durable enough that the aroma always held all the way across the sea.

His pleasure at finding a letter from his aunt dampened only slightly when he heard the scuffling footsteps at the door to the chambers.

Without putting down the envelope, he glanced up. The interruption came from his head guard, Captain Jose Giutterez, who stood at attention at the doorway waiting to be recognized and invited inside.

"What is it, my friend?" Zespedes' good mood relieved the soldier a little, but his news, he felt certain, would change that.

"I have a report, your Excellency, that a large body of men have landed near Rio Indio, south of here. The report says they are British and that they came from the Bahama Islands, although I do not know how it could be ascertained where they are from, only where they are and perhaps who they are."

"Captain Giutterez, do we know how many there are and how well they are armed?"

"I am sorry, your Excellency. The report only said a large body of men. I don't know if that's fifty or five hundred or five thousand. Shall I send a scout to find out?"

"Please do so. Urge the scout to make haste and report back to me as soon as possible."

03 80

Three days later...

Zespedes loved St. Augustine. He especially loved sitting on his high balcony having his midday meal, overlooking the plaza and the Matanzas Bay, accompanied by several glasses of sweet wine from Ribera del Duero, his favorite. His brother always sent him a case for his birthday. As he finished his third glass and began to consider siesta, he heard hoof beats coming down Picalata Road from the west. Three sweaty horses came to a halt below his balcony. All three of the riders leaped off their horses. Two of them came inside the building. One remained to cool down the horses. *So. No siesta today. What's wrong now?*

Shortly, the two riders appeared in his office doorway with Jose Giutterez who introduced them as scouts who had returned from their western investigation of the Creek Indians. "What have you to report?" Eager for his siesta, Zespedes was short with his scouts, whom he usually treated with great respect.

The taller of the two, Etienne Gomez, answered, "A large body of men under the leadership of William Augustus Bowles was identified a hundred miles southwest of St. Augustine. They are moving to the south. We don't know where they're going, but they appear to be on a forced march. We left two of our number to follow them with orders that when it is determined where they are going, one will come to St.

Augustine to report."

"Well." Zespedes waxed thoughtful. "This is getting interesting. A few days ago I had a report that a large body of English landed at the Indian River Inlet. Now another large body of men is headed toward the Indian River Inlet, I suppose to meet the others? Is there an army forming? Is St. Augustine going to be under attack?" Zespedes focused again on the scout. "How many are in this large body of men? Do you know?"

"Several hundred, maybe three hundred men. We saw no cannons. Their armaments consisted of swords and muskets. They don't appear to be regular military, but rather farmers and other laborers. They were not well clothed or well equipped. Some of them saw us and looked fearful. They tried to avoid us."

Zespedes ended the interview, called in his secretary Carlos Howard, and started issuing orders. "Go to the commander at the fort and at the barracks on St. Francis Street. I want three hundred armed dragoons on horseback and riding south at dawn to intercept these two so called 'large' bodies of fighting men. Either kill them or capture them and bring to the Castillo. We will send the lot of them to his Excellency Governor Umzaga in Cuba for trial and hanging. We are not at war. These are just brigands."

⌇ ∞

Daniel McGirtt's fondness for The Indian River Inlet diminished daily while he waited for Bowles to show up. He enjoyed catching plentiful, easily-taken seafood more than he enjoyed eating it. The mosquitoes amazed him. "If you let these bugs have their way, they could drain a man of blood in a single night!"

Patrick Alcorn felt as strongly against the Spanish as did Daniel. His wife Margaret and three children waited for him on Providence Island, hoping they would see him again. "Why do you have to go on another of McGirtt's wild adventures? Haven't you had enough of that yet?" Margaret adamantly objected to his being on the Florida peninsula again. "Your only real protection is that Zespedes doesn't know you by name yet, as he does Daniel. All Zespedes has to do is see Daniel and he explodes."

"Zespedes is reacting to his own guilt." Patrick continued packing the few things he would need and checking on the possibility of a few luxuries, like dried beef. "Zespedes is another whoring politician who does what's expedient for his own good instead of doing what he knows to be right. He should be overthrown. We're going to look into doing that."

Now at the Indian River Inlet, smacking mosquitoes with the rest of them, his reaction to Daniel's comment came quickly. "The mosquitoes seem to be the very worst at dawn and dusk. If we can stay away from the water and vegetation we can protect ourselves through that time. A fire helps a great deal if we can stay in the smoke."

Daniel took a break from scratching to answer, "I wish we had some of that salve that Wakapuchasce's people use. That was very effective. I don't even know how they make it. Most of the two hundred men who came with us are talking about going back to Providence. They have no stomach for these mosquitoes."

"Let them go. If Bowles is as good as his word and shows up with three hundred, we will still outnumber and outgun the Spanish at St. Augustine."

Daniel continued scratching. "I am just about too itchy to fight. I wouldn't be surprised if half or better return to Providence. And I wouldn't blame them for it."

Bowles arrived with only one hundred fifty men, armed but in poor condition from their long journey from Pensacola. Bowles himself seemed exhausted, but he brought with him a good supply of the salve the Creek Indians had for repelling mosquitoes. Daniel was glad to see him, if only because of that. "We must make sure we put plenty of that stuff on the horses. They've suffered just as much as the rest of us with these vampire insects."

The march north began on the second day after Bowles' arrival, giving his men time to sleep, eat and rest. Daniel knew the trails; during his time in Florida he explored as much as he could. The narrowness of the trails rarely permitted more than riding single file, so the line of men and horses stretched for several miles. With thirty miles remaining to St. Augustine, they encountered Zespedes' dragoons. The dragoons suffered from the same inconveniences as McGirtt's party. The narrowness of the trail restricted them to single-file progress as well, but when the Spanish commander realized the men from the south were upon them, he ordered his men off their horses and into organized firing units. A line of men in front knelt, fired, then reloaded while the next line stepped in front of them, after the manner of the English. They too knelt, fired and reloaded as the line behind them stepped forward. They progressed systematically and with deadly effect.

McGirtt's party, at least those in front, saw what was going on before they fell, shot with heavy lead balls. Since the line was so thin, some of them were shot many times. Daniel and Patrick Alcorn were well back in the line more from coincidence than plan. The sounds of the shots made it very clear exactly what was taking place. As they continued toward the front, they began to hear men shouting of surrender.

"Surrender?" Daniel turned to Alcorn. "These intrepid warriors of ours are surrendering after hardly firing a shot. It's time to disappear into the forest. Let's go."

19

Francisco Xavier Sanchez, stomach full from the evening meal, watched the dying embers of the cooking fire in the fireplace. Between forays to Georgia, South Carolina and Cuba with the slave, cattle and lumber trade, his rare presence at home pleased Maria Piedra. Their seventeen years together had produced eight children. Francisco, still pleased with her, didn't mind that her figure was no longer as trim as it had once been. *Eight children could affect the figure of any woman.* He smiled at the thought as Maria brought him a small mug of local wine. "The wild Florida grapes can be sour if they are taken too soon, but the fully ripened ones make excellent wine," he remarked to her. "I wonder that no one has gone into the business of raising these grapes and exporting the wine. Now there's a thought. Maybe I should do that. What do you think, Maria?"

She took a seat next to him. The love seat protected them from the uncomfortable hardwood with thick cushions on the seat and back. She took a sip from the small mug she held in her hand. She placed her other hand in his and answered, "I once read a story about the Germans during one of the Crusades. They were away so long at war that their grape harvest withered and rotted. When they arrived home to harvest the grapes, they were fearful that with the loss of the grape harvest and no wine to sell, they would have great difficulty over the coming winter. You know what they did?"

"What's that, sweetheart?"

"They made their wine from the rotted grapes. They were desperate and they did what they had to do. It turned out that the wine from that harvest of rotten grapes was the best they had ever made. Ever after that, they allowed the grapes to rot a little bit before starting the wine making."

"And your point?" Francisco smiled at her with slightly raised eyebrows.

"You are right about the grapes not being ready until the very last minute. Then they are very sweet, but after they start to rot, their fermentation has already begun, right inside the skins."

Francisco was about to say, "I'll look into that," when a soft knock at the front door on St. Charles Street interrupted them. "Who could that be, this late? It's dark outside. Are you expecting anyone?" He rose and headed for the door as she answered, "No. I don't know who it might be."

Francisco opened the door a crack to peek outside, then threw open the door and quickly dragged Daniel McGirtt into the room. "What are you doing here? If you're caught, Zespedes will have your head on a pike!" Then calming himself a little, he said, "Come in. Have some wine – and TELL me what's going on."

Daniel accepted a chair on the other side of the fireplace, but now with Daniel in the room, Maria no longer felt it proper that she should be there, at least for the moment. Francisco watched her disappear into another room with a shrug of disappointment.

"I slipped into town over the western bridge. There's nowhere else I can go. My brother James, as you know, is in the Bahamas, now. My parents are gone. My other brother, Zach, the last I heard, is in Mississippi."

"Why are you in Florida, at all? I thought you probably had enough of being confined in stone dungeons. That's what you'll get if Zespedes finds out you're here."

"You knew about William Bowles trying to take St. Augustine. He's had a wild hair about that ever since I knew of him. He got information to Providence Island, that I got wind of, to the effect that he was planning an invasion with at least three hundred men rousted from West Florida, Louisiana and other places. He said he had several hundred Indians who wanted to come along as well."

Francisco nodded, with a look in his eye that Daniel had come to recognize meant he knew more than he was saying.

Daniel continued. "His thought is to form an independent Indian state west of the St. Johns River, reaching up into the Alabama and Georgia territories. Some of the boys from the islands wanted to join him. It sounded like it would be interesting, so I came along to watch. Probably not a good idea. Thank you, by the way, for having the supplies delivered to the Indian River Inlet as I asked."

Francisco took a final sip from his mug and said, "De nada, Señor. I heard that most of his men lost heart and surrendered to Zespedes. No one has seen Bowles or if they did see him, they didn't know who he was. This is the first I've heard about you being here. What happened to the men from the Bahamas?"

"They disappeared into the forest when the dragoons showed up ahead of us on the trail. We were badly outnumbered. Less than a third of the men Bowles promised actually showed up and what few came lost heart as soon as they ran into any opposition. I don't know what they expected... the Spanish to lay down their arms and surrender, maybe, thankful to us that they didn't have to manage Florida any longer."

"Life was more prosperous under the British," Francisco reminisced. "Great Britain promoted trade and business. Spain promotes high taxes and regulation of business. The town has gone down since Spain came back. Well... You probably saw all the abandoned storefronts and homes. Everyone is gone. All Spain seems to want us to do is bake bread and ferment wine. The Minorcans are still here. They're an industrious lot. If it weren't for them there wouldn't be much business at all, but they try to stay out of sight with what they're actually doing. My boats pick up produce from them along the St. Johns River and ship it out of the country so they don't have to pay Spain's taxes ...and I'm not the only shipper they do business with."

The two grew quiet for a few minutes. Then Daniel broke the silence with, "I need to find a boat heading for Providence Island and get out of here as quickly and quietly as I can. Do you know of any boats in the harbor now or where they're going?"

"The shippers prefer to stay out of the ocean during hurricane season and as you know, that starts in just a few weeks. Even I spend the summers on shore, with the cattle and lumber business, farming, harvesting. We have been doing well lately with cotton and there is a species of cotton that does very well on the coastal islands. They call it Sea Island cotton. It's good quality, a hardy plant and it brings a good price – better than some other species we've tried. In the fall, I'll have shipments going out and among them, at least a few to Providence Island."

Daniel looked downcast. He remained silent for some seconds then said, "I can't spend the summer hiding here in your house. If I go outside, I'll be arrested. If I try to make my way to Georgia or South Carolina, I'll probably be arrested there, too. I need to find my way back to British territory as soon as possible ...and you know me. I can't sit still very long."

"I have an idea," Francisco ventured. "Some of the Minorcans have made a business out of fishing. They started building a uniquely designed sailing craft. It's beamy, carries one mast with a large sail. They say they like it because its shallow draft allows them to get out to sea and back in easily clearing the sand bars. Since it's so beamy it has a good capacity for cargo, usually fish. We might be able to book passage for you on one of those, if we can keep it secret who you are."

Francisco disappeared early the next morning. When he returned, he said, "It's arranged. Bubo Harkonen agreed to the trip for a large fee, that you will pay him. Do you have money?"

"Can you trust the man?"

"Bubo and I were boys together in this place. His father wove cast nets and we would throw them into the surf to catch schools of fish. We were good friends and I have every reason to believe he's an honorable man when it comes to being paid for a job. I trust him. He can't speak English. Only Spanish. How's your Spanish, Daniel?"

The day dragged on. An hour before what Francisco judged to be first light, he awakened Daniel with , "It's time to go. Walking to the San Sebastian River docks at this time of day, if anyone see us, they will think we are on our way to work with the fishing boats." Francisco took the lead with some distance between them so that if anything went wrong, Francisco would not be associated with McGirtt. "I must protect myself, Daniel. If you go back to prison in El Castillo de San Marcos, I must be on the outside to make sure you have food."

The boat held a small cabin below decks where Daniel could conceal himself. Bubo Harkonen's belly stuck out under his tight pullover shirt. His pants were held up by a rope strung over his shoulders like suspenders. His feet were bare. Daniel thought *the man probably shaves once each month and it's been a few weeks since the last time.* Harkonen greeted them jovially in Spanish, then looked Daniel up and down and signaled sternly for him to go below.

Francisco seemed eager to get away. He hurriedly said to Daniel, "Bubo says the tide will turn in another hour and as soon as it does, he will cast off. Fair winds, Daniel," and he was gone.

McGirtt found the cramped cabin below decks to be very uncomfortable. He could tell when the boat was cast off because it stopped bumping the dock with each ripple of water. He knew when the man had hoisted the sail when the boat stopped rolling from side to side and heeled slightly from the morning breeze. *We're lucky to have any wind at all this early in the morning. St. Augustine's mornings are usually dead calm.* Light though it was, the gentle westerly gave the boat some way in addition to the flow of the falling tide. *At this rate, Daniel moaned to himself, it could take two or three hours to make the open sea.* He hunkered below decks, waiting and commiserating with himself about having come back to Florida at all. *Bowles is an ass to think he could take Florida away from the Spanish with that handful of rabble he brought from West Florida.*

CB ŏO

Lt. Jose Aldana had the duty this morning. Usually, all he did was to sit on the shore a few hundred yards south of the town's plaza, and watch the dolphins playing in the bay before him. Sometimes he would even do a little fishing, just to amuse himself. He used a hand line so as to not be too conspicuous. Zespedes wanted him to give this job his full attention at all times. His job, after all, was to guard the harbor against smugglers and to monitor the traffic in and out of the bay. The job was tedious and dull. Ships came in sometimes and ships left sometimes, but the harbor guards always inspected them when they landed or before they departed. There was no need, that Jose could see, for having someone sitting out here staring at the river all day.

Jose's wife Juanita provided him with a thick portion of bread, some cheese and a piece of dried beef so that when his hunger distracted him from his important duties, he would have nourishment. *What a sweet thing she is!* He liked to think of Juanita. Their marriage of only four months sweetened his life more than he could have imagined. *This is heaven. I sit on the river bank and fish, watch the dolphins and go home at night to that wonderful mujer hermosa. Life is good.* His joy soured for a moment as he remembered his last interview with Zespedes.

"You sit out there wasting time!" Zespedes seldom raised his voice when addressing inferiors. In fact, Zespedes seldom addressed inferiors at all, but this time he did and he was annoyed rather than angry. "I've heard about you sitting out there fishing, flirting with the *muchachas* that pass by. You eat and drink and fish. How do I know you see what's going on in the harbor if all you do out there is amuse yourself. I expect you to be on your feet and actively watching what is going on."

"Si, Señor. You are right, of course. I will see to it that I become more active and that the river has my full attention at all times. I will miss nothing. I promise I will do better."

With that in mind, Jose put the coil of fishing line back in his pocket and stood. He strolled slowly to the north until he reached the buildings south of the plaza. Then he turned and strolled slowly south until he reached St. Francis Street. He was about to turn again and begin his stroll back to the north when he saw the tanned, weather-beaten sail of Bubo Harkonen's vessel, *La Aritza Pequeña*. He had seen the boat in the past and recognized it as one of the fishing fleet that harbored in the San Sebastian River. *Why is he going out this morning? None of the other fishermen are headed out. I wonder if he's going fishing or if he's up to something else.*

Jose turned and hurried north to where other guards languished in the sun, their boredom equal to his own. When he got there, he ordered them to cast off in two of the small rowing craft kept there for that purpose. A team of rowers in each boat quickly and easily headed off *La Aritza Pequeña* and when he was within easy earshot, he called out, "Come about. Luff your sail. You are about to be boarded!"

☙ ❧

This time, Daniel's confinement was solitary. No companions shared his misery in the dark dampness of the dungeon. Its rough stone walls scraped his skin when he had the misfortune to brush against it. Coquina rock, they told him, came from quarries on Anastasia Island. When Queen Marianna, through her regent, ordered that this fortress be built of rock so the Indians could not burn it so easily, the Spanish knew of no rock in Florida. But some adventurous explorers began going from place to place and laying shovel to sand to find out what is beneath it. There, on the island, they found this calcified sand and shell composite that they hoped would act like rock. They were right. When James Oglethorpe shelled the Castillo with his twelve pounders in 1740, the balls sank into the thick walls and stopped. The rock, it turned out, had a springy action to it. When the balls sank in, the hole snapped shut behind it, giving the English the impression that the fort swallowed the balls. It did. Now it was swallowing the cannon ball whose name was Daniel McGirtt.

As good as his word, Francisco made sure Daniel had what he needed. Food arrived daily. Blankets arrived immediately so that Daniel would not have to sleep on the stone floor with no protection or warmth. Francisco, of course, did not deliver these things personally, but through servants whom he hired for the purpose. Daniel and Francisco both knew the servants would pilfer some of the goods and that Daniel would get only a portion of what was sent, so Francisco sent more than he needed. When it arrived, if nothing was missing, Daniel would thank the servant who delivered by giving him the excess.

The days and weeks and months dragged on. Zespedes told him, through a secretary, "I am not going to dispatch a military ship to deliver you to Cuba. I will wait until a merchant ship is going that way who has room in his lowest hold to carry you back to El Castillo de Los Tres Reyes Magos Del Morro. There you will wait for judgment and execution. This time, Señor McGirtt, you are not a misbehaving British resident waiting to decide to immigrate elsewhere. This time you are an enemy invader who attacked New Spain without even the benefit of a sovereignty ordering you to do so. This time, you are recognized for what you are – a criminal – and you will be punished as such."

Generally a very positive man, Daniel could see the end of his life approaching. His wife, the beautiful Mary James, waited for him at Providence not knowing if he still lived. He would never see her again. His children, five of them, some grown, would never present their children to rock on their grandfather's knee. South Carolina, his childhood home, would never again have Daniel McGirtt sink a fishing line into the Wateree River nor would the church he attended as a boy have the chance to fill him with the awe he had once felt when there. He sat on the floor of his dungeon cell, filled with the misery of lost hope. Fooling the guards could not be an option this time. None of them could speak English. Overpowering them to escape remained out of the question. Two always stood guard and they talked endlessly so even during the hours that sleep would afford a temporary and welcome escape, his torture continued. *What was it Dante wrote on that sign? Oh yes, on the sign over the door to Hell:*

> *I am the way into the city of woe.*
> *I am the way to a forsaken people.*
> *I am the way into eternal sorrow.*
> *Sacred Justice moved my architect.*
> *I was raised here by divine omnipotence,*
> *Primordial love and ultimate intellect.*
> *Only those elements time cannot wear*
> *Were made before me, and beyond time I stand.*
> *Abandon all hope, ye who enter here.*

It took Daniel weeks before he remembered all of the words. He had memorized it as a boy thinking that this loss of hope could seldom happen to a real man in a real life. The fantasy of a mad writer was all it could be. Why anyone thought a visit through hell would make interesting reading, Daniel could not imagine at that time. But now, here he sat. There were no brimstone fires. The demons wore Spanish uniforms and spoke unintelligibly. He saw no famous people being punished for their misdeeds, only himself. He worried that his wife would assume he was dead and marry another. He feared his children would forget him or worse yet, judge him harshly and reject him as their father. He rejoiced bitterly that his parents' deaths prevented them from seeing this end to which their son had come. El Castillo de San Marcos! How could such a hell be named after such a saint? Instead of the name of a saint, Dante's warning should be over the door, just above the entrance, at the end of the drawbridge, where all would see it when they entered this hell on the sea coast.

Some day when forts like this are obsolete, Daniel considered, *no one will know or remember the blood and tears that were shed in this place. No one will remember the suffering of the slaves who built it, English, Spanish, negro and indian, alike. No one will remember the prisoners who languished behind these cold stone walls nor hear their supplications to God for rescue or peace. Some, not as fortunate as Daniel to have friends to bring him food, prayed for relief from hunger and from cold. The rats. Oh yes, the rats.* When Daniel first came to this place, he would throw stones at the rats curiously sniffed through the door of his cell. Then he ran out of rocks. He raged at them and they disappeared for a few minutes but when he became silent, they returned. When he slept, he could feel them sniffing close to his body and he would waken and drive them away, but they were very tenacious. Finally he discovered that he slept too long and some of them would gnaw on toes or fingers. He couldn't keep them away for long. His guards thought this was funny. They would laugh as he drove a rat back out of the door, then jeer at him for not liking *"los ratos mejor."*

A day finally arrive when Daniel found himself more than surprised but nearly in shock that his cell door opened. The two guards were now four. The extra two took one of his arms each and marched him out of the door, into the fort's courtyard and over the drawbridge. Not far away, a ship waited for him. As he got close enough to see, he discovered it was one of Francisco Sanchez's vessels, *La Santa Lucia*. He didn't have long to marvel, though, before he found himself chained in the bilge, the lowest possible place on the vessel. Eventually he could hear the crew moving around in rapid activity aloft and then the ship sailed.

The tide began falling about noon that day, so by the time the ship began pitching and tossing in the open ocean, late afternoon had arrived. Someone, one of the crew, Daniel decided, brought him some biscuits and a large tin of fresh water which he consumed eagerly. The time passed as slowly in the ship's bilge as it had in his dungeon, but the newness of the surroundings lifted his mood slightly. *There's something new to see.*

On the second night out, several of the crew undid his chains and led him up the tiny, narrow passageways to the deck of the ship. There stood Francisco Sanchez looking grim. "Come, Señor Daniel. There is a rope ladder over the side of *La Santa Lucia*. Below a boat is waiting to take us to my other ship that you can see just over there." He pointed. "Come. You are saved. His Excellency Governor Zespedes and Governor Umzaga will be told that you died at sea and your body thrown over the side."

"Where is the other boat going to take me, Francisco?"

"You are going home, Señor Daniel, to South Carolina. Our next port of call is Charleston."

"I will be arrested there as well," Daniel groaned.

"No, Daniel. No one will recognize you. You have no idea how much your appearance has changed in the last six months. You will not be recognized. While we make the passage north, I suggest you choose a false name, other than Daniel McGirtt, so that we can make sure no one recognizes you."

"Francisco," Daniel suddenly said. "What is the date?"

"It is January, Daniel. 1789. Zespedes will record your death to have been January, 1789. Please don't jeopardize me by letting him find out the truth. Stay in South Carolina! Don't come back."

"If I survive to see my family again, I will not come back. I have not conversed with another human being in six months. I have had no human contact in six months. It is for me as Mayfield said. I have had enough of stone dungeons."

20

"It's October. Isn't it?"

"Yes, Daniel." Mary James McGirtt rocked beside her husband on the front veranda of Zachariah Cantey, the son of Daniel's sister Elizabeth Cantey and her husband John. The view faced south. The land rolled gently in moderate rises and dips, not really hills. The cotton crop, gleaned clean, left the stocks and branches with tiny bits of white fluff still clinging to them. The brilliant fall colors of the oaks, elms, maples and numerous other species of tree competed in advance with a certain famous Dutch painter who would not be born for another fifty five years. The landscape and foliage prophesied a new era that would be called impressionism. "It's too bad someone can't paint that. Aye Daniel?"

"If somebody painted that perfectly, critics would say it was impossible and that nothing so beautiful could ever happen."

"Beautiful things do happen, though, don't they? What do you say?"

"I would say that one can't properly appreciate such things who has never seen darkness." His face became grim for a moment then brightened again. " I think President Washington was right to declare a national holiday for Thanksgiving. It gives us an extra chance to get together with family, bounce the grandchildren on our knees and thank the good Lord for the chance to do it. I'm looking forward to it."

"We're going to make it feast this year, Daniel. We're going to roast a turkey and we're going to roast enough that the slaves can take a day off and join us."

"Who will do the cooking?" Daniel wanted to know.

"We ladies of the McGirtt and Cantey families are not without our skills, I will have you know."

"You're going to cook for the slaves?"

"Yes! And why not? They cook for us all the rest of the time. If we're going to be thankful, I think we should be thankful to them as well as God. We rely on them just about as much."

"Good heavens!"

ଓଓ ଆ

That evening, Anthony Hampton and his wife arrived at the home of Colonel James Chesnut at the Mulberry Plantation, about five miles south of Camden. Anthony Hampton had served the United States' Continental Army with distinction during the War for Independence. Grown stockier than in his youth, Chesnut refrained from noticing the change in Hampton due probably to age and reduced activity, and he welcomed the visitors warmly. After servants showed the guests to their quarters, they freshened up and came back down the winding staircase to be served dinner.

Chesnut put on a good show for them with maids, servants, cooks and a special servant to pour wine. Mutton, the main course, roasted slowly all afternoon under the watchful eye of Chesnut's favorite chef. His name, "Roland," was selected by James Chesnut when he purchased the eight-year-old child slave. Roland had been a house slave for the Chesnut family for more than thirty years and had been taught to cook.

Hampton and his wife raved over the meal and when it was finished, the ladies went off to the library to chat while the two men retreated to the front veranda for brandy and cigars. There they talked of the war. The chat moved on with good nature, lots of *ooh-ing* and *aah-ing* until Hampton brought up the story of being captured. "I was tied up and lying in the back of an open wagon. The British soldiers were kind enough that when they brought me food, they untied me and stood guard while I ate. Then they would bind me up again. There in the back of that wagon, I slept for three nights, but during the day we bounced over crude dirt paths toward Charleston where I fully expected to be hanged. On about the third night, to my wonder and surprise, I heard a familiar voice say to me, 'don't make a sound.' I, of course, kept my peace but found myself even more amazed to find the ropes binding my wrists had been cut and my hands were free. The man then led me to the edge of the camp and provided me with a horse and safe passage out of the camp. I owe that man my life."

Chesnut took a sip of his brandy and said, "You were fortunate, Hampton. Who do you suppose he was?"

"It was Daniel McGirtt, sir! Daniel, the very son of James and Priscilla who we knew here as boys."

"Well, well. I am glad to hear something good about Daniel. He certainly stirred things up south of Charleston and in Florida."

"Speaking of McGirtt," Hampton continued, "around 1778 I was in a party of cavalry, on a scouting mission, camped on the Santee River. We camped one night in a bend of what the locals there call Jack's Creek, near Vance. You know the place?"

"Indeed I do," Chesnut answered. "I believe I camped there more than once, myself. The land is high enough to be away from the river and low enough to be able to fetch water easily."

"That's the place," said Hampton. "There we were, almost bedded down for the night when a loud hail came from across the water. The voice shouted to us, 'Hello! Is there a Boykin an Irvin or a Whitaker in camp? If so, tell him to come where I may speak to him.' Boykin answered immediately calling out, 'Who are you and what do you want?' The voice then continued, saying, 'Never mind who I am, but take my advice and break camp. Tarleton knows where you are and will be on you by daylight!'"

"What did you do and what happened?" Chesnut asked enthusiastically.

"We broke camp, of course, and moved to the other side of the river and out of sight. Then, would you believe it, within a few hours, Tarleton showed up with a large body of cavalry. Had we not broken camp and moved he would have slaughtered us easily."

"You were very fortunate to get such a warning."

"You know what else, Chesnut? That voice belonged to Daniel McGirtt. I'd know his voice anywhere. We grew up together from the time we were children. He saved my life twice! I wonder whatever became of him?"

Chesnut drew the last sip of his brandy and relighted his cigar which had gone out. "If you would like to know what has become of Daniel McGirtt, Hampton, I suggest you might ask him yourself."

Hampton's surprise continued as Chesnut led him across the boundaries of his home to the plantation land of Zachariah Cantey, right next door. They came down the entry lane on foot, then Chesnut turned off the main road toward a cottage beside the house. He knocked on the door and out stepped an aging Daniel McGirtt. Daniel joined them at the Mulberry Plantation for another brandy and cigar.

Hampton's surprise caused him to forget, temporarily, the stories he had just told James Chesnut, but on the first sip of brandy, he remembered. He turned to Daniel and said, "Daniel, I want to thank you again for saving my life when I was being hauled off to Charleston for hanging."

Daniel smiled and said, "Anthony, I'm pretty sure you would have done the same for me if the roles were reversed."

"I don't know, Dan. I might have let them hang you." Then he laughed and reminded McGirtt of the exchange on the Santee River. "That was you then, too wasn't it?"

"Yes," Daniel sighed. "I did that. I just couldn't stand by and watch friends, especially good old friends like you, Whitaker, Boykin and Irvin, die at the hands of that bloody bastard Tarleton. He was one bloodthirsty man. When he dies, hell will never be the same!"

ෂ ෩

The three had such a good time chatting and sipping brandy on Chesnut's porch that they decided get together again in the spring and go fishing together in the Wateree as they did when they were boys. The Wateree River wound around the farms in the area like a huge snake. The farms, located in the loops and curls of its body, enriched by the silt and nutrients from its occasional floods, produced the best crops in the area because of the rich soil. The Wateree River blessed them often enough to keep the soil rich but not often enough or dramatically enough to force them to build elsewhere. During the ensuing winter months the snows were much heavier than usual. The winter was a cold one. When spring came, the snow melted quickly because the weather became warmer than usual. This, combined with the unusually heavy rains, resulted in rapid and heavy growth of the foliage around the river and on the lands above. Suddenly, though, the rains stopped coming. Drought followed and the foliage died. All this dead vegetation in and around the river gave the water an odd yellowish cast. This is the river the three men visited together for the fishing trip.

Daniel's spirits soared as the three friends strolled down the lane toward their old favorite fishing spot. "We haven't done this together in what – thirty years? What a pleasure to have you two along again!"

It was Hampton who answered first. "This weight I'm carrying doesn't make the walk as easy as it once was. Do you think there will be any fish for us?"

Chesnut came next. "We walked the same paths as boys. As men, our ways certainly diverged. I'm just glad we can all still be friends after all that's passed."

"A man's gotta do what a man's gotta do," said Daniel with a brief grimace. "Enough philosophy and wisdom. Let's catch some fish."

The riverbank, dry from the lack of any recent rain, allowed them to take a seat in the dirt without getting muddy. The night-crawlers they had caught the night before wriggled energetically enough to guarantee them that any fish in its right mind would not be able to resist such a tempting morsel. There they sat, swapping war stories and soaking worms. As the day wore on, they began to grow thirsty. Each had a bottle of water along for just such a need. James Chesnut and Anthony Hampton drank from their bottles but Daniel said, "I haven't tasted the water of the Wateree since I was a boy."

"Best not drink that, Daniel," Hampton volunteered. "That water doesn't look very good. The fish don't even like it much, today."

Daniel dipped his hand in the river, held it to his lips and took a sip. "You're right, Hampton. It tastes poorly as well. No wonder there are no fish. I wonder how long it will take for the river to clean itself up."

The three pulled their fishing lines out of the river and walked back to Chesnut's Mulberry Plantation. There they shared some brandy and chatted about events that took place when they were children, until Daniel mentioned that he didn't feel very well and that he was going to go back to the cottage.

In the morning, Hampton and Chesnut walked over to the Cantey plantation to check on Daniel and as they approached the cottage, Mary emerged looking frantic. "Daniel has growing sick. I don't know what's wrong. I sent for the doctor, but he's down in Sumter and I don't think he's going to be able to get here today."

Author's Note:

The history books say that Daniel McGirtt died at the home of his brother-in-law John James in Sumter, South Carolina, in 1804. The record says only that he died "in misery but not in want." It is known that Daniel spent the evening of his life carefully concealing from neighbors and the town's people who he was. He assumed a name that was not his own. Research has not yet revealed where he is buried or what name he assumed. It's my hope that I may find the grave of his wife, Mary James McGirtt/McGirth/McGirt/McGirit,/McGirith. Historical sources about Daniel McGirtt are not even consistent about the spelling of his name, much less about the dates of his activities, death and location. I found a deed he gave in the sale of a parcel of land in which, in his own handwriting, he spelled his name "McGirtt." So I assume that is correct. He probably knew how he wanted his name spelled. Some accounts say he died in 1789, but sources reporting Daniel's activities in the 1790s deny the veracity of that assertion. Other sources say he died in 1804. There is a Daniel McGirtt buried in St. Marys, Georgia. His date of death is around 1812 and his wife was one Suzanne Ashley. Some sources confuse this Daniel with our Daniel saying that Mary James was a first wife and Suzanne Ashley a second wife. I don't believe this is true. My assumption is that this Daniel was the son of our Daniel's brother James. An interesting complication is the family's continual re-use of first names. James was the name of the father, the brother and at least one nephew, all McGirtts. About a third of the women in the family have the name Mary. Sorting this out was challenging, interesting and fun. I just hope that wherever Daniel McGirtt is now, that he likes the book.

At the time of Daniel's death, there was cholera in the area. I noted a reference to Francisco Sanchez' two sons dying on the same day in 1804, with a passing comment wondering how that happened. It could have been cholera. Francisco Sanchez, by the way, is buried in the Tolomato Cemetery in St. Augustine Florida, together with quite a sizable family.

Stephen Mayfield ultimately left the area for Louisiana. William "Bloody Bill" Cunningham faded from the history books somewhere around the time they got away from El Morro Castle in Cuba. The last information I found on him was his retirement to Providence Island in the Bahamas. Patrick Alcorn is a fictional character I used so that Mc-

Girtt had someone to talk with and the reader could overhear. I'm sure Daniel had plenty of friends I could have used, but the history books didn't mention a single one. The ships' captains, guards and of course other people they met in the prisons are all fictional. I kept to the actual history as closely as possible and stepped away from it only in the interest of fleshing up the scenarios.

Chief Wakapuchasce, a Creek Chief of the Muskogee Nation had two sons of prominence. Payne became King Payne and he is the one Payne's Prairie is named for, near Micanopy (Cuscowilla), Florida. He was succeeded by his brother who became Chief Bolek, known by the white man as Chief Bow Legs. Chief Bolek was the father of Chief Micanopy who was featured in the Seminole wars in the 1820s to 1850s.

Robert G. Makin

BIBLIOGRAPHY

A History of Florida by Charlton Tebeau, University of Miami Press, Coral Gables, Florida 1971

Ahaya (A.K.A. Wakapuchasce, A.K.A. Chief Cow Keeper) from Wikipedia

Augustine Prevost – from Wikipedia

Battle of Kettle Creek (Wikipedia)

Biological Sketch of Stephen Mayfield the Tory of Brown's Creek by Phil Norfleet

Camden Archives and Museum, 1314 Broad Street, Camden, South Carolina 29020
The Camden Archives provided numerous excerpts from their library dealing with the subject of Daniel McGirtt and his adventures during and after the American War for Independence.

East Florida Rangers, Tonyn's Orders, The Online Institute for Advanced Loyalist Studies

Failure and the King's Cause on the Southern Revolutionary War Frontier by Robert Scott Davis

Florida's French Revolution 1793-1795, by Charles E. Bennett, University of Florida, 1981

Fort Tonyn, From Wikipedia

Guide to Historical Sites in Kershaw County/District South Carolina, published by Kershaw County Historical Society 1992

Keiser University – *Biographical Sketch of Daniel McGirtt* Extracted from the book Historic Camden Published 1905 by Thomas Kirkland and Robert Kennedy, Chapter fourteen pages 297-305

Last Days of British Saint Augustine by Lawrence H. Feldman, Clearfield Company Inc, by Genealogical Publishing Company, Inc. Baltimore Maryland 1998

Loyalist Refugees and The British Evacuation of East Florida 1783-1785 by Carole Waterson Troxler, http://www.cyberus.ca/-bharvey/troxler.htm

Major Bloody Bill Cunningham (Wikipedia)

March of the Scopholites, www.southerncampaign.org

Midway Museum and Midway Church, Midway Georgia, Diane Kroell, Executive Director

Old Houses and Plantations in the Stateburg Area of Sumter County, South Carolina, by Charles Broadwell (Charles@fte-i.net)

A Record of the Boykins, by Edward M. Boykin of Camden, South Carolina, printed by Colin McGraw 1876, reprinted in 2009 by the Boykin Tombfield Foundation

Revolutionary War and Aftermath (Chapter 6) Battle at Thomas Creek, www.vernonjohns.org/nonracists/jxrevwar.html

Revolutionary War in Georgia, by Edward J. Cashin, Augusta University

Rootsweb Ancestry.com, Massey & Clarkson Ancestors

South Carolina Department of Archives and History 8301 Parklane Rd, Columbia, SC 29223

Spanish Pathways in Florida / Caminos Españoles in La Florida, edited by Ann L. Henderson and Gary R. Mormino, Pineapple Press, Sarasota, Florida

St. Augustine Historical Society Library on Aviles Street and Charles Tingley

Timeline of the Revolutionary War – www.ushistory.org

Vincente Manuel Cespedes (Wikipedia) ...(usually spelled "Zespedes") Wikipedia

Acknowledgements

The first thank you for the birth of this book goes to Old Town Trolley Tours of St. Augustine, Florida, where I have been working as a tour guide for the last few years. There I provide a historical narrative for the company's guests. My interest in Florida's history initially came from my motivation to provide a better presentation. In interest of that pursuit, I read Charlton Tebeau's book, *A History of Florida*, and it was there that I discovered Daniel McGirtt. A few years later, I read the book again to refresh myself on a few things and again I found McGirtt's colorful and enigmatic character staring at me from its pages. This time, I Googled Daniel McGirtt. The more I read about him the more curious I became. Another Google search introduced me to Francisco Xavier Sanchez in *Spanish Pathways in Florida*. The book dealt with both Sanchez and McGirtt. I found the book on Amazon.com and bought it. That became a slippery slope. I was hooked. Sanchez interested me as much as McGirtt.

My first trip in pursuit of this story took me to The Midway Historical Museum in Midway, Georgia. Next, I went to Camden, South Carolina, and visited several museums. At the Camden Archives and Museum, the archivist, Floride (Windy) Corbett, almost buried me in data about Dan McGirtt. Her amazing help went far in making Dirt McGirtt a real person. After the archives, I visited the Historic Camden Revolutionary War Site where I met some of the descendants of people who had been friends and acquaintances of Daniel McGirtt. What a pleasure!

I owe a debt of gratitude as well to Charles A. Tingley of the St. Augustine Historical Society Library where I visited numerous times on this mission to discover the real Dan McGirtt. Mr. Tingley consistently amazed me with his esoteric knowledge. He would answer the most arcane questions as though the answer rested on the tip of his tongue before I asked. Then he would provide me with a stack of books elucidating his answers. He's an amazing and pleasant fellow. The Historical Society is lucky to have him and I am lucky they do, too.

Another person I am lucky to have met is Jonni Anderson, without whose help this book would not be possible. Jonni keeps me straight on punctuation and spelling, a truly formidable task! She formats the book cover art to fit the impossible pdf formatting that practically makes me go blind every time I see it. Thanks for your amazing help, Jonni, and the numerous and attractive book covers you have designed for me.

Marshall McCullough, whose family comes from the same place as Daniel McGirtt, agreed to allow me to use his face on the book cover. I researched the McGirtt family in Renfrew, Scotland, and the family resemblance is similar, so, for all intents and purposes, Marshall has become Dirt McGirtt in my mind. Thanks, Marshall.

I would also like to thank Sophie Tredor for bravely reading my first draft and Dr. Richard O. Salsgiver for his consistent encouragement and moral support. When I sat in your dorm room long ago at IUP, learning to finger a "C" chord on a six-string for the first time, it never occurred to me that some day you would be editing and endorsing my books. Thank you, Salty.

About the Author

Robert G. Makin graduated from Indiana University of Pennsylvania in Education with a concentration in English. Graduate studies focused primarily in Theology at the Lancaster Theological Seminary of the United Church of Christ in Lancaster, Pennsylvania. Later graduate studies focused on Real Estate and Real Estate Appraising where he earned the professional designation "Senior Residential Appraiser" from the Society of Real Estate Appraisers (later the Appraisal Institute) and "State Certified General Real Estate Appraiser" from the State of Florida. He quips that when his residential appraisal clientele started asking him to write fiction, he chose instead to write fiction the FBI would have no interest in studying.

His first book and first historical fiction, *Return to Masada*, arose from questions he discovered in theological training ... Who were the Essenes? Was Christ an Essene? What exactly does that mean? Exploring those questions resulted in Return to Masada. Five books later and during the writing of the last three, Makin worked as a tour guide in St. Augustine, Florida, where he had done thousands of real estate appraisals over a twenty year period and had already learned much of St. Augustine's history. Giving historical narratives about St. Augustine daily as a tour guide led him to explore more of the history to enrich his tour talks. The discovery of Daniel McGirtt resulted in exhaustive research about Dan's historical period, other important characters of the time and the motivations and concerns of each of them. It was an intriguing study. Some of it has definitely been incorporated into Makin's tours.

While an English Education in a Western Pennsylvania school did not help Makin overcome his Western Pennsylvania dialect, that and his real estate appraisal training certainly prepared him to execute and organize research. *Dirt McGirtt* is a product of that organized research.

Makin can be reached at www.starving-writers.com.

Other Books by
Robert G. Makin
Available at Amazon, Barnes & Noble and other book sellers

Strathnaver Legends

The heart of a quiet, peaceful village, ripped open by the remorseless vitriol of a sadistic predator, drives kith and kin on a hunt for the hunter. Falling in with unknown races and cultures, they are forced to overcome prejudice and distrust in their drive for a common interest, to live in freedom from terror.

The Faces of Inanna

An ancient evil plaguing a small area of the South Pacific has been the focus of an equally ancient, very secret fraternity for hundreds of years. Why were the neighboring islanders driven to insane wars, the deforestation of their islands and illogical religions demanding human sacrifices? "The Watchers" had to resolve the conflict, but could they? Finally, the Ascended Brotherhood designated one man to stand as a fence between the good and the evil. Imagine his surprise upon learning the enigma they so long withstood was a very special woman.

Return to Masada

The historic Battle of Masada has become a symbol of freedom, hope and courage to die, if necessary, for one's principles. Makin delivers a new version of this famous "David and Goliath" struggle of the Jewish people against the Roman Army.

Aleister through the Looking Glass

This is a children's book written for children over the age of 30. Starving-Writer Aleister Smiley takes a job with a literary agent returning unread manuscripts and depositing reading fees. He shortly finds himself whisked into Never Ever Land where he can Never Ever be published. Provinces of Never Ever Land parody the plight of the writer in this new age of formula-loving editors, agents and publishers.

Where the Clouds Sleep

The peaceful hamlet of Copperhead, West Virginia, goes about its business of harvesting rock, raising children and enjoying the rhapsody of life in the mountains -- until dead children begin appearing.

Some believe rape, murder and other evil human foibles are repaid in kind by a justice-loving God. Some call it Karmic Justice. They tell us, "What goes around comes around." They say when it doesn't happen it's like ending a song without resolving its chord progression. It grates on the ear like a fingernail on a chalkboard, offending one's sensibilities on the seventh-chord of outrageous, appalling, injustice. Makin's first venture into writing Crime/Fiction draws the fingernail across the chalkboard of our sensitivities heaping anger upon anger, demanding resolution.

www.ingramcontent.com/pod-product-compliance
Lightning Source LLC
Chambersburg PA
CBHW071159160426
43196CB00011B/2132